OLORADO MOUNTAI
LRC---WEST CA
Glenwood Springs, Co

COLORADO MOUNTAIN COLLEGE
F2521.W671973

.SP
Worcester, Donald Em

D0455456

DISCARDED

F
2521
W 67
1973

Brazil

From
Colony
to
World
Power

COLORADO MOUNTAIN COLLEGE
LRC---WEST CAMPUS
Glenwood Springs, Colo. 81601

Donald E. Worcester

Brazil

From
Colony
to
World
Power

COLORADO MOUNTAIN COLLEGE
LRC---WEST CAMPUS
Glenwood Springs, Colo. 81601

CHARLES   SCRIBNER'S   SONS   •   *New York*

Copyright © 1973 Donald E. Worcester

This book published simultaneously in the
United States of America and in Canada.
Copyright under the Berne Convention.

All rights reserved. No part of this book
may be reproduced in any form without the
permission of Charles Scribner's Sons.

Cover illustration from Theodor de Bry, *America*, Part X
(Frankfurt, 1619). Reprinted with permission of the
Rare Book Division, The New York Public Library, Astor,
Lenox and Tilden Foundations.

Map on p. viii by Harry Scott.

  1 3 5 7 9 11 13 15 17 19 c/c 20 18 16 14 12 10 8 6 4 2
  1 3 5 7 9 11 13 15 17 19 c/p 20 18 16 14 12 10 8 6 4 2

Printed in the United States of America
Library of Congress Catalog Card Number 73-1328
SBN 684-13386-5 (cloth)
SBN 684-13391-1 (paper)

COLORADO MOUNTAIN COLLEGE
LRC---WEST CAMPUS
Glenwood Springs, Colo. 81601

TO MY MOTHER

Contents

COLORADO MOUNTAIN COLLEGE
LRC---WEST CAMPUS
Glenwood Springs, Colo. 81601

Introduction

BRAZIL OCCUPIES A UNIQUE POSITION IN THE WEST-ern Hemisphere for reasons other than its size, which amounts to virtually half the area of South America, and its population, which totals well over half that of the entire continent. Its people represent, as no other people of modern times do, a genuine racial melting pot. Modern Brazilians descend from the Portuguese, Dutch, French, Germans, Italians, Indians, Africans, and Japanese. The United States once claimed to be a melting pot, but it was primarily one of Western Europeans and Britons, not the peoples of four continents; descendants of Africans and Asians are a part of the American population, but the melting process has largely excluded them. In Brazil a virtual biological blending of the various ethnic lines began long ago and continues into the present, and no group has been excluded from the mixing process.

The history of Brazil has been that of a long, slow, often-interrupted climb to national maturity and international prestige. Beginning as a few isolated Portuguese colonies on the coast, Brazil gradually expanded westward across the continent through the efforts of small exploratory parties. At the Andes mountains its westward march was checked by the Spaniards who were firmly established there and beyond. In the seventeenth century Portuguese Brazilians almost singlehandedly drove out the Dutch to secure the land for the Portuguese empire; many Dutch, however, chose to remain within the country and joined their fortunes and families with those of the Portuguese. For a time Brazil became the home of the Portuguese royal family and the capital of an empire extending to Europe, Africa, and Asia. After the proclamation of independence, the government remained a monarchy, the only such successful experiment in the New World. With the fall of the monarchy, Brazil became a republic—troubled almost from the start by the seeming conflict between democracy and effective government.

Part of the country's problem has been economic: how to tap the great natural wealth that exists there. A vast land lying within the tropics, Brazil has a climate governed more by altitude, rainfall, and prevailing winds than by latitude. The Amazon basin is covered by the world's largest rainforest, which until the second half of the twentieth century has resisted virtually all settlement. The country contains the greatest river system in the world, but it has not yet become an important avenue of either commerce or communication. The very magnitude of the waterflow has discouraged human settlement in the river basins because of annual flooding over vast expanses of lowlands.

In natural resources, especially minerals, Brazil is richly endowed. Gold and diamonds were the only minerals exploited to a significant degree in the colonial era. Now, in an age where steel production is essential to modernization and industrialization, Brazil's extensive iron ore deposits have become one of the nation's primary assets. These are supplemented by the presence of metals like manganese, tungsten, and titanium. Bauxite, copper, and nickel are available as well, and there are indications that extensive petroleum deposits exist. Even before the official opening of the Trans-Amazon Highway in 1973, a number of foreign and domestic corporations were already at work preparing to extract the mineral riches of the Amazon basin. One of the obstacles to greater exploitation of mineral resources has been the scarcity of fuels such as high-grade coal and petroleum; the tapping of hydroelectric power has scarcely begun.

For hundreds of years the Brazilian economy was geared to agriculture—indeed, Brazilians were the first to employ large-scale agriculture in the Western Hemisphere. Only a small percentage of the land is arable, however, and of this land only a small portion has been under cultivation. The opening of the West and some portions of the Amazon region will gradually add millions of acres of potential farmland, but many parts of the interior are lacking in fertility and will remain scrubland or, at best, pasture for livestock. The possible hazards to the ecology resulting from the clearing of the forest have yet to be determined.

Brazil has come a long way, however, since its first uncertain days, and the greatness that observers and writers have been predicting for the country for nearly a century may actually be at hand. No longer a "colonial" supplier of raw materials for European commerce, as she was for centuries, Brazil is a modern nation with a rapidly expanding economy and an increasingly significant position among major nations of the world.

Brazil
From
Colony
to
World
Power

1/The Rise of Portugal

AT THE BEGINNING OF THE GREAT AGE OF DIS-
covery, the Portuguese people were endowed with qualities which
aided them immensely in the long, hazardous process of empire
building. Like the Genoese and other Italian merchant-adventur-
ers, they were daring seamen and skilled navigators. They had,
moreover, something these others lacked—an intense pride in their
tiny kingdom, an undying resistance to external pressures, and an
attachment to their homeland which caused the eastern and
western worlds to become dotted with clusters of people representing bits of Portugal. Although spread thinly throughout islands and
lands touched by two oceans, they transmitted their way of life and
their language to the mixed populations that resulted. Today it
seems almost incredible that from a population of about one million
people could have come the builders of eastern and western empires
once the envy of all Europe.

Mobility, adaptability, energy, resourcefulness—these were the
qualities that contributed to the greatness of the Portuguese
pioneers. Part of their adaptability was their uninhibited, unpuri-
tanical attitude toward racial integration. They mixed freely and
without delay wherever their ships made land. An area so vast and
empty as Brazil could never have been populated by a people so few
in number if this were not so. Forgetting their African and oriental
enterprises, the pioneers began life anew and left an unmistakable
stamp on the mixed civilization which emerged. Religion, too,
played an important role. Although possessing a marked capacity
for religious fervor, the Portuguese were quick to oppose intolerance
and bigotry when these were introduced among them.

Portugal had no separate existence from the rest of the Iberian
peninsula until the twelfth century. Like peoples of the neighboring
kingdoms south of the Pyrenees, the Portuguese were the product of
many races and civilizations from Europe, Africa, and the eastern

1

Mediterranean, as invaders from these lands overran the peninsula. Africa begins at the Pyrenees, says the ancient adage, and this historical fact has given the peninsular kingdoms a vastly different history from the more northerly nations of Europe.

As early as the eleventh century B.C. Phoenician merchants established trading posts on the peninsula and opened commerce with Celts and Iberians, who already occupied parts of the land. The Iberians seem to have reached the peninsula from Mesopotamia by way of north Africa, while the Celts, most strongly entrenched in the areas to become Galicia and Portugal, came from central Europe. In the sixth century B.C. Greek and Carthaginian traders arrived to establish posts of their own. Carthage, a Phoenician colony in northern Africa, attempted to conquer and unite the entire peninsula under her rule, but failed. This first attempt at unification ended with the Second Punic War (219–206 B.C.), when the Romans drove the Carthaginians from their posts and began the long effort to extend Roman rule over the entire area.

Some of the tribes, like the Lusitani of the western central region, bitterly resisted the Romans; others succumbed without a fight. Apparently each tribe resisted or surrendered as it chose and no effort was made at united action. Viriatus, the shepherd chieftain of the Lusitani, led his people so effectively against the Romans that their conquest was long and costly. Once their supremacy was assured, the Romans imposed upon the diverse and independent tribes a unified regime, something completely foreign to them. The Romans also introduced their own civilization, completing the process begun by the Carthaginians.

Subordination of the tribes to a central authority was not the only significant change brought about by Roman domination. The Romans left a more lasting imprint than any of their predecessors. As the city was the center of Roman life, municipal development became important. Roads, bridges, aqueducts, and increased commercial activity were some of the material benefits of Roman rule. More lasting than these, however, was the introduction of Roman law, the Latin language, and Christianity. Hispania, as the peninsula was known, became one of the most Romanized areas of the empire. This was especially true of Lusitania, the central area of modern Portugal.

After the fall of Rome in 410 Germanic tribes easily overran the peninsula, for the people of Hispania had grown accustomed to protection by Roman legions. The Vandals, Suevi, and Alani preceded the Visigoths, who established a tenuous rule which was to endure for three centuries. The Visigoths had been under Roman influence before leaving their tribal homelands, so the changes they introduced were minimal. Among the Visigoths succession to the crown was by election, and this often turbulent means of replacing deceased rulers was practiced in Hispania. Unlike the Romans, they preferred rural to city life; the nobles lived more in scattered villas than in the cities.

Roman law, the Latin language, and Christianity survived and were adopted to some degree by the invaders. Though somewhat modified, Roman ideals also persisted. Even a gradual movement away from the elective monarchy toward a hereditary dynasty occurred, because the choice of a successor to the throne became limited to the members of one family. This step made for greater stability in the monarchy and paved the way for the later dynastic successions.

In 711 the Moslem Arabs and subject tribes of north Africa, impelled by the dynamic urge following the rise of Mohammed which changed them from nomadic desert warriors to ardent imperialists, sent raiding parties across the narrow strait separating the peninsula from Africa. The Moslems easily brushed aside the disunited Visigoths. What began merely as raids became campaigns of conquest. The Moslems established their rule throughout the peninsula, save for a few mountain strongholds in Asturias, far to the north, where native mountaineers and some Christian nobles rallied and held onto their lands.

The Arabian and African tribes, clinging to ancient blood feuds, accentuated the disunity prevalent in Visigothic times. An independent Emirate then Caliphate was created in the peninsula, and under these the Hispano-Arab civilization flowered. The literary, philosophical, mathematical, and medical knowledge of the eastern Mediterranean was transplanted to Hispania under the aegis of the Arabs. Córdoba became, for a time, the most important center of learning in continental Europe. While the rest of Europe was plunged into an era of history little noted for its pursuit of knowledge, south of the Pyrenees the wisdom of the ancients survived and was cultivated.

Arab rule also meant changes in agriculture and husbandry, such as the introduction of new plants and plant products, different breeds of livestock, and new farming and stock-raising techniques.

The languages of the peninsular peoples were enriched with a multitude of Arabic words, especially for techniques, officials, and institutions. In art, architecture, and literature, too, the Arabs left an indelible mark on the civilization of the peninsula.

By the eleventh century Moslem disunity was so great that the struggling Christian kingdoms were able to make heavy inroads in their gradual march south. The kingdom of León, mother of both Portugal and Castile, arose in the tenth century. Soon there were five other Christian realms and more than twice that many small Arab states. Gradually the Christian kingdoms were reduced to two major areas: Spain—dominated by Castile, and including León, the Basque province, Navarre, and Aragón—and the kingdom of Portugal. The Spanish realm was, as is obvious, a composite, and it did not escape the special problems inherent in empires. Portugal, on the other hand, was the one peninsular kingdom which successfully resisted domination and fusion. A sense of cohesion and direction appeared early, and Portugal did not change her course suddenly or violently for any reason.

Portugal and Castile first appeared as unimportant counties in León and later claimed kingship for their rulers. The Castilians soon displayed a versatility and talent for innovation which grew with the passing centuries. Portugal, on the other hand, began her career with a conservative outlook and a resistance to external forces reminiscent of the ancient Lusitani in their opposition to Rome.

The Christian recovery of the peninsula initially spread westward from Asturias into Galicia. The northwest corner of the peninsula secure, Christian forces edged slowly southward. Few Moslems had penetrated the area which was to become northern Portugal, and the Gallegos occupied it with little difficulty. The language of Galicia and Portugal were separated in the mid-fourteenth century, but they are still similar in pronunciation.

By the middle of the ninth century this northern area was called *terra portucalis,* after the old town of Portucale on the Douro, near the site of modern Oporto. The name was gradually applied to a wider area, and by the end of the tenth century Portugal was a hereditary county under the king of León.

Alfonso VI of León, whose second wife was Constance of Burgundy, called on Burgundian knights to aid him in extending his conquests of Moslem-held lands. When one of these knights, Henry of Burgundy, brother of the powerful Duke of Burgundy, married Teresa, an illegitimate daughter of Alfonso, he received the county of Portugal as part of the dowry. His tiny domain remained attached to León, serving as a buffer between that kingdom and Moslem raiders from the south. Ambitious Henry extended his authority anywhere he could, more at the expense of Christians than of Moslems. When he died in 1112, however, his ambitions were far from fulfilled. He left as heir his infant son, Afonso Henriques.

The medieval saying, "Woe to the land whose king is a child" is an apt one, for a struggle for power inevitably ensued in these lands. During the childhood of Afonso Henriques his lands were fought over by his mother and her favorite, Fernando Peres, and by Moslems from the south. Afonso Henriques, however, refused to be defrauded of his rights or looted of his lands. In 1128 he rallied a powerful following and seized control of the tiny country. With his reign the national history of Portugal begins.

During the sixty years that Afonso Henriques ruled, Portugal exhibited some of the attitudes of a modern nation. He claimed for himself the title of king under the papacy and independent of Castile, now the major power of the peninsula. Before his long rule ended, he had secured papal recognition of his crown and grudging acknowledgment by Castile. The Portuguese church separated at an early date from the church of León and Castile, and this separation was an additional stimulus to the growth of a feeling of Portuguese nationality.

Aided by European knights on their way to participate in the Crusades, Afonso Henriques besieged and captured Lisbon from the Moslems in 1147. The decline of Moslem power encouraged additional enterprises to the south, while campaigns against Castile proved more costly and less rewarding. Portuguese expansion followed the line of least resistance, and for this reason moved south rather than north or east, and against infidels rather than Christians. By the middle of the thirteenth century the national boundaries of modern Portugal were fairly well set, and the country was free of Moslem competition. The little kingdom was well on the way to becoming a modern nation-state.

The southward expansion was not without setbacks, however, especially when the Almohades invaded the Algarve from north Africa. Much of the Christian conquest and defense was assigned to semi-religious military orders, whose fortified posts were rallying points for the Christian population. The process of settling the conquered lands necessitated relaxation of feudal institutions and obligations; privileges had to be granted to attract settlers. Under Sancho I, son of Afonso Henriques, settlement was completed, and the people were organized into *concelhos* (chartered municipalities). The *concelho* was more than an urban unit, for it controlled surrounding areas. This system, which proved satisfactory in the reconquest, was to be the basic unit of organization employed by Portugal across the seas in later years.

Among the military orders which played so prominent a part in rounding out Portuguese boundaries to the south were the Templars and Hospitallers, which were international in organization. When Pope Clement V condemned the Templars under pressure from France, King Diniz in 1319 established the Order of Christ, a Portuguese order, to assume their place and to accept their possessions. Other military orders active in Portugal were those of São Tiago, which divorced itself from the Spanish order of Santiago in 1290, Crato, and Aviz. The last name was formerly the Portuguese branch of the Spanish order of Calatrava, renamed in 1211 and granted the town of Aviz.

In 1516 Dom Manoel obtained from the pope the right of nominating men to the masterships of the orders—a right which greatly strengthened royal control. Finally, in 1551 the masterships were joined to the crown. As in Castile, where Fernando had earlier gained control over the orders by a similar measure, this was merely an additional step to enhance and strengthen royal authority over the nobility.

By the thirteenth century there was little danger from León, and Castile had not yet reached a position from which to threaten Portugal. Problems were largely internal and concerned mainly the relationship between the king on one side and powerful nobles and the church on the other. In 1246 the pope deposed Sancho II. His successor, Afonso III, former count of Boulogne, although given papal support resumed the clash with the church with more success than Sancho had enjoyed.

It was Afonso III who moved the court from Coimbra to Lisbon—an important move for future development of the country. Lisbon had been the meeting place of traders from north and south, and the crusaders had been amazed at the mingling of races and languages they encountered there after the city's conquest. Commerce flourished and Lisbon's importance grew; serfdom correspondingly declined.

Social organization in Afonso Henriques' time had been simple, based on three main classes: nobles, called *fidalgos* or *ricos homens,* clergy, and peasantry. There was as yet little distinction between ranks of nobles. The Portuguese *Côrtes,* an assembly of nobles, clergy, and a few townspeople, was typical of the meetings of the three estates elsewhere in Europe of that day: The king summoned the *Côrtes* when he desired advice, acquiescence, or assistance. Probably the main concern of the members of the *Côrtes* was in protecting class interests against royal encroachments by reference to custom and appeal to tradition. They were essentially conservative, much more concerned with preserving the status quo than with bringing about political or social change.

By the thirteenth century Portugal had developed a vernacular language of her own based on Latin and similar in sound and speech to that of Galicia. A royal decree that official documents be written in Portuguese stimulated wider use of the language, if not greater elegance. As happened elsewhere in Europe at the time vernacular languages appeared, a type of literary movement followed, launched by troubadours or wandering minstrels who sang the praises of kings or fair ladies. These men greatly enriched the language's phraseology and imagery in a manner and degree wholly alien to the scribes who wrote papers of state. In this same century Afonso III established a course of studies that grew into the University of Coimbra.

In the thirteenth and fourteenth centuries expansion of agriculture led to the production of surpluses, and these in turn to greater commercial activity. An increase in the use of coined money, the holding of great fairs, and the growth of maritime power accompanied the upsurge of commerce. Genoese merchants came to settle in Lisbon to conduct their enterprises, and with the continuing attention to commerce Lisbon became an important seaport. Since overland routes to other European countries were endangered by Castilian hostility, the Portuguese turned wholeheartedly to the sea. In this they were merely continuing an Arab activity of an earlier era. The sea was to be the principal avenue to greatness and wealth for the Portuguese.

The fourteenth century in Europe has been called the "golden age of bastards," and this is justly applicable to Portugal. For Portugal, however, this designation is also apropos of the centuries which came before and those which followed. From the beginning Portuguese monarchs displayed an irresistible passion for members of the opposite sex, which was inspired not so much by high station or noble birth as by certain physical qualities more democratically and dramatically distributed among ·their subjects. This powerful tendency among Portuguese monarchs relegated horse racing to a minor position among the sports of kings. Furthermore, they did not refuse to recognize and claim as their own the fruit of these unions. Thus, a princeling whose parentage was regarded as irregular by conventional standards nevertheless might aspire to the royal succession. Portuguese legends were enriched by a multitude of romantic episodes, and the country seems not to have suffered as a result of considerable deviations occasionally pursued by the royal line of succession. A good king was just that, even from the wrong side of the blanket.

Pedro I, father of Fernando I, last of the Burgundian dynasty, had been a man of unrestrained amorous inclinations. His most famous affair was with Inês de Castro, who rose to the position of royal mistress from the less regal role of lady-in-waiting to the queen. So fearful of her influence were the nobles that they murdered her during Pedro's absence. He devoted most of the remainder of his rule to punishing the murderers and to proving that the children born to him by Inês de Castro were of legitimate birth. He made no similar effort in behalf of his numerous children by other unions.

Fernando I, following in his father's footsteps, threatened the future of the entire country by his rashness. Enamored of Leonor Teles, he ignored dynastic considerations as well as the desires of the nobles and married her. After his death in 1383 she tried to rule Portugal as regent, with the help of the count of Ourem, who quickly replaced her late husband in her affections. Opposed to this arrangement, the nobles looked for a new leader to install on the throne. The chief contenders were Juan I of Spain, two of Pedro's sons imprisoned by Juan I, and João, one of Pedro's sons by a less prominent mistress and also master of the Order of Aviz.

Perceiving an opportunity to fish in waters muddied by the question of succession, the Castilians sent forces across the border. Most nobles rallied around João. The count of Ourem was assassinated, and João organized the defenses of his country. He appealed to John of Gaunt, duke of Lancaster, who had pretensions to the Castilian crown. To aid a potentially valuable ally against Castile, John of Gaunt sent 700 English longbowmen seasoned in England's perennial wars with France.

Soon after the *Côrtes* assembled at Coimbra in 1385 to proclaim him King João I, João's forces defeated the Castilians at Aljubarrota and drove them back across the border. John of Gaunt landed at La Coruña in July 1386 and with Portuguese help tried to conquer Castile. In the same year Portugal and England drew up a perpetual treaty of alliance and friendship. João cemented this alliance by marrying Philippa, daughter of John of Gaunt, and the House of Aviz replaced the House of Burgundy as the royal dynasty.

With the crowning of João of Aviz, Portugal was well on the way to developing a parliamentary body such as eventually checked royal authority in England. Indebted to the *Côrtes* for his crown, João accepted its proposals and lived up to his agreements. If this had been the case with succeeding rulers, Portugal might have become a nascent constitutional monarchy at an early date. But where lack of funds forced English kings to continue calling and yielding to knightly councils, Portuguese monarchs were more fortunate, and the *Côrtes* gradually atrophied. João I assembled the body twenty-two times in forty-eight years and was reasonably responsive to its wishes. Dom Manoel, who ruled in the late fifteenth century, called the *Côrtes* several times early in his rule, but not at all thereafter. In the sixteenth century, João III assembled the *Côrtes* only three times in thirty-six years.

The decline of the *Côrtes* was closely tied to Portuguese expansion overseas. The apparently unlimited wealth which poured into royal treasure chests in the sixteenth century ended the timid reliance upon advice and consent of representative subjects and gave Portuguese kings a sense of kingship and an independence of their subjects' wishes which the impecunious Tudors and Stuarts could never approach. The trend toward royal absolutism and diminished power of the nobility accompanying the rise of nation-states out of the decentralism of the Middle Ages appeared early in Portugal despite the apparent strength of the *Côrtes*. A large part of the nobility had sided with Castile and was destroyed or scattered at Aljubarrota. João I further strengthened his position by attracting the middle class of the towns to his cause. For royal administrators he chose men from this class rather than from the nobility. He also created a new nobility on whose loyalty he could rely, at least temporarily, and he modeled it after English peerage in rank and title. The new nobility gradually took up the causes of the old, however, and later kings were forced to meet its challenge.

In keeping with his policy of expanding royal authority, João I began to summon the *Côrtes* less frequently, and he rejected its demand that it be called annually. Privileges granted to the middle class rewarded and cemented their loyalty to the king and enhanced their power at the expense of the nobles.

The new House of Aviz appeared dynastically secure because five sons were born to João and Philippa. The peace treaty with Castile, however, deprived these young men of the opportunity to win knightly honors in contests with their customary foes. João was persuaded to launch an invasion of Ceuta, the important commercial port of northern Africa from which Arabic invasions had set forth seven centuries earlier. Honors could be won against Moslems as well as Christians, and Ceuta offered not only the prospect of rich booty but future commercial advantages to Portugal as well.

The expedition was organized in great secrecy and at widespread ports, so as to avoid giving the Moslems time to prepare defenses. Neighboring Christian states, however, were greatly aroused at the warlike preparations reported by their informants, and João was obliged to assure them that he had no designs on their lands.

In 1415 the expedition sailed and moved by easy stages to Gibraltar, when it swung suddenly across the narrow strait and bore down on its real objective. João's sons took an active part in the landing and in the assault on the city. Ceuta fell, and Portugal became the first colonial power of modern Europe.

Except for the loot that was captured, seizing Ceuta did not fulfill Portuguese expectations for securing a larger share of Mediterranean commerce. The conquest was important, however, as a harbinger of empire. Ceuta proved to be the first step on the long journey to the Indian Ocean and the fabled wealth of the Orient—and to the closer, though unsought and unknown Brazil.

Henrique, João's third son, devoted his life to untangling the secrets of Africa. He seems to have been content with the almost monkish career he chose for himself. As master of the Order of Christ he had relatively ample funds for his projects. From his headquarters at Sagres, near the high, rocky cliffs of the southern coast, he planned expeditions along the African coast, obtained trained navigators for these voyages, and revised charts as new geographical knowledge was accumulated. Because of his interest in the voyages, Henrique is known to us as "Prince Henry the

Navigator," although he took no personal part in any of the expeditions.

During Henrique's time Portugal discovered and colonized the Madeira and Azores islands. Settlement relied upon a system of concessions to prominent families, who brought colonists at their own expense. The islands were soon producing sugar and wine for export. More valuable still was the experience Portugal gained in conquering and occupying strange lands beyond the seas.

Henrique's efforts were interrupted occasionally by dynastic disturbances. When João I died in 1433, he was succeeded by his oldest son Duarte, who ruled for only five years. Duarte's successor was Afonso V, his six-year-old son, but Pedro, João's second son, governed as regent.

Pedro, one of the generation's ablest men, ruled with ability and severity. He encouraged Henrique to continue his explorations, and the search for the mythical kingdom of Prester John, apparently modern Ethiopia, became one of the purposes of the African voyages. The severity of his rule raised opposition to him. Pedro apparently considered adultery a royal prerogative not open to lesser officials, and he deemed emasculation a proper punishment for transgressors of his code. This attitude excited fears among those who would emulate royalty, and they became parties to intrigues against Dom Pedro.

While plots against Pedro were developing, Henrique's ships began bringing back a few captives to be sold as slaves, thus marking the beginnings of the slave trade in the 1440s. The trade did not become important until tropical plantations were established beyond the seas: slaves taken to Portugal were used more as household servants than agricultural laborers.

When in 1446 the *Côrtes* declared Afonso of age, Pedro was forced to surrender the regency in favor of the fourteen-year-old monarch, who had already been turned against him. In 1449 Pedro's followers and those of the young king clashed in a battle that ended in Pedro's death.

Henrique continued his work at Sagres, but Afonso V lacked interest in the voyages. After Henrique died in 1460, the voyages of exploration and trade he had so long sponsored were carried on by individuals who received monopolies granted by the crown. Despite the king's continuing lack of enthusiasm and support, however, African coastal trade in gold, ivory, and slaves had become too profitable to be neglected.

Afonso's attentions at this time were directed toward Morocco, and the numerous expeditions he sent there won him the title of "Afonso the African." He also yielded to the temptation to meddle in Castilian affairs, hoping to bring that land under his control. His sister Joana was queen of Castile during the rule of Enrique IV, known to his contemporaries by the unflattering but appropriate title "The Impotent." Joana nevertheless gave birth to a daughter, Juana, whom Enrique claimed as his own and named heir to his crown in spite of widespread knowledge that she was actually the child of the Count of Beltrán de la Cueva, who had assumed Enrique's neglected prerogatives. Juana was known in Castile as "La Beltraneja" in deference to Beltrán de la Cueva's virility.

Before his death Enrique sought to secure the crown for his supposed daughter, to prevent it passing to his half-sister Isabel, who against his wishes had married Fernando of Aragón. In the ensuing contest for the throne Afonso V supported la Beltraneja and her partisans. In 1475 he invaded Castile, but was defeated by forces raised by Fernando. Juana la Beltraneja eventually retired to a convent, and the frustrated Afonso lost interest not only in the Castilian crown but in Portugal's as well. Shortly afterwards Portugal conceded Castile's claim to the Canary Islands, disputed since their conquest and settlement by Castile earlier in the century.

João II, who succeeded his father in 1481, had been virtual ruler of Portugal since the invasion of Castile. His first task was to check the trend toward a weakened monarchy and a strengthened nobility, which had set in during Afonso's minority and had grown to alarming proportions. The encroachments on and usurpations of royal lands and authority by ambitious nobles had become threatening. Only an extremely capable, firm ruler could hope to succeed in a fundamental contest with the powerful nobles. João proved himself equal to the task and distinguished himself as one of the greatest monarchs of his day.

He met the problem with vigor and firmness. Instead of wasting time on isolated abuses he went straight to the heart of the matter and ordered the nobles to take a new and detailed oath of allegiance. They resisted, led by the duke of Braganza.

João's cause was aided by the discovery of a treasonable correspondence between the duke and Fernando of Aragón. João carefully gathered information on the plot to dethrone him, then ordered the duke arrested. Portugal's most powerful noble smiled at what he considered merely the empty gesture of a frightened king.

When confronted with the weight of evidence assembled against him, however, he quickly realized that his head must fall and abandoned his efforts at defense.

Other nobles implicated in the plot fled the land while João sequestered their estates as well as those of the late duke of Braganza. The remaining nobles were terrified and sought to relieve their anxieties by plotting to murder the king. News of this plot, too, reached João, and he dealt with the conspirators as summarily as he had with the duke. All doubts as to who ruled Portugal were swept away. Immensely rich lands passed back to the crown, and a large number of vacancies appeared in the ranks of the nobility. Other vestiges of the feudal relationship between monarch and nobles now yielded readily to João's urging.

João did not neglect Portuguese overseas activity even when domestic problems were most demanding. The posts along the African coast were secured by the construction of fortifications. The garrison and fort established at São Jorge da Mina not only served to protect trade with the natives but also provided a valuable station for expeditions farther down the dark continent's unexplored coast. Using this base Diogo Cão reached the Congo River and Angola.

These discoveries raised João's hopes that the southern tip of Africa would soon be reached, enabling Portuguese caravels to cross the Indian Ocean. He dispatched agents to India by land to gain advance information and sent Bartolomeu Dias with three ships to explore beyond the discoveries of Diego Cão. A storm drove Dias' ships far south into the Atlantic. When they swung east to seek land, they found themselves at the continent's end. They sailed along the eastern coast of Africa for a short distance before turning back and rounding the Cape of Good Hope on the return voyage to Portugal.

Dias' success was not followed immediately by an expedition to India. It was necessary, first of all, to design and build a new type of vessel for the long voyage, a task that consumed several years. Domestic affairs also distracted João's attentions. In 1490 Afonso, his only legitimate son, married Isabel of Castile, daughter of Fernando and Isabel. João's last hope of uniting the peninsular kingdoms under a single monarch depended upon this union, but Afonso died a short while later after falling from his horse.

Christopher Columbus visited João's court and proposed a voyage of discovery to the west under Portuguese sponsorship. His expectations of reward were extravagant, and the Portuguese already had many skilled navigators in their service as well as ample reason to believe that the riddle of the African route to the Orient was nearly solved. After careful consideration, João and his counselors declined the offer.

While preparations for the voyage around Africa to India were still in progress, Columbus set out on his famous first voyage under the aegis of the crown of Castile. In March 1493 Columbus in his storm-tossed *Niña* stopped at Portugal on the return voyage and reported to João his success in reaching the Orient by sailing west. Irritated at the prospect of seeing a century of Portuguese enterprise lost as a result of this belated voyage, João's courtiers suggested that Columbus be assassinated. João refused to countenance such a drastic measure—partly, perhaps, because he did not believe Columbus' story—and he permitted the Castilian admiral to continue his journey.

Fernando and Isabel lost no time in seeking support of their pretensions from Rome. Pope Alexander VI, Aragonese by birth, replied by drawing the first line demarking the areas of discovery and conquest open to Castile. In his bull *Inter caetera* he granted the Castilians rights to new lands beyond a line 100 leagues west and south of the Azores and Cape Verde islands. Presumably Portugal was to enjoy similar rights east and north of the line, but these rights were not specifically mentioned. In a later bull, *Dudem siquidem*, Portugal's rights were reduced to posts already held in Africa.

Dom João did not protest to Rome this apparent favoritism, but he applied directly to Fernando and Isabel. Behind his peaceful request for a negotiated modification of the line was the threat of a naval war in which Portugal would enjoy an obvious supremacy. Fernando and Isabel procrastinated, but in 1494 finally agreed to the Treaty of Tordesillas, in which the Line of Demarcation was drawn from north to south 370 leagues west of the Cape Verde islands. East of this line any newly discovered lands would belong to Portugal; west of it, to Castile, regardless of the nationality of the discoverer. Though nothing was known of Brazil at this time, the new treaty was to give Portugal claim to part of the Brazilian coast when that land was discovered six years later. Dom João was concerned mainly with securing for Portugal the sea route to the Orient by way of Africa, which Portuguese mariners had been nearly a century in discovering. It was not until 1529 that Portugal and Castile had learned enough geography to separate their oriental claims by a similar line on the other side of the world.

Soon after the Treaty of Tordesillas had been signed Dom João fell ill, and it became clear that he would not live to see Portuguese ships sail to India and return. He preferred to pass his crown to an illegitimate son, Jorge, rather than to the queen's brother Manoel, duke of Beja. But the queen insisted, and she had her way with the ailing monarch. When Dom João died, Manoel I assumed the crown, and the House of Beja replaced that of Aviz as the royal dynasty.

One of Dom Manoel's first acts was to follow the lead of Fernando and Isabel in expelling from his realms Jews, whose value to Portuguese commerce, arts, and medicine was well known. At first he seemed committed to a lenient policy. Yet when their expulsion was made a condition for his marriage to Princess Isabel of Castile, widow of his nephew Afonso, he called a council to consider the matter. The disadvantages of expulsion were weighed against hopes of securing the Castilian crown for the House of Beja. The Jews lost. In 1496 Dom Manoel decreed that all unbaptized Jews and Moslems must leave his kingdom within ten months.

Before the edict was carried out, Dom Manoel ordered all Jewish children of less than fourteen years seized and prepared for baptism. This inconsiderate act merely increased the legacy of bitterness. The *Cristãos Nôvos* (New Christians, recent converts to Christianity) were likely to harbor deep-seated resentments which would endure for years, even generations. But Dom Manoel ordered that the New Christians be given twenty years in which to become properly instructed and to display the completeness of their conversion, and in this fashion he softened somewhat the general harshness of his policy.

In July 1497 a squadron of four ships was finally ready to sail to India on an expedition originally planned by João II and Admiral Estevão da Gama. Both king and mariner were now dead. Dom Manoel gave command of the expedition to Vasco da Gama, the admiral's son. To gain more favorable winds and to avoid the contrary currents along the African coast, Gama sailed far out into the Atlantic. By November his ships rounded the Cape of Good Hope. After visiting Moslem ports at Mozambique, Mombasa, and Malindi, they turned eastward across the Indian Ocean toward

15

Hindustan. In May 1498 the ships anchored near Calicut. Arab merchants, who dominated the eastern trade, greeted the Portuguese with surprise and profanity.

Only two of the four ships were able to complete the return voyage to Portugal. Two-thirds of the crews succumbed. The cargoes of the two ships were rich, however; the future of Portuguese trade with India promised great gains in spite of competition with the Arabs and the difficulties of the arduous voyage.

In 1500 Dom Manoel dispatched a larger fleet under command of Pedro Alvares Cabral to follow up the initial contact with India. Cabral, profiting from his predecessor's experiences, turned his fleet far westward after leaving the Cape Verdes to take advantage of the more favorable winds and currents.

Heavy winds blew Cabral's ships farther west than he had planned. Early in 1500 Cabral's men sighted land—presumably an uncharted island, but actually the western extremity of the Brazilian coast. Since it fell in the area consigned to Portugal by the Treaty of Tordesillas and because it lay near the flank of the route to India, Cabral decided to delay his voyage to learn more.

Two men carried trade goods ashore. After impatiently awaiting their return for a week, Cabral sent out a search party—but the party returned without finding the missing men. As the men were being rowed out to the ships, one of them remained on the beach, surrounded by a throng of admiring native women. While his initially envious companions watched, the women clubbed him to death, and in a short time carved, cooked, and devoured him. The well-fed women signalled to the shocked Portuguese that they had been equally pleased with the first two men sent ashore.

Cabral, his enthusiasm for the newly-discovered land badly jolted, nevertheless went through the ceremony of claiming it for his monarch, Dom Manoel. He had a report prepared for the king and sent it to Portugal in one of his supply ships. The savage people, misnamed Indians by Columbus, seemed to have no riches comparable to the fabled East. They were sorely in need of Christianizing, but with the wealth of India waiting to be carried home in Portuguese caravels, it would be enough to hasten their conversion at some future and more convenient time.

No one cared to volunteer for the project of learning more of the native customs, for it seemed likely that instruction would end abruptly with the first lesson. Yet such study was necessary. In his fleet Cabral had thoughtfully brought a number of *degredados* (expendable men, such as exiled convicts) to "volunteer" for such projects. Two of these unhappy men were set ashore to learn at first hand the picturesque customs and strange language of the savages who occupied the land. Cabral ordered the fleet on its way to India, leaving further exploration of Santa Cruz, as he named the supposed island, to future Portuguese adventurers.

2/Early Colonial Brazil

CABRAL'S "ISLAND" OF VERA CRUZ OR SANTA CRUZ was found to possess brazilwood, from which a brick-red dye was made. The land came to be called "Brazil," from the name of the tree. Amerigo Vespucci inspected it in 1501 and discovered little that could be exploited, except dyewood, monkeys, and parrots. The king declared brazilwood a royal monopoly and in 1503 granted a profitable concession to exploit the dyewood trade to Fernão de Noronha, a New Christian whom the king ennobled. Many New Christians went to Brazil in the service of Noronha.

The pressures on Jews and New Christians in Portugal forced hundreds to emigrate, much to the advantage of Amsterdam and Brazil. Many sought haven in the New World wilderness, where they could conduct the forbidden rites of their fathers far from the prying eyes of the dreaded familiars of the Holy Office. The majority of the pioneers who made Bahia and Pernambuco the most successful of the early settlements were New Christians. They maintained contacts with friends and relatives in Amsterdam, and these contacts contributed to the commercial success of the colony. They gave a purely agricultural aspect to the conquest of Brazil and thus determined much of its future.

Discovery and colonization of the New World introduced a new phase of European colony planting. Earlier colonies were merely trading posts to facilitate commerce in the products of some region. In Brazil, since there were no such products to be traded, it was necessary to produce trade items, which meant organizing production for the benefit of European commerce. The *fazenda* (plantation), monoculture, and slave labor would become characteristic elements of Brazilian sugar production, and the same system would later be extended to mining. Brazil thus came into being as a producer of goods for international trade, establishing the Portuguese as the first Europeans to undertake large-scale agriculture in the New World.

Planting settlements in Brazil was complicated and costly. The only opportunity for immediate gain was in the brazilwood trade, and since the trees in any area were soon cut down that trade did not result in permanent settlements. In some regions there were Indian wars: even though most of the coastal tribes were of the Tupí-Guaraní linguistic family, common language did not make for peace and friendship among them. The Indians were also cannibals and soon developed a taste for the Portuguese. When Frenchmen, who captured Portuguese caravels loaded with brazilwood, came to the Brazilian coast to collect additional wood, they got along well with the Indians. As elsewhere in the New World, Indians were to be instrumental to opposing sides in colonial wars between Europeans, thus ultimately contributing to their own destruction.

There were no high civilizations in Brazil; life was exceedingly simple. The staple food was manioc, from the Tupí *mandi* (bread) and *óca* (house). This starchy tuber was grown from cuttings which needed practically no care; it could be dug up and stored indefinitely or left in the ground without spoiling. Since the best variety contained a deadly poison, it required some ingenuity to develop a technique for making it safe to eat. Manioc, the source of tapioca, became the main food of the Europeans in the early years of colonization, and the Portuguese made of it a sea biscuit for use on voyages. Europeans adopted the hammock, invented by Brazilian Indians, for use in ships. The Indians' main contributions to Brazilian culture were made largely in the sixteenth century, but the Brazilian vocabulary still contains many thousands of Indian words.

The Indians had two customs particularly distasteful to zealous Portuguese priests—polygamy and cannibalism. When priests tried to convince Indians of the joys of monogamy, the natives asked embarrassing questions about the loose-living Portuguese. Cannibalism, too, was difficult to eliminate if Indians were to serve as allies in wars. Some priests tried to baptize captives, reasoning that saving their souls was better than nothing, but the Indians refused to allow this sacrilege partly on the grounds that baptism spoiled the flavor of their victims.

Between 1500 and 1530 many Portuguese ships visited the Brazilian coast to collect dyewoods and to trade with the Indians,

COLORADO MOUNTAIN COLLEGE
LRC---WEST CAMPUS
Glenwood Springs, Colo. 81601

216

exception of Tiradentes, six of the seven condemned to hang had their sentences commuted to lighter punishments. No poets comparable to the *Escola Mineira* arose during the remainder of the colonial era.

There were sculptors as well as poets in eighteenth-century Brazil, and the most famed was Antônio Francisco Lisboa, or "Aleijadinho" as he was known. Leprosy cost him the fingers of both hands, but he continued his work with hammer and chisel strapped to his wrists. Aleijadinho's work was mostly religious, and his figures of saints won him widespread recognition. He was also a noted architect and designer of churches, and his school of master carvers trained a multitude of disciples. Another famous sculptor of the era was the mulatto Valentín da Fonseca e Silva of Rio de Janeiro, who had been trained in Portugal. Like Aleijadinho, he was an architect as well as sculptor.

Another unique conspiracy occurred in Bahia in 1798. What set it apart was not poets but literate mulatto artisans. So many of them were tailors that the incident was called the "Conspiracy of the Tailors." They talked of liberty, equality, and fraternity, free trade, and similar subversive concepts. For such radical and treasonous talk forty-nine were arrested, four executed, and many exiled. The Conspiracy of the Tailors illustrated the surprising degree to which European revolutionary ideas had spread among the ordinary people of Bahia.

It was not until the end of the eighteenth century that the new learning actually came to be taught in a Brazilian school, the Seminary of Olinda. The seminary was the creation of José Joaquim de Cunha de Azeredo Coutinho, who was born in 1742 near Rio de Janeiro of a *fazendeiro* family. When his father died, he took over management of the family *fazenda* and *engenho*, but Pombal's reform of the University of Coimbra made him determined to attend that university. In 1775, at the age of thirty-three, he renounced his substantial inheritance and departed for Coimbra.

Azeredo Coutinho arrived at Coimbra during the height of ferment over the Pombaline reforms. The methods of Descartes, emphasizing experimentation, and the ideas of the French physiocrats were then widely discussed. Azeredo embraced these ideas and became thoroughly a man of the Enlightenment.

Ordained a priest, Azeredo Coutinho later was appointed to a post with the Holy Office in Lisbon. He wrote a number of essays on the Brazilian economy, including "A Memorial on the Price of

Sugar" (1791), a cogent and convincing argument against the proposal to fix the price of sugar, and "An Economic Essay on the Commerce of Portugal and Her Colonies" (1794). His essays were translated into several languages and his name became well known to European intellectuals. More significantly, his economic ideas were to have an influence in creating a desire for independence among Brazilians, for they made it clear that imperial trade restrictions were injuring the colony for the benefit of the metropolis.

In 1800, shortly after Azeredo Coutinho arrived in Bahia as bishop, he opened the Seminary of Olinda, housing it in a former Jesuit academy. This school, called by some the "New Coimbra," offered a wide range of subjects, including mathematics, mineralogy, and French. Possibly because the prince regent did not approve of the Seminary of Olinda, he recalled Azeredo Coutinho to Portugal to serve in another important post. The school continued, however, and its graduates, mostly priests, would be in the vanguard of subsequent revolutionary movements in Pernambuco and prominent among the martyrs.

Once again events in Europe were to have repercussions in Brazil. After the defeat of the French and Spanish navies off Cape Trafalgar in 1805, Napoleon, abandoning his plan to invade England, introduced his "Continental System" with hopes of closing all European ports to English commerce. His armies were sent into any country that refused to cooperate. Napoleon demanded—and received—permission to send his armies across northern Spain to Portugal. With Marshal Adoche Junot marching rapidly toward Lisbon, Dom João, serving as regent for his demented mother Maria, accepted Britain's offer to escort the royal family to Brazil. The Portuguese nobility, seeing the royal family board the waiting ships and feeling a sudden urge to travel, hurried on board without taking time to pack their belongings. The ships, as a result, were greatly overcrowded; the lack of adequate water or food made the voyage a miserable one for all.

Early in 1808 the refugee court arrived at Bahia. The Brazilians there welcomed Dom João and offered to build a palace for him if he would make the city the capital of Brazil once more. Learning that the people of Rio de Janeiro were preparing the jail for the royal family (no other building was large enough to house the royal staff), Dom João almost accepted the Bahians' offer. Before leaving Bahia for Rio de Janeiro, Dom João paraded the royal family, among them the mad Maria. For all his flabbiness and procrastination, Dom João knew what was expected of a monarch, and he came through on such occasions. Maria was carried unwillingly from the ship and placed in a carriage. As they paraded through the streets she saw people kneeling and concluded that it was a funeral, her own! Her exclamations made this parade the most memorable ever witnessed in Bahia.

Dom João loved Brazil from the start, and he was greatly admired by the Brazilians—a totally new and enjoyable experience for him. Carlota, his wife, detested not only Brazil, but her flabby husband as well. As a fattish youth Dom João had appeared melancholy and monkish, finding his chief pleasure in playing Gregorian chants on the organ. Carlota, flat-chested and hirsute, was "one of nature's marvels"; as one uncharitable courtier remarked, "Her mother must have caught the eye of an ourang-outang." These handicaps did not prevent her from being a notorious and successful man-chaser; indeed, the paternity of all of the royal children except the first was beyond the ability of even a statistician to ascertain. The wife of the French ambassador to Lisbon made the feline comment that "The interesting thing about the royal family is that one child never resembles a brother or sister." Carlota's scandalous behavior finally drove Dom João to confine her in a convent.

The coming of the royal family was the most important event in the whole colonial period, for it marked the end of the colonial era and prepared the way for independence and nationhood. Of all the colonies in the Western Hemisphere, Brazil was the only one to which a European prince came to rule before independence. The presence of the royal family set Brazil apart from her Spanish American neighbors in many ways, especially in transforming it from a sleepy colony to the nerve center of the Portuguese empire. On the recommendation of the Brazilian José da Silva Lisboa, a disciple of Adam Smith, Dom João issued a decree opening Brazil's ports to the ships of friendly nations and revoked earlier decrees against manufacture. Both agriculture and commerce expanded rapidly.

While Dom João and the royal family were settling into their new home, Europeans bore witness to a series of dramatic military and political events. Soon after the royal family departed, Junot occupied Lisbon. Sporadic guerrilla warfare continued against the French, with Britain sending arms and an expeditionary force under Sir Arthur Wellesley, later duke of Wellington, to cooperate with the guerrillas. Wellington soon devised tactics for defeating the previously invincible French armies. Knowing that the French would always attack if an enemy was at hand, his strategy was to maneuver near to a French force and then move into an impregnable defensive position. When the French hurled themselves at his army again and again in futile charges, their ranks were decimated.

In Spain, meanwhile, Napoleon summoned the abdicated Charles IV and Ferdinand VII to Bayonne, where he forced both to surrender their claims to the Spanish throne in favor of his brother Joseph, king of Naples. Joseph was a far better monarch than Ferdinand, but because of their uncompromising attachment to legitimacy the Spaniards refused to accept him, even though he had been imposed by the much-feared Napoleon. The Portuguese and Spaniards were the first Europeans to have the courage to stand up to the all-conquering Corsican. As guerrilla warfare continued in the Iberian peninsula, despite the fact that Napoleon shot a few of his marshals to encourage the others and even went to the peninsula to take command himself, other peoples, such as the Prussians, took heart. The seeds of Napoleon's downfall were planted in the peninsular campaigns.

The Portuguese and British together drove the French out of Portugal and then followed them into Spain to aid the Spanish armies. In 1814 Napoleon surrendered to the allies, and Ferdinand the Desired returned to Spain. He immediately abolished the liberal Constitution of 1812 and persecuted all liberals, including those who had risked their lives to preserve his crown. Too late many Spaniards realized that Joseph the Rejected was much to be preferred to Ferdinand the Desired.

Under Dom João Brazil changed rapidly. He had factories built and established a royal museum, a medical school, a botanical garden, a naval academy, and the *Gazeta do Rio de Janeiro*, Brazil's first newspaper. A cultural commission was invited from France and other European nations for his coronation as João VI in 1816, after his mother's death, and this commission later established the Academy of Fine Arts.

Music was held in particularly high esteem by Dom João and the royal court. In 1808 the prince regent appointed the mulatto José Maurício Nunes Garcia from Rio de Janeiro as inspector of music of the Royal Chapel and later as royal preacher. A priest and one of the most noted musicians of his day, José Maurício wrote sacred music and trained singers. He composed more than two hundred works that were performed in the Royal Chapel. In 1811 Dom João invited Marcos Portugal, the noted Portuguese composer, to Brazil. Perhaps sensing a rival, Marcos Portugal treated José Maurício with scorn and damaged his prestige. In 1816 a famous German pianist and composer who had come to Brazil with the cultural commission was of a more generous nature. He immediately acknowledged José Maurício's talents and declared that Brazilians did not appreciate the great artist in their midst. When he returned to Portugal, Dom João expressed regret that he had not brought José Maurício to Lisbon.

Dom João also founded a public lottery to finance charities, lifted the duty on foreign books, and created the Bank of Brazil. The bank was the first in Brazil, and it became Dom João's private purse. Brazilians were suspicious of banks and reluctant to risk their money in them, so Dom João asked Fernando Carneiro Leão, a member of a prominent Brazilian family, to be the first depositor. Since Dona Carlota was also calling on him for services of a purely social nature, Carneiro Leão could not refuse Dom João's request. He developed an interest in banking and later served as president of the Bank of Brazil.

Britain was the only nation able to take much advantage of the opening of Brazil's ports. Since the French had cut off most British trade with the continent, British merchants flooded the Brazilian market with unsalable goods, such as ice skates and woollen cloth. Many merchants lost money, and they blamed their losses on Brazilian ingratitude. In 1810 Dom João and Britain signed a commercial treaty giving the British an advantage over others who might trade with Brazil: British goods incurred a maximum duty of 15 percent while others were subject to a minimum of 20 percent. Lord Strangford, who negotiated the treaty, also insisted that British subjects have the right of trial by British judges in Brazilian courts. Gradually an antipathy for the British arose, which increased when they began pressuring Brazil to end the slave trade. Brazilians found that having Britain for a step-mother was no great improvement over having Portugal as a mother.

Although there were many capable Brazilians, Dom João did not appoint any of them to high office, for he had an excess supply of Portuguese nobles available. This exclusion of Brazilians, together with Portuguese pretensions of superiority, kindled the fires of anti-Portuguese feelings that would persist until Brazilians cast off all allegiance to the mother country.

When the Spanish American Wars of Independence began in 1810, Dom João perceived an opportunity to fulfill an old Portuguese ambition by extending his rule over the *Banda Oriental.* In 1811 he sent an army into the area, but the British persuaded him to withdraw it the following year. Dona Carlota was also plotting to get control of the whole Río de la Plata region, but her plans came to nothing. Late in 1816 Dom João sent an army into the *Banda Oriental* again, which early the next year entered Montevideo. In 1821 the whole region was incorporated into Brazil as the *Cisplatina* province (the province this side of the Plata).

In 1815, in order to receive proper recognition at the Congress of Vienna, Metternich suggested that Dom João raise Brazil to the rank of kingdom, coequal with Portugal. For Brazil this was a crucial step, and Brazilians were determined never again to assume the status of colonials. Although British and Portuguese troops had liberated Portugal several years before he succeeded to his mother's crown in 1816, Dom João was still in no hurry to return to the troubled kingdom. In Brazil he was highly regarded; he would not be in Portugal.

When it was time to find a bride for Dom Pedro, his oldest son, Dom João sent the marquês de Marialva to Europe to see what match could be arranged. Dom João loosened the royal purse strings, and Marialva spent so freely in Vienna that he convinced the Austrians Brazil was a veritable gold mine. The prize for whom this ostentation was intended was Archduchess Leopoldina Josepha Carolina of Hapsburg, daughter of the Austrian emperor, sister of Marie Louise Bonaparte, and niece of Marie Antoinette. There were French and Russian princesses available, but the Austrian connection was most important as a counter to British influence.

Leopoldina was favorably impressed by Dom Pedro's portrait and what Marialva had to say about him. Dom Pedro was equally impressed by the portrait of the blonde beauty that Marialva sent to Brazil, but unfortunately it was not Leopoldina's portrait. They were married by proxy. When Dom Pedro saw his bride for the first time he could scarcely conceal his shock and disappointment. Leopoldina was plumpish of figure, and she made no use of beauty aids. She was kind-hearted and intelligent, however, and Brazilians loved her. The royal couple performed their dynastic duties and produced a number of children, beginning with Maria da Glória in 1819. But Dom Pedro, who had inherited his mother's amorous inclinations, sired another dynasty outside of wedlock.

Opposition to Portuguese rule in Pernambuco continued to grow. There were many sources of discontent with the Portuguese, some as old as the War of the *Mascates* a century earlier. Cotton planters had enjoyed a brief period of prosperity during the War of 1812 between Britain and the United States, and they realized how much better it would be if they could grow what they wished and sell to the best market. Furthermore, since Azeredo Coutinho's founding of the Seminary of Olinda, many had learned to speak French, and French books and ideas circulated freely throughout the captaincy of Pernambuco. In 1814 a Masonic lodge had been established in Recife, and it became a center for discussing liberal and republican ideas.

In 1817 there was a republican revolt in Recife led by priests and Masons, most of them graduates of the Seminary of Olinda. Governor Caetano Pinto of Pernambuco was warned of the conspiracy, but before he could suppress it he was seized and sent to Rio de Janeiro. The rebels declared a republic and sent agents to Argentina, Britain, and the United States to obtain arms and support. The provinces of Alagoas and Paraíba threw in their lot with Pernambuco, but the royal navy blockaded the ports while a sizable force marched from Bahia. The rebellion was crushed with severity, but republican ideas could not be eliminated by repression.

Dom João lingered on in Brazil, although the French had long been expelled from Portugal and Napoleon's fate had been sealed on St. Helena. He had little desire to return to the intrigues of the Portuguese court and he dreaded the return voyage. Meanwhile, the Portuguese became increasingly jealous of Brazil and ever more insistent that he return.

European events finally forced the monarch's return to Portugal. In the year 1820 there was a rash of rebellions against absolute monarchies in southern Europe. In January Spanish troops under Colonel Rafael Riego mutinied and forced Ferdinand VII to restore the Constitution of 1812. Frightened, Ferdinand complied, but secretly begged the French for help. Three years later a French army rescued him and restored Spanish absolutism. Inspired by the Riego revolt, Portuguese liberals rebelled in Oporto late in 1820 and demanded a constitution. The movement spread to Lisbon, and Dom João was faced with the choice of returning to Portugal to fight for his crown or of losing it. Reluctantly he chose to return. Before leaving Brazil, however, he called for the election of deputies to the *Côrtes Gerais,* which the liberals had scheduled to meet the following year. A Brazilian mob demanded that he swear allegiance to the Portuguese constitution, which had yet to be written. When the deputies-elect of the *Côrtes* met, they demanded that Brazil have a separate constitution and forced him to proclaim the Spanish Constitution of 1812 for Brazil. The army dispersed the assembly, however, and demanded that Dom João again proclaim the Portuguese constitution.

Late in April 1821 Dom João and Dona Carlota embarked for Portugal, the former sadly, the latter with glee. For a decade Dom João had watched the breakup of the Spanish American empire as one colony after another threw off royal authority and gained its independence. He suspected that some Brazilians might harbor similar desires. Before leaving Brazil, therefore, he gave Dom Pedro some fatherly advice. If the Brazilians should demand independence, Dom Pedro should take the lead and retain control of the government. It seems likely, too, that they agreed that in this event Dom Pedro would, when the opportunity arose, reunite the two kingdoms. Within a year he was to heed his father's sage advice.

4 / The First Empire

DOM PEDRO, TO WHOM BRAZIL'S FATE WAS ENtrusted, was in many ways an excellent leader, although he was often torn between conviction and impulse. Despite his lack of formal education, he was convinced that constitutional monarchy was the best form of government for Brazil, but having been raised in an absolutist household, his immediate reactions, unfortunately, were always those of an absolutist prince. He perceived the growing sentiment for independence, especially when the Portuguese *Côrtes* tried to force Brazil back into a position of colonial inferiority; before committing himself unequivocally to independence, however, he wanted assurance that Brazil would become a monarchy rather than a republic. In 1821, the very year he became regent, Agustín Iturbide established an empire in Mexico, but the shortlived fiasco did not make prospects for the institution of monarchy in the New World seem very promising.

A Brazilian recently returned from Portugal became Dom Pedro's chief adviser and the "Patriarch of Brazilian Independence." He was the *Paulista* José Bonifácio de Andrada e Silva, the brilliant and renowned scientist who had studied law at Coimbra. The Portuguese government sent him and two others to study mining techniques throughout Europe, and he arrived in Paris during the second year of the French Revolution. He also studied in Saxony, Bohemia, Hungary, Prussia, Sweden, Norway, Scotland, and Spain, before returning to Portugal in 1800.

José Bonifácio was authorized to create a course in metallurgy at Coimbra, and was named intendant general of mines and metals for all of Portugal. When the French invaded Portugal in 1807 he joined the resistance and distinguished himself as a guerrilla warrior. In 1819, at the age of fifty-six, he returned to Brazil after an absence of thirty-six years. At first José Bonifácio favored a dual monarchy, but when Portuguese intransigence made this impossible, he embraced the cause of complete independence. His knowledge and experience aided him in skillfully guiding Brazil through the difficult steps to independence without serious turmoil.

In planning for independence José Bonifácio was well aware of the pitfalls to avoid. In 1820, "The Terrible Year Twenty" in Buenos Aires, that anarchic Argentine province had twelve governors, and the national government experienced complete disintegration. By using Dom Pedro as the instrument for securing independence under a stable and orderly monarchy, José Bonifácio was certain that Brazil could avoid the republican anarchy that plagued Argentina. Dom Pedro appointed him minister of kingdom and foreign relations, making him the first Brazilian to reach the rank of minister.

Dom Pedro set about governing Brazil as if it were already an independent kingdom, lifting the duty on foreign books and abolishing censorship. He ordered the teaching of law courses in São Paulo and Olinda and called for introduction of the Lancastrian system of education, a method of using students to help with instruction to compensate for a shortage of experienced teachers. He also encouraged immigration, which added a number of small colonies of Europeans to those established after the coming of the royal family. Among the immigrants were ex-mercenary soldiers, primarily Germans, who were given tracts of land as payment for their services.

The Portuguese were not at all pleased with Dom Pedro's actions, and trouble soon started. In 1821 the *Côrtes Gerais* of Portugal met after an interlude of more than a century, and for the first time included Brazilians as well as delegates from other Portuguese colonies. Only forty-six of the sixty-nine Brazilians authorized to attend arrived in Lisbon, and they were rudely treated by the public and the press. The *Côrtes,* for all its professed liberalism—it favored constitutional monarchy—was also extremely hostile toward Brazil and determined that it should be deprived of its coequal status with Portugal. The members of the *Côrtes* attempted to abolish the privileges granted by Dom João and devised other ways to weaken the kingdom, such as ordering military commanders to report directly to Lisbon rather than Rio de Janeiro, limiting commerce, permitting the creation of juntas of government in place of provincial governors, and abolishing the institutions Dom João had established when Brazil was the center of the empire. The *Côrtes* also commanded that Dom Pedro's ministers be appointed from Lisbon. To counteract these efforts José Bonifácio declared all provinces under the authority of the government in Rio de Janeiro. São Paulo and Minas Gerais agreed, but such cities in Maranhão, Bahia, and Cisplatina, in which there were still Portuguese garrisons, adhered to the *Côrtes*.

Late in 1821 the *Côrtes* ordered Dom Pedro to return to Portugal to "complete his education," but the Masons circulated a petition asking him to remain. The first Masonic lodge in Rio had been established in 1800, and it included eminent men from civil, military, and ecclesiastical circles. The Grand Orient, with three lodges, was the principal Masonic organization, but it was sharply divided into liberal and conservative factions. José Bonifácio headed the conservatives and Gonçalves Ledo led the ultraliberal group, which was numerically the stronger of the two and preferred a republic or a limited monarchy. José Bonifácio was grand master of the Orient but Ledo, as senior warden, usurped control. Both factions endeavored to gain influence over Dom Pedro. When the Masons called on him to remain in Brazil he was willing. "Fico," he replied. "I will remain." From this time on Brazil was virtually independent, but José Bonifácio and Dom Pedro sought some event to dramatize independence and win popular support for the government. The Portuguese garrison in Rio was determined to seize Dom Pedro and ship him to Portugal, but the aroused *cariocas,* together with local militia units, forced the garrison to embark without him. There were also Portuguese garrisons in other cities, and these would have to be dealt with before all of Brazil became independent.

Dom Pedro created a council of *procuradores* (representatives of the provinces) to serve as an advisory body and to bring about greater unity of purpose in the country as a whole. Only a few provinces appointed delegates, for some feared to do so and others were opposed. Without waiting for others to arrive, the three provisional delegates from Rio de Janeiro passed a resolution asking the prince regent to call for the election of delegates to a constituent and legislative assembly, which he did immediately. This was perhaps the most decisive of the various acts in the process leading to Brazilian independence. All that was lacking was a formal declaration announcing the rejection of Portuguese authority. The *Côrtes* regarded the meeting of provincial delegates as a revolutionary action, which it was, and revoked its measures. The *Côrtes* also ordered the arrest and trial of the São Paulo junta and others that had disobeyed its edicts.

The Brazilian deputies to the *Côrtes Gerais,* feeling the intense hostility toward them in Lisbon, did not advocate Brazilian interests, nor did they reflect the growing anger in Brazil over the actions of the *Côrtes.* In February 1822, however, the São Paulo delegation arrived and the situation changed, for with it was Antônio Carlos Ribeiro de Andrada, brother of José Bonifácio and the most effective Brazilian orator of his time.

Antônio Carlos immediately assumed the role of spokesman for the whole Brazilian delegation. He presented a plan, drafted by his brother, calling for a dual monarchy of Portugal and Brazil, but the Portuguese rejected this out of hand. The Brazilians became stubborn and their outbursts were frequent. By summer it was clear that there was no hope at all of a reconciliation. In September a delegate from Bahia lost his temper and shouted that if the *Côrtes* continued its policies toward Brazil that country would be justified in becoming independent, cutting off trade with Portugal, and allying with Austria, whose powerful minister, Metternich, was the archenemy of constitutional regimes such as the *Côrtes* sought to introduce. *"Passe muito bem, o senhor Brasil"* (Fare thee well, Mr. Brazil), the Portuguese deputies replied. Neither they nor the Brazilians knew that Dom Pedro had already declared Brazil independent.

Some of the Brazilians sought permission to return to Brazil, but the *Côrtes* refused. It was an awkward situation for those who felt that Brazilian independence was near: if they remained they would be expected to sign and swear to the Portuguese constitution, which had been the *Côrtes'* chief accomplishment. Seven deputies, including Antônio Carlos and Father Diogo Feijó, secretly boarded the Falmouth packet and sailed to England. The packet had the reassuring name *Duke of Marlborough,* and the captain was none other than John Bull.

The Brazilian press had begun demanding independence early in 1822. Dom Pedro wrote to Dom João, "It is impossible to keep Brazil and Portugal united by armed force; commerce and mutual reciprocity, on the other hand, make union a certainty. Business interests and a zeal for cooperation form the real basis on which the Luso-Brazilian monarchy must rest." But Dom João was virtually a prisoner of the *Côrtes* and unable to act independently. In May, when Dom Pedro accepted the title "Perpetual Defender of Brazil," José Bonifácio sent letters to foreign nations asking them to open direct relations with Brazil.

The conservative *fazendeiros* preferred to retain some form of union with Portugal providing their economic requirements were met. Because independence seemed certain to come, they saw in monarchy the only hope of maintaining unity, and they were fortunate in having a European prince already at the head of the government. The troublesome question of legitimacy would not arise. The Portuguese were not, however, willing to accept Brazilian independence without a struggle.

When a Greek agent arrived in Lisbon to offer Dom Pedro a crown so that he could lead the struggle for independence against the Turks, the *Côrtes* saw an unexpected opportunity to lure him away from Brazil. It forwarded the request to Dom Pedro, but he did not, as the *Côrtes* hoped, find the offer too flattering to refuse. Too much was happening in Brazil for him to think of leaving. In June Leopoldina described the situation to her father: "Everything here is confusion," she wrote. "On all sides the new principles of liberty and disorder seem to dominate, working toward the formation of a confederation of peoples, patterned after the democratic system of the free states of North America."

Because Minas Gerais and São Paulo were the most populous provinces and did not have Portuguese garrisons, it was vital to José Bonifácio's plans to know the attitudes of the *Mineiros* and *Paulistas* toward monarchy. He persuaded Dom Pedro to visit the two provinces to test reactions. Despite opposition to him in Minas Gerais, where the governing junta refused to recognize his authority, he rode boldly into Vila Rica with a small party, ignoring warnings that his life was in danger. His courage and openhandedness won over the *Mineiros,* who promised him their support. Early in September 1822 he set out for São Paulo, where there had also been disorders.

While Dom Pedro was absent, insulting dispatches arrived from the *Côrtes,* further reducing his authority. On September 7 a messenger overtook him with the dispatches and letters from José Bonifácio and Leopoldina suggesting that the time was ripe for declaring independence. After hastily reading the dispatches Dom Pedro agreed. Ripping the Portuguese colors from his uniform he exclaimed, "The hour is now! Independence or death!" Since he was at the Ipiranga River when the messenger arrived, this declaration is known as the *"Grito de Ipiranga"* (Cry of Ipiranga).

In the same week as the *Grito de Ipiranga* Dom Pedro met and was captivated by Domitila de Castro, a beauty of São Paulo. She had been married at an early age to a narrow-minded officer of the royal guard, by whom she had had two children. Returning from extended duty elsewhere, her husband found her again with child and when quick calculation convinced him that this one was not his, he stabbed her and fled. Thoroughly enamored, Dom Pedro could not wait to install her in Rio. Since Leopoldina said nothing, he believed that his precautions had been successful. But "Titila" wanted the world to know of her exclusive position, and even her ex-husband came to share her good fortune and had to be bought off. The news of Titila's arrival, however, was not kept from Leopoldina, for they shared the same hairdresser and were fitted for maternity dresses the same week. Dom Pedro rewarded his favorite mistress by elevating her to the rank of marquesa de Santos.

Although Titila was the most famous and enduring of the royal mistresses, the list of those sharing the royal couch was impressively long. Among them was the actress Ludovina Custódia, who gave a benefit performance in the emperor's honor and was ravished between acts, causing the curtain to be rung down early.

On December 1 Dom Pedro was crowned emperor of Brazil in a coronation ceremony patterned after that of his hero and brother-in-law, Napoleon. Europeans were scandalized at this deference to the recent scourge of Europe, but Dom Pedro was happily indifferent to European prejudices. He controlled only the southern part of his empire—Rio de Janeiro, Minas Gerais, São Paulo, and Rio Grande do Sul—for Portuguese garrisons and pro-Portuguese groups still controlled or neutralized the other provinces.

The first questions to be resolved concerned the form of government, monarchy or republic, and what branch was to predominate, executive or legislative. Many Masons and others favoring a republic had been disappointed when Dom Pedro decided to remain in Brazil, because this meant that the government would be a monarchy, at least temporarily. There was still the possibility of limiting the monarch's powers, and some of the Masons schemed to achieve this goal.

Because there were no political parties and few organizations of any kind, José Bonifácio persuaded Dom Pedro to become a Mason and join the Grand Orient of Brazil in Rio de Janeiro. Ledo and his ultraliberals, hoping to limit Dom Pedro's powers, engineered Dom Pedro's election as grand master, thus demoting José Bonifácio to assistant grand master. At Dom Pedro's installation Ledo's speech was virtually an ultimatum from the ultraliberals, who, having failed to establish a republic, wanted a limited monarchy in its place.

Ledo's plans included obliging Dom Pedro to swear to uphold the still unfinished constitution, after which the embryonic constitution would be modified sufficiently to give the legislature the leverage it needed to control the emperor. Willing to consider swearing to uphold the constitution, Dom Pedro even gave Ledo three sheets of blank paper with his signature on them. José Bonifácio opposed the scheme, however, and Dom Pedro was furious when Ledo's machinations were explained. He sent for Ledo and demanded the signed sheets. In December 1822 he dissolved the Grand Orient and exiled its leaders. If any check was to be placed on his power, it would have to be provided by the constitution.

Dom Pedro was greatly aided by Lord Thomas Cochrane, tenth earl of Dundonald, the Scottish naval genius who had recently commanded the Chilean naval squadron in that colony's successful bid for independence. As in Chile Lord Cochrane had to improvise a naval force. After one indecisive action with Portuguese warships off Bahia, however, the Portuguese did not again threaten Brazil by sea, and the Bahians finally drove the Portuguese garrison from the city in July 1823. Ridding Brazil of the other Portuguese garrisons from Maranhão to Montevideo was largely Cochrane's work, and as a consequence Brazil became independent without being saddled with militarism. By February 1824, when the Portuguese government ordered its Montevideo garrison to withdraw, royal authority had been established in all of the coastal cities, and the political unity of Brazil had been achieved. The problem would be to maintain it, for the new empire was composed of twenty separate provinces held together by the fragile thread of their attachment to the emperor.

Because he believed in the necessity of a constitution for Brazil, Dom Pedro had called for election of a constituent and legislative assembly in May 1823. The ninety-member body was composed of lawyers and judges, priests, army officers, and a scattering of physicians, landowners, and officials. Most were inexperienced in the legislative process, though a few had served in the *Côrtes*. José Bonifácio and his brothers were active in both the ministry and the assembly. When the delegates met, Dom Pedro informed them bluntly that he would approve of their work only if it was worthy of his respect. Some men doubted that he really wanted a constitution. When the official gazette published decrees signed by Dom João and praised the absolutist movement that had overthrown the Portuguese constitution, their suspicions seemed to be confirmed.

José Bonifácio was cautious about self-government for Brazil, for he feared the anarchy characteristic of Argentina and other Spanish American republics. The more radical Brazilians regarded him as an arch conservative, while the *fazendeiros* considered him too radical because of his opposition to the slave trade and his desire to raise the general standard of living of Brazilian workers. He was, in addition, overbearing and harsh toward his opponents. Dom Pedro, surrounded largely by Portuguese friends, received many complaints against José Bonifácio's high-handed methods. This "kitchen cabinet" finally succeeded in undermining Brazil's ablest statesman.

In July 1823 Dom Pedro annulled a series of José Bonifácio's police measures, driving the Andrada brothers into the opposition. This was one of his first serious mistakes, for he badly needed José Bonifácio's assistance and counsel. Anti-Portuguese feelings increased, and the three Andrada brothers led such an effective attack against Dom Pedro's Portuguese ministers that they resigned. Dom Pedro angrily replaced them with others who were even more pro-Portuguese in outlook.

Relations between Dom Pedro and the assembly worsened rapidly, for the legislators determined to rid Brazil of Portuguese influence by limiting the emperor's power. As his resentment grew, Dom Pedro's patience vanished. Fearing some surprise action, the delegates declared the assembly in permanent session. Dom Pedro retaliated by sending troops to dissolve the assembly and exiling the Andrada brothers to France. The absolutists, who were largely Portuguese, were delighted at the dispersal of the assembly, but in the provinces opposition to Dom Pedro intensified.

In 1823 also, Dom Miguel, Pedro's younger brother, organized a counterrevolution in Portugal to overthrow his father's constitutional regime and restore absolutism under his own rule. Dom João cannily snatched leadership of the movement from Dom Miguel and retained his crown while ridding himself of the obnoxious constitution. Miguel, who had been egged on by Dona Carlota, sought sanctuary in Vienna. By June the *Côrtes* had been disbanded.

The Portuguese assumed that Dom Pedro had sought independence as a result of the ill-considered acts of the *Côrtes* and that he would now be inspired to dissolve the Brazilian assembly (which he did), assert himself as an absolutist prince, and return Brazil to the Portuguese empire. The king sent the Count of Rio Maior to Rio de Janeiro on a "mission of pacification," but he was not allowed to land without first acknowledging Brazil's independence. He returned to Lisbon, his mission a failure.

Since he had promised a constitution, Dom Pedro appointed a committee of Brazilians to complete the assembly's unfinished work. The assembly's constitution had delegated power from the people to the emperor; Dom Pedro's version was granted by the emperor to the people. The constitution, modeled after the French Constitution of 1816, was submitted to the municipal councils for approval, and promulgated in March 1824. The government it established was composed of four branches, the fourth being the "moderating power." The legislative branch or General Assembly included the Senate, whose members the emperor appointed for life from lists submitted by the provinces, and the Chamber of Deputies, the lower house whose members were elected for four-year terms. There was also the Council of State, which served as an advisory body to the emperor. Presidents of provinces, ministers, and bishops were appointed by the emperor.

Under this arrangement the emperor represented both the executive and the moderating power, which made him responsible for preserving balance and harmony in the other branches and in the provinces. He also had veto power and the right to call or prorogue the Chamber of Deputies and the Senate.

Suffrage was limited, but the constitution guaranteed individual freedom and equality before the law. For its day it was liberal as well as flexible, for it could be amended fairly easily. That it was reasonably designed and workable for Brazil is indicated by the fact that it endured until 1889.

The constitution declared Roman Catholicism the religion of the empire; other faiths were permitted if the places of worship did not have the external appearances of churches. The emperor had the right of patronage—the right to appoint bishops and other clergy. The constitution also gave him the authority to approve or disapprove of papal letters and decrees—without his approval these were without effect in Brazil. Dom Pedro sent an emissary to Rome to seek accord with the pope concerning the church in Brazil; he also sought to transfer the dioceses of Pará and Maranhão from dependence on the archbishopric of Lisbon to that of Bahia, and have the emperor named grand master of the Order of Christ, which included the right of patronage.

Regalism, a legacy of Portugal, permeated the Brazilian clergy as well as every political faction. After the Holy See recognized Brazil's independence, a papal bull established the Order of Christ in Brazil and named Dom Pedro grand master as requested. The Chamber of Deputies refused to approve the papal grant to Dom Pedro, resolving that his right of patronage was based on the constitution and not on the fact that he was grand master of the Order of Christ. To the members of the Chamber, Roman control over the Brazilian church was too reminiscent of colonialism.

In 1824 there was another republican revolt in Recife, which proclaimed the "Confederation of the Equator." As in 1817 several currents were involved—regionalism, anti-Portuguese sentiments, and dissatisfaction with both the provincial president Dom Pedro had appointed and the new constitution. The uprising indicated that to the people of the northern provinces subordination to Rio de Janeiro was no improvement over subordination to Lisbon, and that at this early date in his reign Dom Pedro had already lost the confidence of some of his subjects. General Francisco de Lima e Silva and the naval genius Lord Thomas Cochrane made short work of the rebels.

For all his excellent qualities and good intentions Dom Pedro succeeded in alienating one group of Brazilians after another. From the outset he fought with the legislature, especially the Chamber of Deputies, which was trying to lay the basis for true cabinet government with ministerial responsibility placed with itself. It is only fair to say, however, that there was blame on both sides. Some Brazilians were as uncompromising as Dom Pedro. The constitution and parliamentary government were both new to them, and Dom Pedro interpreted the constitution as if he were an absolute monarch. He surrounded himself with dissolute Portuguese, and Portuguese held the principal posts in the administration, judiciary, and army, constantly reminding Brazilians that he had been born in Portugal. Once Brazilians took the view that Dom Pedro was Portuguese rather than Brazilian, they began to identify many of his actions as inspired by Portuguese ambitions. From that time on

Dom Pedro could do little that pleased them. He was able to offend them in many ways, however, causing them to overlook his good qualities and his valuable contributions to the new nation.

After the constitution had been promulgated, the next major problem was recognition. As in the winning of independence, Brazil was again much more fortunate than most Spanish American republics. In January 1824 Dom Pedro sent José Silvestre Rebello to Washington to seek United States recognition, which was granted less than two months after that diplomat's arrival. By itself American recognition signified little, for the United States was no power on either land or sea, and the government was determined to avoid foreign involvement. The real importance of American recognition was that it impelled the British to take the same step for fear of losing trade advantages to the United States.

Obtaining Portuguese recognition was a complicated process, because Portugal was a pawn in a gigantic diplomatic struggle between Britain and the Holy Alliance. In Portugal and Brazil between 1820 and 1825, the "whole European and British diplomacy was exhibited on a miniature stage." Three groups were involved—the absolutists, led by Dom Miguel; the pro-French group, which urged intervention by the Holy Alliance to restore the Spanish and Portuguese empires; and a pro-British group, which turned to Britain for help in finding a solution to the dilemma of Portuguese-Brazilian relations.

The *Miguelistas* were eliminated after their failure to overthrow Dom João. The French party in Lisbon was stronger than the pro-British group, and this complicated the task of British Foreign Minister George Canning. The British had been taken by surprise in 1823 when a French army, with the blessing of the Holy Alliance, crossed the Pyrenees and crushed the Spanish liberal-constitutionalists, restoring Ferdinand VII to absolute power. Canning was determined to check the French, but was committed to his government's policy of nonintervention in Portugal.

If Britain did not intervene in Lisbon, it would mean a triumph for the pro-French party, and if Britain did not recognize Brazilian independence it would be denying an obvious fact and likely would cost the British much of their profitable trade with Brazil. When Portuguese attempts to open negotiations with Brazil were rebuffed because they refused to acknowledge Brazilian independence, Canning reluctantly concluded that he had no choice but to intervene. It was clear that the two countries were committed to irreconcilable positions and that restoration of any form of official relationship between them was impossible. Brazil refused to negotiate without prior recognition of its independence; Portugal refused to negotiate without Brazil's acknowledgment of Portuguese sovereignty.

Dom Pedro turned to Britain for help, while Portugal turned to France and Austria. Metternich tried unsuccessfully to organize a conference of major powers in Paris to deal with the problems of both Spain and Portugal, but Canning refused to participate. Canning then suggested joint Austrian-British mediation, which was accepted, although Austria played only a passive role.

Everyone but the Portuguese regarded Brazilian independence as an accomplished fact. Metternich and Canning agreed to recognize Brazil's independence, but after Portugal had done so. It was left to Canning to persuade the Portuguese government to take this disagreeable step. He was especially concerned with preserving constitutional monarchy in Brazil as a countertrend to the growth of republicanism in the New World. He also wanted to safeguard British commerce against the restoration of colonial mercantilism and to prevent the Holy Alliance and its members from intervening in the former colonies. This complex operation required a hand skilled in diplomatic surgery, but Canning was equal to the task.

In August 1825 the treaty of independence was accepted—for a price to be sure. The price was a secret clause in which Dom Pedro accepted for Brazil the debt of £1,400,000 that Portugal owed Britain, and the payment of £600,000 to Dom João for palaces and other properties left in Brazil. Within a year most of the other European powers had also recognized Brazil, and this recognition was an important factor in maintaining Brazilian stability.

After the treaty for independence was signed, Dom João assumed the title "Honorary Emperor of Brazil," which he resigned in favor of Dom Pedro, and at the same time named his son the heir to the Portuguese crown. Brazilians were outraged by these acts, but they were even more furious when they learned that Dom Pedro had agreed to pay Dom João for his palaces and to assume the Portuguese debt to England. The Chamber of Deputies censured him and the press criticized him in strong language. In all of his treaty-making Dom Pedro showed poor judgment, for the constitution required him to share the negotiation of treaties with the parliament. He understood this to mean that he did the negotiating, signed the treaty, and then allowed parliament to approve it.

He would have been far wiser to have allowed members of parliament to wrestle with some of the sticky problems and to have shared responsibility for the decisions, for they probably could not have obtained better terms. As it was, the agreements were "Dom Pedro's treaties," and the anger they generated was directed at him.

In 1826 France and Brazil concluded a commercial treaty which contained some perpetual clauses, a sure source of future disagreement. In March 1827 a new commercial treaty between Britain and Brazil was signed, reconfirming the Anglo-Portuguese agreements of 1817 concerning the right of British cruisers to search slave ships and the establishment of an Anglo-Brazilian admiralty court at Rio de Janeiro. Brazil agreed to end the slave trade three years after ratification, which meant that after 1830 slaves could no longer legally be brought to Brazil. Brazilians were fearful that the end of the slave traffic would mean the ruin of agriculture, and that three years was much too short a period to make an adjustment to free labor. Because of an upswing in the sugar trade the number of slaves imported increased substantially after 1830, reaching as high as 50,000 a year. Dom Pedro, as usual, negotiated the treaties and presented them to parliament after ratification, which meant that the lawmakers had no part at all in making the treaties and they were not held responsible for the unpopular aspects of the agreements. Only in 1831 did this situation change.

Dom João died in March 1826 and the regency proclaimed Dom Pedro as Pedro IV of Portugal, although there were justifiable doubts as to the legality of the act. After consulting the Council of State, which opposed his acceptance of the Portuguese crown, Dom Pedro accepted it, confirmed the regency, and proclaimed general amnesty. If he had hoped to reunite the two kingdoms, as seems likely, he soon found that there was no possible way to accomplish this. The assembly's unfinished constitution had contained a clause stating that if the Brazilian emperor accepted the Portuguese crown, he forfeited that of Brazil. Although this clause was deleted from Dom Pedro's constitution, it was clearly the intention of the Brazilian people. If he was to retain the Portuguese crown, he must reside in Lisbon; but if he returned to Portugal, he would surely lose the imperial crown of Brazil.

Caught in this dilemma Dom Pedro reluctantly abdicated in favor of his daughter Maria da Glória on two conditions. The first was that his brother Miguel, whom he named regent, would marry her. The second was that the constitution he granted Portugal would be accepted by the Portuguese people. Neither of these conditions was ever fulfilled, for there was a legitimist-absolutist revolt against Dom Pedro. In 1828 Dom Miguel usurped his niece's crown and began persecuting liberals. Dom Pedro's efforts in behalf of Portugal further antagonized Brazilians, and he also roused the resentment of all European governments except Britain's for granting Portugal a constitution. Metternich declared that it was "in the highest degree improper that a New World potentate should introduce a constitution into the Old World, turn[ing] a strict monarchy into a limited one."

Another source of conflict between Dom Pedro and Brazilians was the war with Argentina over the *Cisplatina* province. Early in 1825 Juan Antonio Lavalleja and the "Thirty-three Immortals" crossed the Paraná River into Cisplatina and raised a revolt. The rebels declared the *Banda Oriental* incorporated into the United Provinces of Río de la Plata, and the Argentines accepted it, which meant a war with Brazil for which the United Provinces were totally unprepared. Dom Pedro sent his fleet to blockade Buenos Aires, but the war was costly and thoroughly unpopular. To Brazilians it signified the spending of their blood and money to fulfill a Portuguese ambition. The blockading squadron committed many violations of international law, and in July 1826 French warships sailed into Rio de Janeiro's harbor to force the government to modify the blockade and to press the claims of French citizens for damages suffered as a result of it. Brazilians held Dom Pedro responsible for the humiliating experience.

The Chamber of Deputies resolutely rejected Dom Pedro's requests for funds and troops enough to prosecute the war effectively. The war continued for three painful years. In the end the cost and sacrifices were in vain, for in 1828, at Britain's urging, the *Banda Oriental* became the independent, orphan state of Uruguay, an unhappy buffer between two large and unfriendly neighbors. To Brazilians the war was a calamity: men and treasure had been wasted in trying to retain a poor province, and that province had been lost.

In 1826, while visiting the war theater, Dom Pedro learned that Dona Leopoldina was gravely ill and hastened back to Rio de Janeiro, but he arrived too late. Before she died, the popular Leopoldina admitted to friends that she had been deeply hurt by Dom Pedro's infidelities, especially his flagrant affair with the marquesa de Santos. Because Dom Pedro was "too Portuguese" to please Brazilians, they frowned on him for what they would have envied and admired in another. Ugly rumors spread that her death had been caused when Dom Pedro allegedly kicked his pregnant wife during a violent quarrel over the marquesa. During the long, chaste, and boring reign of his son Dom Pedro II, however, many Brazilians were to recall the spicy life of the father with nostalgia.

Dom Pedro's exclusive control over the ministry contributed to the Chamber's hostility toward him. In the year of Leopoldina's death the parliament held its first session, and the *Mineiro* Bernardo de Vasconcelos presented a bill in the Chamber requiring ministers and secretaries of state to submit annual reports on their administrations and to attend budget sessions. Although he resented the Chamber's initiative in such matters, Dom Pedro appeared to accept this change in good grace.

In November 1827 he appointed a liberal cabinet selected out of the Chamber of Deputies, according to the wishes of that body. It was headed by Pedro de Araújo Lima and included Antônio Carlos and Martim Francisco de Andrada, who had returned from exile. (José Bonifácio was not restored to grace for another two years.) The ministers willingly submitted reports to the Chamber as requested and appeared before it to answer questions when it summoned them. For a short time it appeared that harmony between Dom Pedro and the Chamber had been achieved.

German and Irish mercenary troops had been lured to Brazil on false promises, and the incredibly brutal treatment they received finally led to violent reprisals. In June 1828, when a German soldier in Rio de Janeiro received 230 lashes for failing to salute an officer, the soldier's company left the barracks and searched for the commandant throughout the city. The Irish troops happily joined in the search, and for the next few days the city was given up to looting, rape, drunkenness, and murder. Eventually the troops were subdued. Most of the Irish were sent back to Ireland, though a few settled elsewhere in Brazil. Many of the Germans joined the German colony of São Leopoldo in Rio Grande do Sul.

After the mutiny Dom Pedro dismissed the minister of war, and the rest of the ministry resigned—an unfortunate event, because it had been well on the way to reconciling the people to Dom Pedro's rule. When the ministers resigned Dom Pedro ignored the Chamber and appointed men of his own choosing without even consulting the deputies.

Financial troubles plagued Brazil throughout Dom Pedro's

reign, for when Dom João and the court departed for Lisbon in 1821, they had carried off most of the banknotes. When these banknotes were presented for redemption, the Bank of Brazil nearly collapsed. Dom Pedro knew nothing of financial matters, and it seemed to him that making money was simply a matter of bringing paper, ink, and a printing press together. Budget deficits were met by fresh issues of paper money with nothing to support it. The problem was aggravated by newly minted copper coins issued at higher than face value. The coins were crude and easy to counterfeit. Eventually the treasury had to call them in, counterfeit along with the genuine. The value of Brazil's currency in foreign exchange declined steadily; gold and silver were driven from circulation. Despite the financial troubles commerce was thriving, in part because of the commercial credit provided by the Bank of Brazil.

In 1829, however, reflecting the usual frontier suspicion of financiers, the parliament ordered the bank liquidated. It had been the only source of commercial credit in Brazil and because nothing was done immediately to replace this vital element for economic development, commerce suffered. Since the treasury now printed worthless paper money, currency continued to depreciate.

After Leopoldina died, Brazilians insisted that Dom Pedro get married again, but not to the marquesa de Santos. The task of finding a suitable bride was entrusted to Felisberto Brant Pontes, marquês de Barbacena. Metternich made this assignment as difficult as possible by pressuring the most likely candidates not to marry Dom Pedro. Barbacena also discovered that no European princess would marry Dom Pedro unless he sent the marquesa away. With the latter an accomplished fact, Barbacena found the ideal bride for his emperor. She was the seventeen-year-old Amelia de Leuchtenberg, of second-rate Napoleonic royalty, but a blonde beauty who made Dom Pedro forget Titila de Castro.

Dom Pedro had not forgotten the fake portrait of Leopoldina that Marialva had sent from Vienna, but he trusted Barbacena implicitly. When he saw the attractive blonde princess, he was so delighted with her and especially with Barbacena for choosing her that in December 1829 he called on Barbacena to form an all-Brazilian ministry. This had been the suggestion of José Bonifácio, who had just returned from exile and had been immediately reconciled with Dom Pedro; thereafter, the statesman made a strenuous effort to restore the emperor's popularity and to safeguard the throne for him.

In the Barbacena ministry nearly all the members were titled, but since all were Brazilians, the public did not resent them. Barbacena and his ministers governed strictly by the constitution, and they won much popular support for the government, particularly when, with great difficulty, they persuaded Dom Pedro to dismiss his "kitchen cabinet" of low-born Portuguese friends, from whom he too frequently received bad advice. Unfortunately, he continued to correspond with them, so that their influence was only weakened, not destroyed. By 1829, however, only eleven of thirty-three Brazilian newspapers favored the government, and Dom Pedro was frequently under attack. Evaristo Ferreira da Veiga, the ablest journalist of his day, led the campaign in the *Aurora Fluminense,* which he had established in 1827.

News of the July 1830 revolution in France reached Brazil in mid-September. The year 1830, like 1820, was a time of revolution in Europe, for there were also uprisings in the Netherlands, Poland, and Italy. The revolt in France, however, was the one in which Brazilians saw the closest parallels to their own situation. Since the Brazilian constitution had been patterned after the French one, Brazilians were especially interested in events in France. Like Charles X, who had been toppled by the Parisian mob in the July revolution, Dom Pedro was suspected of planning to restore absolutism because he too had ignored the constitution. In the *Aurora Fluminense* Evaristo da Veiga made a telling remark: "Charles X had ceased to reign, and may the same thing happen to any monarch who, betraying his vows, shall undertake to destroy the free institutions of his country."

All Brazil was aroused; the news from France, together with comments in the Brazilian press, stirred men to action. Only Dom Pedro remained unmoved, for he alone apparently saw no connection between his actions and those of Charles X. He knew that he had no secret desire to restore absolutism, and on the basis of his record he felt justified in believing that Brazilians knew his true feelings. His own absolutist upbringing made it seem improper and unnecessary for him to explain anything to the multitude. Brazilians, however, had forgotten his expressed belief in constitutional monarchy and suspected him of the darkest motives.

Dom Pedro's background, his lack of formal education, and his impulsiveness made it impossible for him to make the adjustment necessary to cope with a constitutional regime. When he was informed that the best way to dissipate the crisis was to appoint a ministry of Brazilian liberals, he was irate—he considered himself the leading liberal. Insensitive and incautious, Dom Pedro, influenced by his distant Portuguese friends, turned against the Barbacena ministry which had served him so well. The parliamentary session had been fruitful, producing the first budgetary statute and a law regulating the armed forces. It also produced a criminal code devised by Bernardo de Vasconcelos, the first legal code prepared by a Latin American nation, which later served as a model for the Spanish code of 1848 and other codes in Latin America and Russia. Barbacena's forced resignation, however, brought a demand from the radical press that the monarchy be abolished.

Another episode increased opposition to the monarchy. When Libero Badaró—an Italian journalist of extremist views who had defended some São Paulo law students arrested during a demonstration—was murdered, the government was suspected. Because police made no apparent effort to apprehend the murderers, the suspicion seemed to many to be confirmed.

A conservative group planned to organize a society called the "Pillars of the Throne" to defend the emperor, Dom Pedro would have no part of it, and his disapproval was enough to kill it. Even though the society never actually existed, the idea of it continued to inspire wild rumors, the wildest of which was that it was preparing an armed force to make Dom Pedro absolute monarch. Another fertile source of rumors was Dom Pedro's "secret cabinet," simply a group of friends who handled his personal correspondence. Since the group's work was confidential and no one knew exactly what it did, there was nothing to discredit the bizarre rumors that were invented and circulated about it.

Among the new ministers Dom Pedro named was José Antônio da Silva Maia of Minas Gerais, whose reelection to the Chamber of Deputies was necessary if he was to remain in his post. Feeling his personal pride at stake, Dom Pedro decided to travel to Minas Gerais early in 1831 to influence the outcome of the election. The Chamber's efforts to dissuade him from making the trip only strengthened his determination. The Chamber then sent agents to Minas to generate opposition to the emperor and his candidate.

Bernardo de Vasconcelos opposed Silva Maia in the press, and Dom Pedro's candidate was defeated.

Nine years earlier Dom Pedro had been warmly received despite warnings that he was unwelcome in Minas. On this occasion, however, the *Mineiros* were cool and distant, for they were much agitated over the Badaró affair. Dom Pedro offered various honors and titles to prominent *Mineiros,* who publicly rejected them. He was accused of trying to buy friends through the distribution of honors. Much discouraged by the cold reception, he issued a somewhat incoherent blast at the opposition, accusing it of deceiving the people and trying to change the constitution illegally. This demonstrated again his determination not to make concessions to his opponents. They accepted it as a declaration of war.

As he reentered the capital, people in the streets shouted as he passed, "Long live the emperor as long as he abides by the constitution!" Street fights broke out between his adherents and opponents. The night of March 13 saw the greatest violence, with the capital's streets becoming a veritable battleground. This was remembered as *"a noite das garrafados"* (or the night of the bottles) in deference to the choice of weapons. It widened the chasm between Brazilians and Portuguese still farther, and some consider it the opening battle of the Revolution of April 7. Evaristo da Veiga suggested that true Brazilians wear the national colors on their sleeves, and those wearing these badges were so numerous that the emperor's supporters were awed into silence. On March 20 Dom Pedro took a step in the direction of conciliation by appointing a ministry of moderate Brazilians, but they were not members of the Chamber and he did not consult that body. The emperor was sent a blunt but timely warning: obey the constitution and forbid your followers to use violence or face the certainty of deposition. He made no reply.

Opposition to Dom Pedro continued to grow. Of the fifty-three newspapers then being published in Brazil, more than half opposed the emperor, but they offered no consensus on what was to be done. Some maintained a moderate tone, but others were inflammatory and irresponsible. These latter papers were especially influential in the provinces, where anything in print was likely to be accepted as true.

Three factions had crystallized during Dom Pedro's rule: the absolutists, comprised of men in most governmental posts, who wanted a monarchy without a constitution; the *moderados,* liberals who favored a constitutional monarchy; and the *exaltados,* ultraliberals who wanted to create a federal republic. It was the *exaltados* more than any other group who brought about the so-called Revolution of April 7, 1831. Although they had accepted the monarchy in 1822, they regarded it as a temporary obstacle to be eliminated when the opportunity arose. The time now seemed ripe.

In March the *moderados* and *exaltados,* meeting at the Chacara de Floresta, a country estate that belonged to a *Mineiro* deputy, decided to subordinate differences between their two groups. In order to check Dom Pedro they knew they would need the support of the army. Fortunately, there were both *moderados* and *exaltados* among the officers, and army discipline had deteriorated. Furthermore, the war with Argentina had changed the army by increasing the number of Brazilians among the officers, thus giving it a strong anti-Portuguese prejudice.

The Chacara de Floresta group did not agree on what it would do if Dom Pedro were ousted or abdicated. It merely decided that when the session of the General Assembly opened on April 3 one of its number should introduce a motion declaring Dom Pedro disqualified as emperor of Brazil. Neither the army nor the *exaltados* was satisfied with this bland method of attack.

As the revolution was taking shape in Rio de Janeiro news of the *"noite das garrafados"* and other disturbances was agitating the provinces. By early April Bahia and parts of Minas Gerais were in open rebellion, but the rebels had no clearly defined goals, except that they opposed disorder and absolutism. It seems likely that some revolutionary movement would have been launched if Dom Pedro had not abdicated when he did.

April 4 was Maria de Glória's birthday and Dom Pedro planned to celebrate with a concert at the São Cristovão palace outside the city. Most of the ministers thought it unwise, but Minister of War General José Manoel de Morais assured the emperor that he would maintain public order. During the evening a dispatch telling of disturbances in the city reached Dom Pedro. He read it aloud and publicly berated the ministers of war and justice for incompetence. The Ministry of March 20 was dismissed, although news of the act was not widely circulated until the next day.

Dom Pedro appointed a new ministry of aristocrats, the

"Ministry of Marquêsas," most of whom had been his allies in 1823. To Brazilians this was unmistakable evidence of Dom Pedro's absolutist tendencies. Early on April 6 protests were rising, and by midday crowds had gathered at the Campo de Santa Ana. The *exaltados* were calling loudly for a republic and federalism. Evaristo da Veiga and others were convinced that the revolution must be resisted, for fear that it would lead not only to the downfall of Dom Pedro, but to the destruction of political institutions as well.

Dom Pedro and his new ministers remained closeted for most of the day, then proclaimed that the government would abide by the constitution. When the proclamation was read to the sullen crowd assembled in the Campo, the paper was trampled in the dirt. Tell the emperor to reinstate the Ministry of March 20, the crowd demanded.

Early that evening the people presented a petition to the emperor to restore the ministry, but Dom Pedro's absolutist upbringing made it impossible for him to listen to the voice of reason if it came from the multitude. With growing anger he insisted that he was acting in a constitutional manner and quoted the article in the constitution that gave the emperor the power to appoint his ministers. "I will do everything for the people," he concluded, "but nothing by the people."

General Francisco de Lima e Silva then tried to convince the emperor of his error. With growing impatience Dom Pedro refused to make any concession and recklessly dismissed Brazil's ablest officer. As he left the palace, General Lima e Silva signaled to his brother, the commander of the Imperial Battalion, and this unit soon joined the gathering at the Campo, followed by the Imperial Guard. Because of his stubbornness, Dom Pedro was left totally deserted—the only military support remaining were the sentries at the gates. A German battalion he expected from Rio Grande do Sul never arrived, and so bloodshed was avoided.

At midnight, his confidence shaken by the defection of the army, Dom Pedro had a change of heart. He sent a message to Senator Vergueiro, asking him to form a ministry satisfactory to Brazilians, but the message never reached Vergueiro. When General Lima e Silva sent an officer to report the worsening situation at the Campo, the emperor handed him the Act of Abdication. Some of those present were certain that the people would reject the abdication, but Dom Pedro knew that it would be accepted. They had not accepted him, he said, because he was not Brazilian. His son would be well received, he added, and he wanted to save the throne for him.

Initial surprise at the abdication was followed by an enthusiastic demonstration of people and troops. Next morning Dom Pedro dismissed the ministry, except the marquês de Inhambupe, the minister of empire. Rejecting French or British offers of military escorts as "unconstitutional," he rode to the waterfront accompanied by three officers and two sentries and followed by a crowd of weeping Negroes. He boarded H.M.S. *Warspite,* but after four days he transferred to H.M.S. *Volage,* which sailed on April 13. With him went as much of the Brazilian treasury as was within reach.

A French *chargé d'affaires* remarked of Dom Pedro that "He knew better how to abdicate than to reign. . . . On this unforgettable night the sovereign rose beyond himself, and revealed a presence of mind, a firmness and a dignity, that declared what this unhappy prince might have been, with a better education, and if more noble examples had come before his eyes."

Brazilians owed Dom Pedro more than they realized or cared to admit in their time of anger, for despite his mishandling of foreign relations and his total inability to adjust to a constitutional regime even of his own devising, he had made possible an easy and inexpensive transition to independent nationhood. Under a monarchy in which the perplexing issue of legitimacy did not arise, Brazil had become independent with virtually no bloodshed and no trace of militarism. Compared to most of the former Spanish colonies, Brazil was exceedingly fortunate, and much of her good fortune revolved around the presence of Dom Pedro. Unlike Spanish America, Brazil did not disintegrate into a dozen small states, for the emperor's presence provided an invisible but elastic bond between the various provinces and Rio de Janeiro. Furthermore, despite his autocratic reactions, Dom Pedro gave a liberal tone to the constitution and Brazilian politics. All in all, he gave Brazil an enviable start toward nationhood and self-government.

In the remaining three years of his life Dom Pedro drove Dom Miguel from Portugal and installed Maria da Glória on the throne as Maria II. Before he died in 1834 at the age of thirty-six, he wrote his young son, Dom Pedro II, a letter displaying remarkable insight and understanding that, had they emerged earlier, would have made his reign far happier and more effective:

The time when princes were respected simply because they were princes is past. In the century in which we are living, with the peoples fully informed as to their rights, it is necessary that princes should be equally well informed and realize that they are men and not divinities; it is indispensable that they should have broad knowledge and the good opinion of their subjects in order that they may be loved even more than they are respected—the respect of a free people for their ruler should spring from the conviction that he is the leader capable of enabling them to attain that degree of well-being to which they aspire; if this is not the case, then it is unhappy leader, unhappy people!

This was the soundest of counsel. The pity is that Dom Pedro himself had not received similar words of wisdom and followed similar advice during his stormy decade as emperor of Brazil.

5/The Regency: A Republican Experiment

THE SO-CALLED REVOLUTION OF APRIL 7 WAS AN expression of resentment against the Portuguese, especially because of their interference with Dom Pedro's government. In this sense it was a second *Grito de Ipiranga*, but it left Brazil without a ruler—there was no adult member of the royal family to serve as regent for the infant prince. The constitution provided that in such cases the General Assembly could elect and regulate a three-man regency to serve until the then five-year-old emperor was of age.

Many Brazilians were apprehensive about the monarchy, fearing that it might be swept away and a federal republic established in its place, which would cause the country to disintegrate, as had happened in parts of Spanish America. There was no panic, however, for Brazilian political leaders closed ranks to save the monarchy. They called a council of notables, which met the same day Dom Pedro abdicated. As had happened in France in 1830, it was the moderates who captured control of the government, rather than the radicals who had incited the movement. The council of notables elected a temporary three-member regency composed of the marquês de Caravelas, who was the main author of the constitution, Senator Nicoláu Pereira dos Campos Vergueiro, and General Francisco Lima e Silva.

The regents immediately assumed control of the government and reappointed most of the ministers Dom Pedro had dismissed on April 5. A few days later they had Dom Pedro II brought from São Cristovão to the city palace to calm the people by showing them he was still in Rio de Janeiro. During the procession the troops left their ranks to join the crowd following the carriage—an indication that the army was still undisciplined and more inclined to engage in disruptive acts than to preserve order. In a burst of enthusiasm the people unhitched the horses and pulled the carriage themselves.

In the meantime H.M.S. *Warspite* lay at anchor in Guanabara bay, and knowledge of Dom Pedro's presence there excited the absolutists and alarmed those who had opposed him. He freely received visitors and sent messages, one of which named José Bonifácio as tutor for the royal children. Although there were widespread fears that the ex-emperor plotted a return to power, he countered those who offered to support such a move by asking them to defend his son instead. Fears were finally set to rest when he sailed on H.M.S. *Volage*, never to return.

The presence of demoralized and undisciplined troops in the capital was also a cause of alarm, for the 1828 mutiny of German and Irish troops was still fresh in many minds. Dom Pedro had never concerned himself with military organization and discipline. The unpopularity of the war with Argentina had led to increased recruitment of Portuguese and foreign mercenaries, and the troops were arrogant and irresponsible, a ready source of violence. Minister of War José Manoel de Morais, himself a general, urged the soldiers to observe proper discipline and to cease their insubordination, then dismissed most of the remaining foreign mercenaries, both officers and enlisted men. The state of the army was such, however, that it took more than a polite admonition from the minister of war to restore discipline.

Although the people of the city participated indirectly in politics through street demonstrations and mob action, a small elitist group monopolized political power. The constitution limited the franchise to less than ten percent of the population. As a result, although the press stirred up considerable debate on political problems, the bulk of the population had no say at all in their solution.

Brazilian society was still divided into three general groupings, and only the first and a fraction of the second of these could vote. First in importance and at the apex of government, society, and the economy were the large landholders, a group of rich Portuguese merchants who prospered after Dom João lifted restrictions on commerce in 1808, and a number of top bureaucrats. The heterogeneous middle group—composed of small landowners, lesser bureaucrats, officers, and priests—was racially mixed, almost totally lacking in cohesion, and not really a genuine middle class, for its members did not regard themselves as a distinct group with interests of its own. Its economic opportunities were greatly restricted by the universal dependence on slave labor. At the bottom were the slaves, who composed half of the population.

The political factions present in 1831 had changed somewhat from the days before the abdication. *Exaltados* favored a federal republic and had been mainly responsible for forcing the emperor's abdication; *moderados* upheld constitutional monarchy; and absolutists or restorationists wanted Dom Pedro restored and the constitution abolished. There were as yet no political parties, but the formation of political clubs by the three groups was a step toward party organization. The first of these was the *Sociedade Defensora da Independência e Liberdade do Brasil*, which became the stronghold of the *moderados*. It included such key figures as Senator Nicoláu Pereira dos Campos Vergueiro, José Bonifácio and Martim Francisco de Andrada, and General Francisco Lima e Silva. The prime mover and organizer of the *Sociedade Defensora* was Evaristo da Veiga, the noted journalist who played a vital part in the formation of public opinion through his newspaper, the *Aurora Fluminense*. Although at one time he sided with the *exaltados* in their demands for federalism, his greatest efforts were spent in behalf of a liberal constitutional monarchy and moderation in political affairs. His reasoned writings differed greatly from the irresponsible rantings of the radical press, and because of him many Brazilians developed a respect for constitutional government. *Exaltados* and restorationists also published newspapers in order to place their views before the public.

On May 3 the General Assembly met under rather tense conditions: the deputies elected in 1829 were largely liberal, while the senators supported Dom Pedro. The Assembly was authorized by the constitution to select the regency and to limit its powers, and the liberals quickly took advantage of this, hoping eventually to gain enough power to adopt a new constitution based on liberal principles. The Assembly voted to deprive the regents of the power to veto bills, to dissolve the legislature, to appoint men to the Council of State, and to pardon offenses of ministers or councilors. The regents were also prohibited from suspending a citizen's individual liberties, granting titles of nobility, and making treaties without the approval of the Assembly prior to ratification. The senators, not at all happy with these provisions, realized that they had no public support and acquiesced; they were satisfied to retain their positions, for there had been talk of abolishing the Senate. While these limitations on the regents calmed the fears of those who dreaded an absolutist takeover, they made the regency an impotent government and exposed the country to the danger of anarchy.

The *exaltados,* resenting their exclusion from power by the *moderados,* stirred up public demonstrations in favor of such extreme measures as the creation of a federal republic. The Assembly countered with a law prohibiting more than five persons from congregating in public and another that kept sailors off the streets after dark. It also passed a law giving itself the right to name the royal tutor, but José Bonifácio declared that he could not surrender the responsibility given him by Dom Pedro.

In July the Assembly elected José Bonifácio royal tutor, as a way of asserting its authority in the the matter. Later it enacted a law prohibiting the royal tutor from engaging in any manner of political activity, a law that José Bonifácio ignored. An attempt to deprive him of the office was defeated in the Senate by only a single vote. José Bonifácio was implicated in restorationist disturbances in 1832 and the following year, and after the second episode his service as royal tutor was ended.

Before April 7 the main issue had been liberty. After the abdication public order was the foremost problem; riots and street fights became chronic. Because the Assembly had deprived the regents of the powers needed to suppress or prevent disorders, the government had little popular support, and its task was difficult, virtually impossible. Too many politicians were concerned more with personal or factional interests than with the welfare of the nation. The frequent public disturbances even convinced some that Dom Pedro should be recalled to serve as regent for his son. To the liberal factions, however, the thought of Dom Pedro's returning was completely unacceptable, and the possibility was enough to hold them together. Because the army remained insubordinate and undependable, Minister of Justice Diogo Feijó created a national guard to suppress disorders. Commissions were distributed liberally to supporters of the government, especially rural landowners. So many landowners were commissioned *coronel* (colonel) that as a result the word became virtually synonomous with *fazendeiro.* A rural militia was formed by the *agregados* (free working class), who served as *capangas* (henchmen) to the *fazendeiros.*

The permanent three-man regency elected by the Assembly was composed of General Francisco Lima e Silva, one of the temporary regents, José da Costa Carvalho of Bahia, and João Braulino Muniz of Maranhão. None of them was a member of the *exaltado* faction, for the *moderados* were convinced that it would be impossible to govern with the *exaltados.* Even though they had precipitated the abdication, the *exaltados'* demands for sweeping changes induced the *moderados* to exclude the group in hopes of preserving political institutions. Bitterly disappointed, the *exaltados* were determined to embarrass the *moderado* government at every opportunity.

Because senators had been appointed by the emperor, the Senate was the center of restorationist power, and it was able to prevent the *moderados* from enacting reforms. After the Senate prevented the dismissal of José Bonifácio, at Feijó's urging the *moderados* turned to extralegal ways to achieve their goals. Feijó, the energetic and liberal priest who had been a delegate to the *Côrtes* and was then minister of justice, regarded the Senate's action as a personal affront, for he had denounced José Bonifácio. He was determined that constitutional changes would be made in spite of Senate opposition, and he was quite willing to eliminate that body if necessary. He planned to have the ministry resign, then to have the Chamber of Deputies declare itself a national assembly for the purpose of adopting a liberal constitution.

On July 26, 1832 the ministry resigned, ostensibly in protest against José Bonifácio's continuing as royal tutor. When the chamber met, with Feijó still at his ministerial post despite his resignation, General Pinto Peixoto asked permission to leave the Chamber to take command of the national guard, which was being mobilized to break up street brawls. The moment for the Chamber to declare itself a national assembly had arrived.

The revolutionary plan, however, went down in defeat. Honório Hermeto Carneiro Leão, later the marquês de Paraná, wielded enough prestige and good arguments to convince a number of *moderados* to draw back. Legality had been, after all, the basic *moderado* principle, and enough of them were still committed to it to defeat the revolutionary move. Feijó's plan was abandoned, and the regents continued in office at the Chamber's request. The abortive *coup,* however, undermined the *moderado* position at a time when the government needed all the strength it could muster. Feijó did not return to the ministry, and his loss was sorely felt. The *exaltados* rejoiced, for they wanted constitutional changes far more radical than anything the *moderados* might have proposed. The restorationists, too, were encouraged by the *moderado* failure, and the Senate was saved from extinction.

In October 1832 the Assembly passed a law enabling those who voted for deputies for the next legislative session to grant or oppose authorization for amending the constitution. The voters granted the authority, and in August 1834 the *Acto Adicional* (Additional Act) was passed by the Chamber of Deputies, an apparent victory for the liberals. After lively debate it had been decided that only the Chamber should vote on it, for the Senate probably would have blocked it. The act reduced the number of regents from three to one, who would be elected for a four-year term, and it abolished the Council of State, which the liberals considered the bulwark of convervatism. It also gave the government the right to appoint provincial presidents, and authorized the provinces to replace their provincial councils with elected legislative assemblies. The powers of these provincial assemblies to regulate local affairs were vaguely defined and not expressly limited—an oversight that provoked many disputes over jurisdiction. The responsibility for public schools below the university level was transferred to the provinces, which proved generally damaging to the development of education. The act also abolished entail, the medieval rule against breaking up large estates. The *Acto Adicional* was, above all, a reflection of the excessive fear of absolutism, and it went too far, as Bernardo de Vasconcelos, its principal author, was soon to point out. Dom Pedro's death in the following month should have dissipated the fear of absolutism, but the act was neither modified nor repealed until it had done its damage.

After passage of the *Acto Adicional* Feijó—strongly supported by Evaristo da Veiga, and equally strongly opposed by Vasconcelos—was elected as single regent by a narrow margin. The choice reflected a deep-seated desire for public order, for Feijó had been instrumental in putting down disorders in Rio de Janeiro in 1831 and 1832. Feijó was never able to work harmoniously with those around him and alienated many who otherwise would have supported him. An uncompromising political warrior, he could neither appreciate nor accept opposing views. Indeed, he aroused such fury in his enemies that they were quite willing to endanger the country in order to avenge themselves against him. Although he had been an able and effective minister of justice, his health began to deteriorate, and he suffered the first of several attacks of paralysis shortly before he took office in October 1835. He was, therefore, ailing and despondent at the very time his best efforts were needed to deal with insurrections all over the country. A dedicated patriot and one of the great men of his era, he held preservation of public order and obedience to law as his major goals, caring not at all for honors and rewards. His treatment of the General Assembly was no more tactful than Dom Pedro's, however, for in 1835 and 1836 he refused to select his ministers from the Chamber of Deputies.

Feijó generated strife between church and state, for he favored abolishing clerical celibacy and resisted papal authority over the church in Brazil. Vasconcelos, who opposed him on almost every issue, defended the church with his usual effectiveness. When Father Antônio Maria de Moura, a liberal priest who also supported the movement to abolish celibacy, was named bishop of Rio de Janeiro, the pope refused to confirm him unless he changed his views concerning celibacy. In 1835 the minister of justice ordered him not to recant, for that would compromise the nation's sovereignty. Later in the same year a bill to separate the Brazilian church from Rome was defeated in the Chamber by only two votes. When Moura withdrew his name as bishop and Feijó rejected a similar appointment, the friction disappeared.

The death of the ex-emperor caused a general reshuffling of political assignments. Evaristo da Veiga, Father Feijó, and others created the Liberal party out of the *moderados* and the *exaltados,* along with a few former restorationists such as the Andrada brothers. Vasconcelos and others, seeing the need to calm the country, founded the Conservative party, which took a position midway between the absolutists and the federalist *exaltados.* Experience with the *Acto Adicional* demonstrated convincingly that any further move toward federalism would be disastrous. The *exaltados,* however, continued to agitate for federalism, and it was necessary to combat their arguments. Logically, deliberately, and so effectively did Vasconcelos shatter their stand, that they attacked him viciously at every opportunity. He also constantly badgered Feijó, contributing to the latter's difficulties by turning the Assembly against him.

In 1838 and 1839 Vasconcelos conducted a campaign to prevent the *Acto Adicional* from becoming a permanent threat to Brazilian nationhood, just as he had worked earlier to eliminate flaws from the constitution. Taking the lead in defining the exact meaning of the act's provisions, he demanded that the powers of provincial assemblies be made explicit and that the authority of the imperial government not be dangerously restricted. His views prevailed over all opposition. The Law of May 1840, "interpreting" the *Acto Adicional,* was largely his creation. It restored the Council of State and deprived the provincial assemblies of many powers they had claimed owing to the act's vagueness. Certain administrative and judicial changes were introduced to give the executive the power needed to govern effectively.

The regency had already suffered from a rash of rebellions before Feijó became regent—in Maranhão (1831–32), Bahia (1832–35), Minas Gerais (1833), and Mato Grosso (1834). The *Cabanagem* revolt in Pará began in January 1835 and continued until 1837, leaving that province in ruins. At the outset it was only a feud between *filantrópicos* (nativists) and *caramurús* (Portuguese), but it degenerated into a senseless orgy of murder and pillage. Later in 1835 the most serious revolt of all began—the *Farroupilha*, or War of the Ragamuffins, in Rio Grande do Sul. The *Farrapos*, so-called because of the fringed leather they wore on the cattle ranges, were influenced by some of the separatist currents of the Río de la Plata region, for Rio Grande do Sul bordered on Uruguay, and neither side paid much attention to international boundaries. *Riograndenses* and *orientalistas* (Uruguayans) mingled freely in each other's feuds. Underlying these revolts were separatist tendencies as well as a lack of respect for the central government. The *Acto Adicional* had whetted provincial appetites for greater autonomy and had thereby contributed to the insurrections.

When Feijó became regent, most of the government's efforts were concentrated on crushing the *Cabanagem* in Pará, leaving few troops available for combatting the *Farrapo* rebels in Rio Grande. Feijó was apprehensive about committing errors that would compromise the government and injure its prestige, for the *Farroupilha* had political overtones absent in most of the other rebellions. His first move was astute. Early in 1836 he appointed the popular José de Araújo Ribeiro president of Rio Grande do Sul. Araújo Ribeiro, who had many friends and relatives in Rio Grande, was supposed to be inaugurated in the presence of the provincial assembly, but fearing that the assembly would refuse to let him take office, he simply assumed his duties. The assembly declared him suspended, and warfare intensified. Araújo Ribeiro's appointment had a salutary effect, however, for it won over Bento Manoel Ribeiro, his relative and the rebels' ablest officer. The situation improved rapidly thereafter, and government troops recovered Pôrto Alegre, which the rebels had taken in 1835.

Other lost ground was regained, but Araújo Ribeiro still needed powerful support from the regent. For reasons never explained Feijó dismissed him, but such a storm of protest arose that he reinstated the president within three weeks. In September 1836 the rebel forces won a significant victory and proclaimed the "Republic of Piratinim." The rebels were probably more federalist than separatist, but their declaration of the republic was a challenge the government had to meet, because other provinces might be tempted to imitate it.

Despite the rebel victory of Piratinim, Araújo Ribeiro was making progress. By early 1837 Rio Grande was nearly under his control, but Feijó again abruptly dismissed him. His dismissal was viewed as an undeserved punishment. Bento Manoel Ribeiro returned to the rebel cause, and the republicans soon regained the ground they had recently lost.

Feijó suffered other blows in 1837. In May his close friend and invaluable adviser, Evaristo da Veiga, died. Bento Gonçalves da Silva, a *Riograndense* leader elected president of the Republic of Piratinim while a prisoner of the government, escaped from Bahia, returned to Rio Grande do Sul, and in his first action inflicted a serious defeat on government troops. Uruguay, envisioning the addition of Rio Grande do Sul to its territory, supplied the rebels with money, horses, and arms. Depressed, discouraged, and unable to cope with the situation, Feijó sought more troops, but the Chamber of Deputies—then controlled by his enemies—took pleasure in denying his request.

Feijó might still have saved himself by appointing Vasconcelos minister of empire, but he could not bring himself to appoint so implacable a political foe, preferring to resign instead. Pedro de Araújo Lima, whom Feijó had persuaded to accept the post of minister of empire not long after Bento Gonçalves' escape, rightfully took over as temporary regent when Feijó resigned. In elections held the following year Araújo Lima was chosen as regent and the Conservatives won a majority in the Chamber of Deputies. Later, when Feijó was named a senator, he was accused of trying to avenge himself on all who had opposed him as regent.

In November 1837 the *Sabinada* revolt broke out in Bahia, and it was at least indirectly related to the *Farroupilha*. Its leaders were suspected of having helped Bento Gonçalves escape, and the revolt had begun, in fact, when a crowd applauded news of rebel victories in Rio Grande do Sul. The leaders of the *Sabinada* declared that Bahia would be independent until Dom Pedro II was of age, a declaration similar to one made by the *Farrapos*. In both revolts a measure of local autonomy with less interference by authorities in Rio de Janeiro, rather than separation from Brazil, seems to have been the major goal.

Although Araújo Lima appointed as ministers men of outstanding ability, including Vasconcelos as minister of empire, they were no better able to pacify and govern the country than Feijó had been. Furthermore, Brazilians looked upon the regent as merely an elected figure who served for a short term, not as a genuine substitute for the emperor.

Araújo Lima was granted funds and troops that had been denied Feijó, but he made little progress in restoring the Republic of Piratinim to the empire. The government's prospects for ending the *Farroupilha* remained gloomy. The widespread need for troops to combat disorders in many provinces made it impossible to concentrate a sufficiently large force in Rio Grande. Money and supplies provided by the Uruguayans continued to encourage rebel resistance. In 1839 the rebels even invaded Santa Catarina, established a short-lived republic there, and again laid siege to Pôrto Alegre. Araújo Lima was determined to crush the rebels, and later that year the army was systematically reorganized and thereafter improved. The minister of war visited the war theater, accompanied by Major Luís Alves da Lima e Silva, son of the famous general and later the famed duque de Caxias, the greatest military figure of the empire. Lima e Silva made a thorough study of the military situation in Rio Grande do Sul, gathering information that would be useful a few years later when he was given command there.

The question of majority—that is, of declaring Dom Pedro or his older sister Januária of age—first arose in 1836 when Vasconcelos suggested the idea to the assembly of Minas Gerais. Vasconcelos planned to declare Dom Pedro of age, but there was also talk of doing the same for Dona Januária, so that she could serve as her brother's regent until December 1843 when he would be eighteen. Following the death of Dom Pedro I, the Portuguese had declared fifteen-year-old Maria da Glória of age, so the precedent was clearly established. Brazilians were aware of this Portuguese solution, for the Assembly had already excluded Maria da Glória from succession to the Brazilian crown. She had been next in line after Dom Pedro II, but Dona Januária was named imperial princess, which placed her after her brother in the line of succession.

The majority movement in Brazil was completely political from its outset to its conclusion. When Conservative Vasconcelos first proposed it, the Liberals, who controlled the government, were opposed because they knew it was then simply an attempt to unseat or embarrass Feijó. They remained opposed as long as they were in power. Once out of power, they took the opposite view.

The Conservatives and Liberals easily changed positions on the majority issue as well as on others, for they were by no means doctrinaire. Their differences were not great, and the stand either party took on an issue was determined largely by the advantages that might be derived from it.

In 1838 and the following two years the Liberals were looking for any means of regaining control of the government. Senator José Martiniano d'Alencar organized the secret Society of Invisible Patriarchs to promote the Liberal cause, but the society failed to produce results. He and others then turned to the majority movement as the surest method of regaining Liberal control. In the early months of 1839 the movement was already well advanced in Rio de Janeiro, but it still centered around Dona Januária.

In April 1840 Liberal leaders and the Andrada brothers organized a secret club to promote the majority of Dom Pedro II. The essential requirements for success were Dom Pedro's consent and the General Assembly's approval to give the action at least a veneer of legality. Seeking to declare the majority was, of course, a violation of the constitution, but the club made it possible for those in favor to band together, pooling their ideas and strengths. Even the Conservatives accepted the fact that the majority movement was too strong to be delayed much longer. In the Senate a widely respected elder statesman declared that the immediate crowning of the emperor was a national necessity, whether or not it was constitutional. Brazilians, despite Vasconcelos' efforts, had not yet developed the attitude that the constitution was a sacred document; they did not shrink from violating it when it was clearly in the national interest to do so. Such precedents are, of course, dangerous for constitutional regimes because, among other reasons, there is rarely nation-wide agreement on what is clearly in the nation's best interest.

The Andradas began to organize public demonstrations in support of the majority, and the press engaged in lively debate, heightening public interest. On July 22 Araújo Lima issued a decree proroguing the General Assembly, which caught the Liberal *Maiorista* deputies off guard. Quickly recovering, they charged off to the Senate, where an excited rump session of deputies and senators became a revolutionary convention. By this time the only basic disagreement between Conservatives and Liberals was over the appropriate date. The Conservatives, ably led by Vasconcelos, held out for December 2, Dom Pedro's fifteenth birthday. This would give them time to enact laws which hopefully would give them a foothold in the government after the emperor assumed power. The Liberals were too impatient to wait another four months, and public opinion supported them. Vasconcelos, despite his famed powers of persuasion, could not check the tide in favor of an immediate declaration of the majority.

The *Maiorista* Liberals were not to be denied because of a mere obstacle such as the lack of a quorum. Disregarding Araújo Lima's pleas for postponement, a joint session of the Chamber and Senate invested Dom Pedro with imperial authority on July 23, 1840. He took the oath to uphold the constitution, and three days of wild celebration followed. The whole business was strictly unconstitutional. It was merely a legislative *coup d'etat* strongly supported by public opinion, but this aspect disturbed only a few men. The regency was at an end and most Brazilians breathed easier, feeling that the nation had been saved from chaos. Brazilians embraced the Second Empire with renewed enthusiasm and hope. The new monarch was to reign nearly half a century.

The regency period was a crucial era for Brazil, since the country had been in grave danger of breaking up. Above all, the period was an experiment in republicanism and federalism, for the regent was elected for a four-year term and the provinces were granted the authority to create provincial assemblies. Joaquim Nabuco, one of the ablest statesmen of the century, called the regency a "provisional republic" which had the opportunity of demonstrating to Brazilians that the monarchy was no longer needed. What made the statesmen of the regency great, according to Nabuco, was not what they had accomplished positively but the fact that they were able to prevent the country from falling into a state of complete anarchy.

Although the republican experiment failed, the regency had not been an unmitigated calamity. There were many positive accomplishments despite the fact that the government's main efforts were directed toward restoring and maintaining peace. Freedom of the press had been established in 1830, and it was preserved throughout the decade regardless of the irresponsibility shown by some journalists and publishers. During the same period Portuguese law was replaced by a new criminal code, the treasury was reorganized, the public debt funded, and a sinking fund created.

Under the regency's auspices many Europeans were attracted to Brazil. In 1835, after the most serious slave revolt of the century occurred in Bahia, the *Sociedade Colonizadora* was organized to protect colonists brought from Europe. In the following year the marquês de Barbacena induced a few British and Swiss to emigrate to Brazil. In 1840 Senator Vergueiro devised a plan to bring in colonists under the *parceria* (partnership contract arrangement), which worked so well that in the ten years after 1845, in São Paulo alone 60,000 colonists had been settled. Many others came to Brazil under the same arrangement, and those who acquired land of their own brought in still others of their own countrymen under the same plan.

In 1837 the *Colégio de Dom Pedro II* was created and, owing to Vasconcelos' attention, it began operating the following year. The academy became a famous preparatory school for sons of the wealthy. Also founded during the regency were the *Instituto Histórico e Geográphico Brasileiro* (1838), a national archives, and a school of agriculture. Journalism became an important means of forming public opinion. Furthermore administrative practices were simplified, a two-party system worked out, and the tax system greatly improved.

Failure of the republican experiment greatly revived support for the monarchy, which had waned in 1831 and previous years. For most Brazilians the monarchy was still a powerful symbol, and—as leaders had hoped in the less "political" moments of the majority movement—its reestablishment provided the cement necessary to preserve national unity.

Unlike his father, Dom Pedro II had been born and educated in Brazil, and he was Brazilian to the core. His tutors exposed him to heavy doses of Enlightenment thought, for they were sworn to mold the perfect emperor. No word of scandal was ever uttered about Dom Pedro. More than half a century after his death it was discovered that he had exchanged letters with a lady of the court, but the relationship appears to have been purely platonic.

The search for a bride for Dom Pedro had begun soon after his coronation in 1841. It was no longer easy to convince European monarchs to allow their daughters to depart for the empire in the tropics, because Latin American political instability was now well-known. A bride was finally found in Naples—Tereza Cristina, daughter of Frederick I. Her brother was Frederick II of the Two Sicilies, and her mother was the sister of Dom Pedro's grandmother. Hers was not an impressive family as European royalty went, but the dowry she brought was substantial and made up for other shortcomings. She was twenty-two and no beauty. Dom Pedro was a handsome, blue-eyed young man of eighteen. As was the case with his father, Dom Pedro was sent a false portrait. Upon seeing her for the first time, he could not conceal his consternation; hence, Tereza's brother did not leave his side until the nuptials were completed. In time Dom Pedro and Tereza became good friends. They produced two sons, who died in infancy, and two daughters.

Emperor Dom Pedro was dignified but not given to pomp and ceremony, and, as if pledged to atone for his father's joyous infidelities, he was a model of domestic virtues. He was widely admired and respected in Europe and the United States as the ideal emperor. Victor Hugo somewhat extravagantly called him the "grandson of Marcus Aurelius"; others referred to him as the "philosopher king" and as the best "republican" in all Latin America. Less flattering was the description of him as a "Queen Victoria in trousers."

Those who promoted the majority received their rewards as expected. Five of them, including Antônio Carlos and Martim Francisco de Andrada and the brothers Calvalcanti, were named to Dom Pedro's first ministry, the Ministry of the Majority, appointed by the new emperor on July 23, 1840.

The new ministry was headed by Antônio Carlos as minister of empire. Though an eloquent orator, he was impulsive and occasionally unscrupulous, hence not an able administrator. His mishandling of the *Farroupilha*—he entered into correspondence with the rebels without informing the commander of the imperial troops—caused the latter to resign in disgust. Those appointed afterwards were inept failures. This embarrassed the ministry and was one of the causes of its resignation.

The year 1841 was the last in the four-year term of the deputies, and Antônio Carlos used every possible method to guarantee a Liberal majority in the Chamber of Deputies. The Liberal ministry had already aroused much resentment by its unrestrained dismissals of provincial presidents and other officials, and its fraudulent and corrupt manipulation of the Chamber election intensified the opposition and produced nation-wide protest. Torn by dissension within and blocked by the Conservative majority in the Chamber, the ministry resigned after eight months in office.

Dom Pedro next turned to the Conservatives who quickly modified some of the constitutional changes of the *Acto Adicional*. They restored the Council of State, limited the powers of the provincial assemblies, and introduced judicial and administrative reforms to strengthen the imperial government. During the regency judicial and police powers had been invested in locally elected judges. The Law of December 3, 1841 assigned the judicial functions to police authorities controlled by the government in Rio de Janeiro—a harsh device that helped to maintain the solidarity of the empire, but led to many abuses.

The Liberals did not anticipate remaining out of the government for very long, since the new legislature elected under their control would meet early in 1842. The Conservative ministry, however, convinced Dom Pedro that the election had been exceedingly corrupt, and he ordered the Chamber of Deputies dissolved before it met.

The infuriated Liberals launched rebellions in Minas Gerais and São Paulo, but these were easily crushed by Luís Alves Lima e Silva, then the barão de Caxias. Caxias was next sent to Rio Grande do Sul as president and military commander. By the end of the following year the rebels were on the run, and in March 1845 a peace agreement was signed. Rio Grande do Sul returned to the empire. Soon after this Caxias was named a life senator from Rio Grande.

The Liberals returned to power from 1844 to 1848. Although they had protested bitterly against the Law of December 3, 1841, once they were in control of the government they found it a useful means of maintaining control of the country and of elections. A new currency law was passed and a number of new banks were opened which facilitated the growth of commerce; another law permitted the duty-free importation of machinery to stimulate industries.

In July 1847 the Liberal ministry created the post of president of the Council of Ministers, in effect prime minister—an important step in the development of Brazil's parliamentary system. As there had been rumors of a "palace clique" gaining control of the young emperor, this move was designed to give him greater political independence. He named the president, and together they selected the rest of the ministry. The change gave greater unity to the ministries and greater responsibility to parties and party leaders. It was one of the elements that made Brazil's parliamentary system function reasonably well for half a century. The parliamentary system, whatever its imperfections, was the greatest political achievement of the reign of Dom Pedro I, the regency, and the first decade of the reign of Dom Pedro II.

Although members of the General Assembly consciously sought to emulate the French and British systems, the Brazilian parliamentary system was not thoroughly an imitation of any European model. Outwardly the system appeared to be smooth-functioning and effective, but it was actually intricate and complicated, and, in the final analysis, its success depended heavily on the judgment of one individual—the emperor. When he believed it was in the country's interest to change the party in power, he dismissed the ministry and appointed a president of the Council of Ministers from the other party. A new ministry would be named, and following the example of the Liberals in 1841, it would conduct elections in such a way as to guarantee it a majority in the Chamber. Dom Pedro's judgment was not infallible; because so much depended on him, his errors were to contribute to the downfall of the monarchy. If it had not been for his exercising the moderating power, however, one party might well have maintained itself in power throughout the empire.

In the February Revolution of 1848 in France, Louis Philippe was overthrown. As usual, events in France reverberated in Brazil. In that year the Liberal ministry was dismissed, and the outraged Liberals staged the *Praieira* revolt in Pernambuco, a revolt that meant many things to many people. It was, first of all, an expression of the Liberals' resentment of the dismissal of their ministry. It also contained elements of anti-Portuguese sentiments, factional rivalries, and urban-rural hostility characteristic of Pernambuco society since the War of the *Mascates*. Unavailability of land was another cause of protest; the rebels demanded that a heavy tax on uncultivated land be levied in order to force the breakup of the *fazendas*. After the revolt was suppressed in 1850, the distribution of uncultivated land to the wealthy was ended. This revolt so thoroughly discredited the Liberals that they did not return to power until the 1860s.

The slave trade was a problem left unsolved by the regency despite the 1831 law abolishing the traffic, called for in the 1826 treaty with Great Britain. Although some officials were eager to end it, the *fazendeiros* who dominated the government regarded the slave trade as essential to agriculture. It took only a few years to work out a system for evading British cruisers and officials and to set up slave-trading posts near the northeast coast where the demand for slaves was strongest. When the ministry introduced a bill to appropriate money to repatriate newly arrived slaves, the Chamber of Deputies rejected the measure, so resentful were they of high-handed British efforts to eliminate the inhumane traffic.

In 1837 the marquês de Barbacena returned from Europe and launched an attack on the trade. The bill he introduced provided severe punishment for slavers but left the slave brokers and *fazendeiros* unscathed. The law's only effects were to make the slavers more cautious and to increase the price of slaves. The British became even more vigilant, and their cruisers sailed the coasts of Africa and Brazil in search of *tumbeiros* (floating coffins), as the slave ships were called. Most of the slave ships were Portuguese rather than Brazilian, and a few were of Spanish or American origin. The fact that the Portuguese made the profits while Brazilians suffered humiliation at the hands of the British navy gradually turned Brazilians against the trade.

Relations with Britain were increasingly strained over the slave trade, since the British were convinced that only by harsher measures could they induce Brazilians to end the traffic. In 1845 the agreement permitting British cruisers to search ships in Brazilian waters and providing for joint Anglo-Brazilian admiralty courts in Africa and Brazil to try the cases expired. The British decided on severe, unilateral action. Lord Aberdeen, the British foreign minister, submitted a bill to Parliament. The Aberdeen Act authorized the British navy to treat slavers as pirates and to try them in British admiralty courts. There was a tremendous outburst of protest in Brazil, and the number of slaves brought illegally into the country doubled in 1846. By 1848 the number had tripled, rising to upwards of 60,000 that year.

In 1850 the Conservatives were again in power, and Minister of Justice Eusébio de Queiroz Coutinho Mattoso da Câmara presented a bill to end the trade that was simply a modification of the Barbacena bill of 1837, which had attempted to remove the obvious loopholes. The Queiroz bill proposed that special courts to try slavers be set up and that all ships sailing to Africa from Brazil post bonds covering the value of the ship and its expected cargo. If any ship was found to be involved in the slave trade, its bond was forfeited. Lord Aberdeen was not convinced the Brazilians were serious, and he ordered British cruisers to enter Brazilian waters and seize all ships fitted out as slavers. His inconsiderate action temporarily delayed passage of the Queiroz bill, but in September it became law. Within three years the trade was completely stifled.

Abolition of the slave trade was of the utmost significance for Brazil. It meant, among other things, that vast sums of money previously allocated to the purchase of slaves were available for investment in other enterprises. This wealth became available at a most opportune time, the year the *Praieira* revolt ended in Pernambuco, and the entire empire was at peace for the first time in decades. Except for the abolition of slavery itself, Brazil's major problems had been solved. It was during the next decade that the Second Empire was to reach its high tide.

6/ The Second Empire: Towards Republicanism

THE 1850s WERE THE GREAT YEARS OF THE EMpire. Brazil entered the decade with optimism and expectation inspired partly by an expanding economy. All of the provinces were at peace; the monarchy had preserved Brazilian unity as well as territorial integrity. Republicans and federalists were silent, for at the time they could not oppose the monarchy without appearing unpatriotic.

The law schools created in São Paulo and Olinda in 1827 had become unusually important as centers of intellectual activity and political reform. Both were located in former convents, symbolic of the change from the ecclesiastical spirit and religious conservatism of the colony to the judicial and revolutionary spirit of the empire. Through these law schools the influence of French and English philosophers entered Brazil. Programs for achieving justice and social reform were born and nurtured, and many revolutionary ideas were forged there. Law students were ever in the vanguard of political movements, and the schools themselves were instrumental in freeing Brazilian culture from dependence on Portuguese models. As Brazil had no separate college of arts and sciences until 1934, when the University of São Paulo was established, the two schools grew to become educational centers for the elite, teaching not only law but arts and sciences. Journalists, politicians, and businessmen alike were trained in law, and Brazil became a thoroughly juridical culture.

Since students came to study law from all regions of Brazil, the law schools helped develop and diffuse a sense of nationality. They provided the governing class of the empire. Unfortunately, because the schools could provide only meager scientific training, none of the brilliant statesmen concerned themselves with the economic development of the country. In 1832, for example, a law was enacted authorizing the establishment of a school of mines in Minas

Gerais, but the school was not opened for forty-four years, and only then because of the interest in it expressed by foreign scientists. Of the three great classical traditions upon which Brazilian culture was molded, the Roman heritage of rational law predominated strongly over the sense of mission characteristic of the Judaic-Christian tradition and the cult of pure intellect pursued by the Greeks.

There was, among educated Brazilians, a great zeal for literary prestige—professional men felt that their careers were incomplete unless they were also members of the literati. Doctors, lawyers, and statesmen doubled as men of letters; some of their work was excellent, but much of it was better forgotten.

Romanticism, which originated in Germany during the last two decades of the eighteenth century, flourished in Brazil at that time. The movement reached Brazil by way of France, where it first appeared in the preface to Victor Hugo's *Cromwell* (1827). Romanticism's broad goal was social, political, and artistic freedom; its ideal, universal brotherhood. The movement was thus well suited to Brazilians of the era, for it provided a literary form and mood appropriate for the nascent Brazilian nationalism. It also offered Brazilian writers and artists dissatisfied with classicism a comprehensive literary pattern. To the romantics all men were naturally good. As manifested in the "noble savage" motif characteristic of the era, the commonplace and the vulgar were explored and exalted for their underlying aspect of goodness and beauty. Often viewed as "poets of nature," the romantics did not revel in their love of earth and sky. Melancholy, doubt, and sometimes even despair were among their prominent moods.

The most important romantic poet in the first half of the century was Gonçalves Dias, whose *Suspiros poéticos e saudades* (Poetic Sighs and Longings, 1836) accelerated the revolt against classicism. Virtuous Indians and the beauties of the Brazilian landscape were among his favorite subjects; his poems manifested a taste for the picturesque and a feeling for nature that were characteristic of the movement. His "Song of Exile," written at Coimbra in 1843, is one of the most popular romantic poems; its opening line—"My country has palm trees, where the *sabiá* sings"—was known by several generations of schoolchildren.

Among the great romantic poets in the latter half of the century was the Bahian Antônio de Castro Alves. The son of a physician, he was educated in the São Paulo law school and was a gifted poet, painter, and playwright. Known as the "poet of slaves," he dedicated his short life to making his countrymen painfully aware of the misery and suffering of the slaves at a time when other poets devoted their verse to the color of their mistresses' eyes or to their own sorrows and infirmities. Unlike most literature written to support a particular cause, the poems of Brazil's first socially conscious poet were not forgotten once abolition had been won. His erotic love poems as well as his abolitionist verse were much admired by Brazilian and Portuguese writers throughout the century.

The novel also began to flourish during the Brazilian era of romanticism. Among its first notably successful practitioners were Joaquim Manoel de Macedo and José de Alencar. Macedo's *A Moreninha* (The Little Brunette, 1844), Brazil's first best-seller, gives an excellent glimpse into Brazilian life in the 1840s, and it is still read today with pleasure. The talented and imaginative José de Alencar, like the poet Gonçalves Dias, favored idealized Indians possessed with an excess of virtues. His *Iracema* (1865) is the story of an Indian maid who loved a Portuguese warrior. With *O Guaraní* (1857), the love story of a courageous and virtuous Indian warrior and the daughter of a wealthy *fazendeiro*, Alencar placed himself on shaky ground, even for a romantic: prevailing social attitudes dictated that his hero and heroine could not marry, yet his readers would rebel if he killed either of the noble pair. He solved this problem with the aid of a great flood, described in the most graphic terms as it swept away the plantation house. The hero, with the strength of a modern bulldozer, uproots a huge palm tree, and on this makeshift raft he and his love float away with the flood, leaving readers to supply whatever ending suited them.

Alfredo Escragnolle de Taunay, a Brazilian of French descent, wrote *Inocência* (1872), a more sophisticated work than earlier provincial or regional novels. *Inocência* is the tragic love story of a young girl of the interior, where fathers still had the power of life or death over members of their families. A link between romanticism and naturalism, which was to supersede romanticism in the last three decades of the century, the novel made literary history and was translated into many languages. Taunay's fame rests mainly on *The Retreat from Laguna* (1871), a gripping account of a disastrous overland expedition in which he participated during the Paraguayan War.

The availability of funds previously channeled into the slave trade enabled Brazilians to invest in many new economic enterprises. Among these were banks, textile mills, food processing, clothing, railroads, and coffee plantations. One of the most remarkable men of the century was Ireneu Evangelista de Sousa, barão de Mauá—a manufacturer, builder of railroads, and financier. Sousa took his titled name from the Indian village of Mauá, which suggests that Dom Pedro may not have held him in as high esteem as a *fazendeiro*. Wealthy, influential, and not a member of the oligarchy, Mauá was always viewed with some apprehension by Dom Pedro, government officials, and landed aristocrats, all of whom were still oriented toward a slave-based economy. Later, when Mauá's financial empire was about to crash in 1875, a government loan could have helped him weather the storm, but partisan opposition prevented it. He spent the rest of his life paying off his debts, and died less than three weeks before the empire fell. Mauá was the transitional figure between the manorial economy of the colonial era and modern capitalism. His Banco Mauá was more successful than the Bank of Brazil. He provided Rio de Janeiro with gas lighting, introduced steam navigation on the Amazon river, and supervised the laying of a trans-Atlantic cable. Mauá was the only Brazilian who could keep pace with foreigners in the domains of industry and commerce, although others had begun to invest more actively.

In an effort to eliminate costly friction and to support a program of administrative reform and economic development, Liberal and Conservative leaders cooperated with Honório Hermeto Carneiro Leão, marquês de Paraná, and formed a temporary "Party of Conciliation," headed by a "Ministry of Conciliation." Carneiro Leão died in 1856; the Ministry of Conciliation was to survive him by three years. It was not until the Liberal victory in the election of 1860 that urban middle-class groups took over the economic and political management of the nation. The statesman Joaquim Nabuco commented, "With this victory the tide of republicanism, which had been ebbing since the monarchical reaction of 1837 and was at its lowest ebb after the majority, began to turn . . . and the victory assumed the proportions of a peaceful revolution against the oligarchy in their senatorial stronghold." Others later looked back on it as the "dawn of a new age."

The coming of the new age was delayed, however, by the long and costly Paraguayan War (1865–70). After 1851, when Brazilian troops helped the Argentine Justo José Urquiza of Entre Ríos province overthrow Juan Manuel de Rosas, tyrant of Buenos Aires, temptation to interfere in the Plata region must have been reinforced by that easy victory.

The *Colorados* and *Blancos* (Reds and Whites), Uruguay's two warlike parties representing Montevideo and the countryside, alternated the presidency by exchanging bullets rather than by counting ballots. In 1854 at the request of the Uruguayan president, a *Colorado*, Brazil sent 4,000 troops who remained in Uruguay two years. Mauá, earlier commissioned to provide secret subsidies to the besieged government in Montevideo, established branches of Banco Mauá there and in Buenos Aires. He became deeply involved in trade, industry, and finance in the two countries—an involvement that contributed to his later ruin.

Chronic political turbulence in Uruguay led to frequent raids across the border into Rio Grande do Sul, which the embattled government was unable to prevent. In 1864, when the *Blanco* Atanasio Cruz Aguirre seized power, Brazil presented him with an ultimatum—restore peace and satisfy those with claims, or Brazil would take military reprisals. Francisco Solano López, Paraguay's ambitious young dictator, promised to support Aguirre. He warned Dom Pedro not to upset the balance of power by interfering. Dom Pedro ignored the warning.

When Brazilian troops joined *Colorado* rebels against Aguirre, López retaliated by seizing the Brazilian steamer *Marquês de Olinda* en route to Mato Grosso, and sent his troops into that Brazilian province. The invasion of Mato Grosso, the site of a large Brazilian arsenal, was necessary because Paraguay, despite the frequent assertion that it was "armed to the teeth," was woefully short of military weapons. The campaign was successful, but by the time López was ready to aid the *Blanco* government, it had already fallen. His request that President Bartolomé Mitre of Argentina allow him to cross the thickly populated Corrientes province to reach Uruguay was denied. In March 1865 López declared war on Argentina and threw his forces across Corrientes, thereby alienating Urquiza of Entre Ríos, who might otherwise have supported him, and indirectly helping Mitre unite Argentina.

The Allies—Argentina, Brazil, and Uruguay—agreed not to make peace until López had been removed. Paraguay was to indemnify them for the cost of the war, as well as to suffer the destruction of its forts and a loss of territory. Secretly Argentina and

Brazil agreed to partition Paraguay, but a British consul obtained and published a copy of the secret clause, stirring sympathy for Paraguay and widespread criticism of the two large nations intent upon carving up a small neighbor. Until 1867 Mitre was nominally commander-in-chief of the Allied forces, but Caxias, the superb strategist, commanded Brazilian troops and became commander-in-chief when Mitre withdrew.

The Paraguayan force sent to the aid of Uruguay was destroyed at Uruguayana, and thereafter Paraguay was on the defensive. The river fort at Humaitá, the "Gibraltar of South America" that was built under the supervision of Brazilian engineers, checked the invading armies and navies until July 1868, but by the end of that year the Paraguayan army, now composed of women and young boys, had been scattered. When the Allies entered Asunción in January, they discovered that the city had been abandoned. Caxias, in ill health and irritated by partisan criticism of his method of conducting the war, was unwilling to continue the war merely to dispose of López; he declared it ended and resigned his command. After his return to Rio de Janeiro he was named "duque," making him the only Brazilian ever to receive that title usually reserved for princes.

Believing the fighting over, Dom Pedro allowed his son-in-law, the conde d'Eu, to assume command in Paraguay. López, however, raised yet another army of women and children and resumed the fighting. Brazilian troops finally ran him to earth and killed him at Cerro Corá in March 1870. López' earlier offer to destroy the defenses, accept the frontiers demanded by the Allies, and pay the expenses of the war had been rejected because Dom Pedro refused to compromise unless López agreed to leave Paraguay. But López had become the symbol of a nation fighting for its very existence, and he would not abandon his people. Because of his unsavory and cruel character, it has been easy for Brazil and Argentina to make him appear responsible for the war; but Dom Pedro and, to a lesser extent, Mitre must also bear a heavy share of responsibility.

The war was extremely costly for Brazil and Paraguay in lives as well as in money. Argentina, however, profited from the sale of provisions to Brazil. Dom Pedro had called the war a "good electric shock to nationality," but it nearly ended Paraguay's existence. When it was over, Dom Pedro, with his white hair and beard, appeared to be a broken old man, although he was not yet forty-five. Among the positive results of the war were the acceleration of industrial production and the freeing of some of the slaves who had served in the army. While the war was in progress, the United States and other nations urged Brazil to open the Amazon to international commerce. Dom Pedro signed the necessary decree, setting September 7, 1867 to be the opening of the great river and some of its tributaries.

On the negative side, the first military intervention occurred during the war, touching off a chain of events that was to culminate in the overthrow of Dom Pedro in 1889. The events leading up to this crisis are complicated: abolition and the emperor's use of the moderating power were also factors. After the "Party of Conciliation" disintegrated, moderates and Liberals banded together in 1862 to form the Progressive party. Progressive rule (1863–68) reached its high point in the ministry of Zacarias Góes e Vasconcelos (1866–68). Since the constitution allowed officers on active duty to hold political office, Caxias had served in both the Chamber and the Senate. His political activity in behalf of the Conservatives had generated enmity among the Liberals. Realizing, however, that Caxias was the only Brazilian officer capable of commanding the army in Paraguay, Zacarias offered him the command. When Caxias refused because Minister of War Angelo Muniz da Silva Ferraz, later marquês de Uruguayana, was his personal enemy, Zacarias, believing that Caxias was indispensable, replaced Ferraz.

Soon after Caxias, angered by Zacarias' failure to defend him against partisan attacks, resigned his command, the ministry fell. Its demise was presumably over the question of proper procedure in selecting a senator to fill a vacancy, but the underlying cause was Caxias' displeasure with the ministry. The province of Rio Grande do Norte had submitted three names, as prescribed by the constitution. The Council of State recommended a Conservative. Zacarias, hoping to maintain his party's strength in the Senate, protested to Dom Pedro. The emperor upheld the Council of State, and the ministry resigned. Conservatives and Liberals alike, however, viewed the incident as an overthrow of a ministry due to military pressure.

Zacarias, refusing to consider reconciliation with Caxias, remained resentful and eager for vengeance. Following his custom, Dom Pedro asked Zacarias for advice as to his successor, for the Progressives had a substantial majority in the Chamber. Zacarias remained silent, which was tantamount to saying that no member of his party was capable of organizing a new ministry. Ignoring the

Progressive majority, Dom Pedro violated parliamentary practice and called on the Conservatives to form a government.

The Progressives regarded the appointment of a Conservative ministry as a palace *coup d'etat* and accused Dom Pedro of being "Machiavellian." The Progressive majority in the Chamber immediately returned a vote of no confidence in the new ministry. Dom Pedro dissolved the Chamber and called for a general election, which the Conservatives conveniently won by the usual methods. From this time on Dom Pedro followed the advice of the ministry in selecting senators, but the damage had been done: thereafter, when it was convenient to blame him for their failures, he was criticized by both parties.

In 1869 the Liberals issued a manifesto, beginning with the words "Either Reform or Revolution" and calling for sweeping governmental changes. Among other things, the Liberals wanted to abolish the moderating power, the Council of State, the national guard, and slavery. They called for direct elections and extension of the franchise, limited terms for senators, an independent judiciary, popular election of provincial presidents, and religious freedom. Their goal, as exemplified by these proposed reforms, was substantial decentralization of the imperial government.

After the Paraguayan War the empire, responding to growing interest in nonagricultural enterprises and rising opposition to slavery, set new goals and began to move in new directions. Abolition became the most important issue facing the empire. Since independence there had been occasional protests against slavery, but the dominant *fazendeiros* refused even to discuss abolition. Noting the contempt of Argentine and Uruguayan intellectuals for slavery, Dom Pedro determined to end it in Brazil as gradually and painlessly as possible. In 1865 he informed the French Council for Emancipation that emancipation would be considered when the Paraguayan War ended.

In 1864 Dom Pedro suggested the advantages of freeing children born of slave mothers, and the following year he asked the lawyer Pimento Bueno, marquês de São Vicente, to prepare a project for progressive emancipation. In his "Speech from the Throne" in 1866 the emperor gently alluded to the matter: "The servile element in the empire," he said, "cannot fail . . . to merit your consideration. While respecting existing property rights . . . the important interests involved in emancipation must receive your careful attention." Mild as it was, this statement infuriated the *fazendeiros,* who regarded it as an unprovoked attack on their cherished institution.

Zacarias and a few other Liberals also became convinced that slavery must be ended. He appointed a commission headed by Senator Nabuco de Araújo to frame a law providing for gradual emancipation, and the assignment was completed in August 1868. Zacarias had firmly protested the appointment of a Conservative to fill the vacant Senate seat from Rio Grande do Norte because of his concern to maintain the strength of antislavery forces in the Senate.

Conservative ministries remained precariously in power for a few years after 1868. José Maria Silva Paranhos, later visconde do Rio Branco, headed the ministry in 1871, and though a Conservative, he was a confirmed abolitionist. He proposed the bill that Nabuco de Araújo had drawn up. In September it was passed as the so-called Rio Branco Law of Free Birth, while Dom Pedro was traveling in Europe. The law required registration of all slaves and their children. All children born after the date of its passage would be free, with the provision that when a child was eight years old, its former master could accept either a payment from the government or the labor of the child until its twenty-first birthday. The slaveholders, grudgingly reconciled to gradual emancipation, accepted this as a compromise. Most of them chose the children's labor rather than cash payment.

In January 1878 the old and infirm duque de Caxias resigned as president of the Council of Ministers, and Dom Pedro called in the Liberal Cansanão Sinimbú. The Chamber was dissolved, and the subsequent election gave the Liberals a sizable majority. Among the newcomers in the Chamber was Joaquim Nabuco, son of the former senator and an ardent abolitionist. The Law of Free Birth did not satisfy him, for he regarded slavery solely as a moral and religious issue, not an economic one. He condemned it for failing to free the present generation. When the Chamber rejected Nabuco's bill to end slavery in ten years, he realized that the abolitionist campaign would be long and difficult, but he was willing to devote his life to the cause if necessary. He founded the Brazilian Antislavery Society and gradually built up a following through public lectures and newspaper articles. He also wrote *O abolicionismo*, the Brazilian counterpart of *Uncle Tom's Cabin*.

The antislavery campaign was not the only current movement. The Liberals still demanded reforms to make elections meaningful. As long as the Conservatives controlled the government, however,

nothing more could be done about abolition; and until the power of
the slaveholders was broken, these other reforms had little chance of
passing and becoming effective.

In 1878 the Liberals came to power pledged to introduce
needed changes in the electoral system. Dom Pedro was also
concerned about electoral reform. Previously the voters chose
electors who chose deputies—a system open to all manner of
irregularities. The only political error under these circumstances
was losing an election that one's party controlled. This system
obviously did not reflect the wishes of the people. Dom Pedro tried
to overcome this deficiency by rotating parties in power, but this
was an artificial solution at best, for it depended entirely on the
judgment of one man who was not infallible.

Sinimbú, who proved a poor choice to head the ministry
because he lacked prestige, was forced to resign, and Dom Pedro
called on Senator José Antônio Saraiva to form a ministry. Saraiva
was convinced that electoral reform could best be accomplished by
ordinary legislation rather than by the slow process of constitutional
amendment. He also believed that direct election of deputies by
districts would eliminate the opportunity for fraud—as if law alone
could change human morality. In January 1881 the Saraiva Law
was passed, providing for direct elections and lower property
qualifications for voting.

The next election was conducted honestly and with restraint,
resulting in the defeat of two of Saraiva's ministers. He was honored
as being above political dissent, but that did not help his party stay
in power. Subsequent elections made it painfully clear that the
empire's major parties preferred conventional to reformed electoral
procedures. The electorate was still ridiculously small, fewer than
150,000 out of a population of 15,000,000, and the new law was
effective only as long as Saraiva was in a position to enforce it. The
solution to the electoral problem was human, not legal, for more
depended on the intentions of the president of the Council than on
statute. In January 1882 Saraiva was out, and the next few
ministries were short-lived. In a desperate effort to check the
abolitionist tide, the Conservatives returned to the former methods
of conducting elections, insuring that abolitionists were eliminated
from the Chamber. The failure of electoral reform was evidence
that no basic changes could be made until the power of the
fazendeiros was broken, and there was only one way to accomplish
that—immediate emancipation without compensation, which

would ruin them financially. Gradually those who were seeking any change threw their weight behind the abolitionist movement.

As sentiment for emancipation spread, largely through the efforts of Nabuco, Rui Barbosa, José Patrocínio, and a host of other dedicated abolitionists, confusion intensified and few ministries were stable. Both factions blamed their difficulties on the emperor. The Conservatives held him responsible for stirring up abolitionist agitation in the first place. The abolitionists, for their part, were dissatisfied with his moderate but indecisive approach.

After several ministries had fallen, the emperor, on consulting Liberal leaders, called abolitionist Manoel Pinto de Souza Dantas to head the ministry in 1884. Dantas was pledged to free all slaves aged sixty or older. He approached the issue with great caution; although the provinces of Ceará and Amazonas had freed all slaves within their borders without waiting for the imperial government to act, in the General Assembly abolition generated little enthusiasm. Dantas' bill called for an increase in redemption funds, a prohibition of the transfer of slaves from one province to another, and emancipation of all slaves at age sixty. When the bill was announced, a resolution was presented: "The Chamber of Deputies, not accepting a solution of the slavery problem that does not include indemnification, refuses to give its support to the cabinet's policy."

Despite Dantas' immense popularity, a vote of no confidence in the ministry passed the Assembly by two votes. Dantas was ousted, and Dom Pedro called again on Saraiva to replace him.

Saraiva was prepared to compromise, thus incurring the wrath of the most ardent abolitionists, who called his agreement a pact between "the timid and the obstinate" and "the happy medium between the minimum and nothing." In September 1885 the new ministry pushed through a bill similar to that of Dantas except that, as a compromise, sixty-year-old slaves were obliged to work for their masters for three years after they were "liberated." Convinced that his work was done, Saraiva resigned, and the emperor named Conservative João Maurício Wanderly, barão de Cotegipe and president of the Senate, to head the ministry.

The fact that Dom Pedro called the Conservatives to power, however wise the move may have been, greatly irritated the Liberals, who had been close to victory. Joaquim Nabuco, in a pamphlet entitled "The Error of the Emperor," criticized Dom Pedro for replacing Dantas with Saraiva. "On the previous day," he wrote, "emancipation was in power, while on the following day, slavery was triumphant." The emperor's error was changing his mind, thereby reversing the tide.

This abolitionist law, like the Law of Free Birth, was finally passed by a Conservative government after the Liberals had prepared the way. Since Dom Pedro alone could determine which party would be in power at any time, he presumably preferred this party relationship to abolitionist legislation. The Liberals, seeing their efforts usurped by unwilling Conservatives, resented the emperor's action. The Conservatives, faced with the unavoidable necessity of damaging their own interests, were equally resentful. Dom Pedro's exercise of the moderating power may have been fair and honest, but on occasions it showed him lacking in political wisdom. Gradually he alienated his chief supporters, and the monarchy came to hang by a thread. During the last years of his reign diabetes seriously impaired his capacity for work; the monarchy's health declined simultaneously.

From mid-1887 on the abolitionists were certain of eventual victory, for the slavocrats had exhausted every delaying tactic. Toward the end of the year Joaquim Nabuco, while in Europe, conceived a brilliant stratagem for forcing through emancipation. Isabel, who had been named regent while the gravely ill Dom Pedro went to Europe seeking medical advice, was known to be profoundly devout—some called her bigoted—and Nabuco intended to exploit this trait for the cause of emancipation. He obtained letters of introduction to Pope Leo XIII and in February 1888 visited Rome.

Nabuco pointed out to the pope that everything thus far accomplished for the slaves was owing to Dom Pedro's intercession. The pontiff agreed to speak out in behalf of Brazilian slaves, but Conservative diplomatic agents realized what was transpiring and protested to the pope. As a result of their pressure the papal encyclical was not directed specifically at conditions in Brazil. Leo XIII announced his support of the enslaved everywhere and canonized Father Pedro Claver, the seventeenth-century "Apostle of the Negroes" in Venezuela. When the news reached Brazil, Cotegipe realized his ministry's precarious position, but he grimly hung on, delaying emancipation as long as possible.

Various other currents were to converge in 1888 and 1889 contributing to the overthrow of the monarchy. Positivist ideas had entered Brazil in the 1850s by way of the military and technical schools, where men became interested in Auguste Comte's philosophy through study of his works on mathematics. Positivism appealed to many of Brazil's educated elite, only a fraction of the free population. The new interest in science and material progress made this intellectual minority receptive to a philosophical system that promised a well-ordered society which was to be dominated by the wealthy and provide a progression of steps leading to utopia. The philosophy was also attractive to army officers and republicans, for it upheld republican dictatorship as the ideal government.

Brazilian positivists were soon split into two groups—the orthodox party, controlled by Miguel Lemos and Raimundo Teixeira Mendes, and those who accepted only those aspects of positivism that were useful to them. The former had little impact on political events, while the latter, inspired by Colonel Benjamim Constant Botelho de Magalhães, were instrumental in replacing the monarchy with a republic. Constant, a mathematics professor at the Military School and a veteran of the Paraguayan War, exerted a profound influence on a generation of cadets. Dom Pedro, who admired Constant, chose him as a tutor for the royal grandchildren. When Constant reminded the emperor that he was a republican, Dom Pedro replied, "That won't hurt—you may be able to convert them."

Republican ideas spread during the 1860s. In 1863 James W. Webb, United States Minister to Brazil, predicted that Dom Pedro would be the last emperor, and that Brazil would become a republic without a violent struggle. In 1870 the Republican party was organized by dissident Liberals and others who were disenchanted with the empire. Its formation in this year echoed the fall of the French empire and the rise of the Third Republic. On December 3, the day after Dom Pedro's birthday, the party issued the "Republican Manifesto," demanding an end to the monarchy and many reforms that Liberals had proposed earlier. Although a Republican party was an exotic party in a monarchy, Dom Pedro regarded it benevolently and did little to check its growth. The godfathers of the new party were the Frenchman Gambetta, who sent greetings, and the Spaniard Castelar, who sent an expert in conspiracies to deliver practical advice. The secret of revolutions, the latter informed the Republicans, was to have an infallible means of escape.

Many Republican clubs and newspapers were founded, but the party was never large. Six years after it was founded, in 1876, the first Republican deputy was elected, and in the following year three Republicans were elected to the São Paulo provincial assembly. The spread of republican ideas reflected the decline in the relative importance of the *fazendeiros* and the rise of urban commercial and industrial groups. The party was never influential enough to be a threat by itself, but over the years it accustomed Brazilians to the idea of a republic. The Liberals were determined that the moderating power should be transferred from the emperor to the president of the Council of Ministers, but Republicans preferred to wait until a republic had been established and then delegate the moderating power to the president.

When the Liberals returned to power in 1878, Dom Pedro demonstrated political acumen by suggesting that a prominent Republican be included in the ministry—a shrewd device to lure away an effective leader from the Republican party. Despite pleas from a number of prominent Republicans, Rodrigues Pereira accepted the post of minister of justice, thereby depriving the party of his leadership. The Republicans resented the emperor's interference, but they had no serious complaint against him. Except for this one instance, he did not interfere with them in any way, nor did he bear grudges against those who attacked him in the press.

Another current that contributed indirectly to the fall of the monarchy by alienating one of its former supporters was the conflict between church and state in the 1870s. Dom Pedro, his cabinet members, and many priests were regalists, and the constitution gave the emperor the right to sanction or exclude papal decrees. As Joaquim Nabuco described the emperor's attitude: "The mind of Dom Pedro II was steeped in anticlerical prejudice. He was not exactly anticlerical—he saw no real danger in the existence of the clergy; he rather failed to find attractive the actual religious vocation. For him . . . the soldier and the priest were two social phenomena with no future, two temporary necessities which he would have liked to put to better use." The emperor also favored civil marriage, and he encouraged Protestant missionaries to come to Brazil. On his trips to Europe he enjoyed visiting Protestant shrines and Jewish synagogues, which caused some of the devout to suspect his faith. His own feeling in the matter he summed up by saying, "I am religious because morality, which is a quality of intelligence, is the foundation of the religious idea."

The Brazilian clergy had generally been tolerant and understanding, and had adapted itself well to the patriarchal society. As minister of justice (1854–57), Nabuco de Araújo, with the backing of the bishops as well as the emperor, tried to suppress the disorders characteristic of the convents and to restore monastic discipline. As the bishops had tried and failed, they did not consider it an unwarranted intrusion for the government to help solve this ecclesiastical problem. In 1857 Nabuco abolished appeals to the crown in cases in which bishops had pronounced suspensions or interdicts. These events are merely illustrative of the cordial relations that existed between church and state.

In 1864, however, a papal syllabus asserted the church's right to control all cultural activities, including education. It rejected liberty of conscience, demanded that the church be completely independent of state control, and maintained that it was the government's duty to carry out papal instructions. An encyclical of the same year denounced the Masonic order and instructed Catholics to abjure membership, but Dom Pedro refused to sanction it. In Brazil Masons were regarded as one of the arms of Christianity. They played an important role in charitable organizations and, furthermore, Dom Pedro and many leading statesmen, among them the barão do Rio Branco, were members. The Brazilian Masons had not been involved in revolutionary disturbances since 1848.

In March 1872 the Masonic lodges of Rio de Janeiro staged a celebration honoring the Rio Branco Law of Free Birth of the previous year. When the press published a sermon delivered by Father Almeida Martins at a meeting of the Grand Lodge, the bishop of Rio de Janeiro ordered him to renounce Masonry or face suspension. Almeida refused, for the papal encyclical was not legally binding in Brazil.

In Pernambuco the newly appointed bishop, Vital Maria Gonçalves de Oliveira, a Capuchin friar who had been educated in France and whose attitude toward Masons was colored by his experiences there, was determined to put the encyclical into effect in his diocese. In a pastoral letter he denounced the Masons and challenged the emperor's right to *padroado* (patronage). He ordered the *irmandades* (semi-religious brotherhoods) to expel their Masonic members. When the *irmandade* of Santissimo Sacramento refused, he suspended its religious functions and put its chapel under the interdict. The *irmandade* appealed to the emperor, who referred the appeal to the Council of State. The latter ordered Vital to lift the interdict and, when he refused, brought him before the Supreme

Court of Justice. Vital declined to defend his actions, declaring simply that the government had no right to interfere with spiritual functions of the church. In February 1874 he was sentenced to four years at hard labor.

The bishop of Pará, Antônio de Macedo Costa, a Sulpician friar also educated in Europe, took up the same cause and received a similar sentence. Dom Pedro commuted both to simple imprisonment, but he considered the bishops' actions as serious offenses. Before sentences had been passed, Dom Pedro sent the barão de Penedo to Rome, where he reached an agreement with Pius IX, who expected that the trials would be dropped. When news of the harsh sentences handed the two bishops reached Rome, all was confusion. Peace was restored when Isabel, serving as regent while her father was on his way to the United States for the 1876 centennial celebration, declared amnesty; the pope in turn ordered the bishops to lift the interdicts. The Masons were never completely excluded from the *irmandades,* but the affair left wounds that were slow to heal.

The monarch lost prestige as a result of the conflict. Clergy and Conservatives were embittered over the treatment of the two bishops, although neither man was actually punished. The Liberals were resentful because Dom Pedro had turned back instead of pushing on and separating church and state. The clergy never forgave the emperor. Later, when the bishop of Rio de Janeiro learned that Dom Pedro had been deposed and confined to the palace, he exclaimed: "Exactly as he did with the bishops! And Macedo Costa exulted, "The throne disappeared . . . and the altar? The altar stands."

Although many currents contributed at least indirectly to the decline and fall of the monarchy, the rise of militarism and the growing animosity between army officers and the *casacas* (politicians, literally "frock coats") were paramount. The fall of the Zacarias ministry in 1868 followed by the formation of a new Conservative ministry prompted José Bonifácio "the Younger" to introduce a resolution in the Chamber of Deputies. The Chamber, it read, had no confidence in a ministry installed after "something other than a parliamentary question has caused the fall of its predecessor." The Conservatives were also aroused at interference by the army in the person of Caxias.

After the Paraguayan War the army had been reorganized. Recruiting by force was replaced by conscription, whipping was abolished, and officers' pay was increased by one-third. Neverthe-less, the army considered itself neglected, and the idea that the *"políticos* are the enemies of the military" began to spread. At the same time army officers were becoming convinced that they were destined to save the nation from the *políticos*. The division between civilians and the military was widened in 1874 when the Central School was divided into the Military and Polytechnical Schools; thereafter cadets were no longer educated with civilian students. The cadets, however, were much more interested in studying nonmilitary subjects than in learning the art of war. They embraced abolitionism, positivism, and eventually republicanism; like the Paraguayan War veterans, they were intensely interested in politics.

Caxias had been involved in politics since 1840, when he was elected to the Chamber of Deputies from Maranhão. He also served as a life senator from Rio Grande do Sul, minister of war, and president of the Council of Ministers. A leading Conservative, he was able to keep the army from getting out of line as long as he lived. His counterpart among the Liberals was Manoel Luiz Osorio, marquês de Herval, another hero of the Paraguayan War. Osorio died in 1879 and Caxias in 1880. Thereafter the Conservatives courted Deodoro da Fonseca as the "new Caxias," while the Liberals turned to Correia da Câmara, visconde de Pelotas. Remembering the lesson of 1868, the *casacas* competed for allies among the officers. The situation had changed, however, for in the long contest with Paraguay the veterans had developed an *esprit de corps* and a touchy sense of honor. Army officers entering politics could not comprehend the *políticos'* lack of a sense of professional honor. As it turned out, it was a grave error to allow these officers to hold political posts while on active duty; they were not at all prepared for the rough give and take of Brazilian parliamentary debate or for the *políticos'* custom of insulting their opponents at every opportunity. When their "honor" was impugned, the officers could not rest until the stain was wiped away; in turn, the *políticos* could not fathom that to the military class an insult to one was an insult to all.

In 1883 the marquês de Paranaguá introduced a bill in the Senate that would provide pensions for retired soldiers and widows of servicemen. On the surface this seemed an overdue action to protect military families, but it included the provision that service-men could be retired or dismissed "when the good of the public service" demanded it. This was simply a skillful device to give the government an advantage over politically-minded officers, for "the good of the public service" was not defined and therefore open to the government's interpretation in any situation. Lieutenant Colonel Senna Madureira, a brilliant officer with a reputation for insubordination, analyzed the flaws in the bill and warned the military against the possibility of *presente de grego* (Greeks bearing gifts). The outcry that followed led to the bill's defeat and put the army more than ever on guard against the *casacas*.

In the spring of 1884 Madureira, commanding officer of the military school at Campo Grande, permitted abolitionist propaganda to circulate freely. When the adjutant general inquired whether newspaper accounts of abolitionist celebrations were correct, Madureira replied that he was unaware that the adjutant general had the right to inquire into what had happened at the school. For this he was relieved of his command and reprimanded, "for the good of the discipline of the army." In December the government reissued a ban on army or navy officers' discussing political events in the press without prior approval from the minister of war.

In July 1886 Colonel Cunha Mattos was "insulted" in the Chamber of Deputies after submitting an unfavorable inspection report on an officer who was a friend of Deputy Simplício Coelho de Rezende. The colonel and the deputy traded insults until Minister of War Alfredo Chaves took umbrage at one of Cunha Mattos' remarks against him. He ordered Cunha Mattos restricted to the waiting room of his regimental headquarters for forty-eight hours, calling attention to the *aviso* prohibiting officers from discussing political or military matters in the press.

Alfredo Chaves was a *casaca*, not a career officer, and the military ignored Cunha Mattos' violation of regulations on the grounds that his "honor" had been at stake. The punishment, no matter how mild it was, was viewed by the military as a clear-cut endorsement of the insults Coelho de Rezende had made in the Chamber. This rift between Cunha Mattos on one side and the minister of war and Coelho de Rezende on the other was to blossom into a bitter war between army officers and civilian ministries.

The visconde de Pelotas, veteran of the Paraguayan campaign and a senator from Rio Grande do Sul, defended Cunha Mattos in the Senate. An insult to one officer's honor, he declared, was an insult to all. "I place my honor above everything," he concluded. As the barão de Cotegipe ruefully remarked a few years later, "A seed produced a great tree and the words of Pelotas have been the seed of the question." The Cunha Mattos affair produced much heat but little light. New wounds were inflicted and old ones reopened. The breach never healed.

Senator Franco de Sá, minister of war at the time of the Madureira affair, once again justified the measures taken against Madureira. When the latter's angry reply to Sá's statement was published in the press, Minister of War Chaves censured him for violating the *aviso* prohibiting discussion of political or military matters in the press. Madureira, insubordinate as ever, published a protest of the censure and a request that he be relieved of his command. His declaration that members of the military had the legal right to defend their honor was favorably received by army officers everywhere in Brazil.

Pelotas, in a letter to a Republican paper in Rio Grande do Sul, declared that the government seemed determined to destroy what the army guarded most zealously—its honor. "Yesterday," he concluded ominously, "it was Colonel Cunha Mattos. . . . Today, it is Lieutenant Colonel Madureira. . . . Who will it be tomorrow?" This widely publicized letter deepened the growing chasm between the ministry and the military. It may also have awakened Republicans to the potential advantages of intensifying conflict between the army and the civilian ministers. The Republicans, willing to gain their goal with bayonets, soon began supporting the officers and stirring up trouble between the latter and Liberal and Conservative *casacas*. The main obstacle to military revolt, they discovered, was Deodoro da Fonseca's devotion to the "old man," Dom Pedro.

In 1883 Deodoro, the most popular officer in the army after Caxias' death, was sent to Rio Grande do Sul as military commander, serving part of the time as acting president of the province. He, too, spoke in behalf of Madureira. Pelotas and Deodoro, the first a Liberal and the second a Conservative, had been political opponents in the past, but they now embraced and forgot their differences because their beloved army was under attack. When Deodoro made clear to Cotegipe, then head of the ministry, that he sided with those involved in the disorders in Rio Grande do Sul, Cotegipe removed him as acting president, pointing out at the same time the army's growing lack of discipline.

The constitutional legality of the *avisos* issued by the minister of war was settled by an imperial resolution: "According to the Constitution, officers, like other citizens, have the right to manifest their opinions through the use of newspapers." The ministry submitted the question of the censures to the Supreme Military Council, which ruled that the cases of Cunha Mattos and Madureira involved discussions between officers and civilians, not between officers. The *avisos* had, therefore, been illegally applied to them.

The issue was thus apparently settled in favor of the army, but the ministry was reluctant to acknowledge its error by revoking the censures. It announced that the censures would be rescinded when the censured officers requested it. The two officers, knowing that the ministry was on the defensive and encouraged by Republicans, refused to request removal of what should not have applied to them. There was no spirit of compromise on either side.

The abolitionists and Republicans added fuel to the flames by loudly reiterating the military's demands that the ministry revoke the censures. Deodoro was detached from Rio Grande do Sul and returned to Rio de Janeiro, where he called a meeting of officers; out of it came a petition to the emperor. Deodoro also wrote an appeal to Dom Pedro for justice for the military. The *casacas* were aroused, for the appeals to the emperor had the ring of pressure and coercion. On the same day he received Deodoro's appeal, Dom Pedro met with his Council of Ministers and dismissed Deodoro as quartermaster general of the army. They probably expected Deodoro to resign his commission, but instead of resigning Deodoro wrote yet another appeal to Dom Pedro for justice.

Minister of War Chaves urged Cotegipe to retire Deodoro and close a number of the military schools. As Cotegipe commented later of this request, "It is all very well to advise 'punish, imprison, cut off heads,' but in practice many times we see ourselves obliged to moderate in order not to sacrifice higher interests," meaning the monarchy itself. Chaves resigned.

Ribeiro Luz, the new minister of war, did not revoke the censures, so the agitation continued in the spring of 1887, encouraged by abolitionists and Republicans. A military rebellion now seemed likely, and Republican leaders came to Rio de Janeiro from São Paulo to discuss the possibility of Pelotas' proclaiming the republic. Pelotas demurred. "That will come later," he said. "For the present it is necessary to have the agreement of all the comrades."

After discussing with Deodoro, Constant, and others the matter of proclaiming the republic, Pelotas decided that they should appeal to the General Assembly to settle the issue peacefully. The appeal, really an ultimatum, was published in May 1887. Cotegipe still opposed lifting the censures until either the two officers requested it or the minister of war revoked the censures on his own, but he sent the barão de Lucena to placate Deodoro. Deodoro, with pledges of support from all of the provincial garrisons but those of Pernambuco, informed Lucena that the ministry would soon fall, but assured him that Cotegipe would not be harmed.

Liberals interceded with Pelotas. They agreed, along with Cotegipe, that the Senate should request the ministry to revoke the censures, though the latter was convinced that the Senate resolution would be considered a censure of his government and topple the ministry. Some Brazilians believed that the republic was assured the moment the Senate passed the resolution inviting the government to "terminate the effects of disciplinary punishment . . . for use of the press without prior approval. . . ." After much debate the Senate passed the resolution. The ministry did not fall; as Cotegipe wryly remarked, however, it came out of the affair "with its dignity somewhat scratched."

The "military question" was far from settled, and military crises, both real and imaginary, continued to disturb the peace. Most of the older officers still respected the emperor, but the younger ones were openly antimonarchical. Early in 1888 in Rio de Janeiro the arrest of Leite Lobo, a naval officer who was not in uniform, prompted still another incident. When the final report discredited the testimony of the adjutant general of the navy and of an army officer who tried to secure Lobo's release after his arrest, the Naval Club, backed by the army, demanded that the chief of police be dismissed. Clashes between military personnel and the police became so serious the government was obliged to call in the police and ask the army to patrol the streets. Under pressure from the Naval Club the regent Isabel asked Cotegipe to dismiss the chief, but the ministry resigned instead.

Isabel turned to João Alfredo Corrêa de Oliveira to form a new Conservative ministry. For the moment, concern over the hazardous situation with the military was laid aside. The General Assembly convened on May 3. Five days later, at Isabel's request, João Alfredo submitted a bill to end slavery which passed the Senate and Chamber almost without opposition. On May 13 Isabel

123

came down from Petrópolis to sign it. The law stated simply that "Slavery in Brazil is declared extinct. All dispositions to the contrary are revoked." There was no mention of compensation. The regent was named "Isabel the Redeemer," and the nation joyfully embarked on an eight-day celebration.

The Liberals were bitterly disappointed, for once again the realization of a goal for which they had labored and sacrificed was to be achieved by the Conservatives. Indeed, all three emancipation laws had been passed under Conservative ministries—a paradoxical situation that did not endear Dom Pedro to either Liberals or Conservatives. Only Nabuco and a few others who put emancipation above party interests approved and supported the Conservative ministry. "Our obligation," Nabuco observed, "is to free the slaves. They are neither Liberals nor Conservatives. . . ." Cotegipe, on the other hand, opposed abolition to the end. When Isabel asked if it would not have been wiser for him to have voted for the law, he replied: "Your Highness has redeemed a race but lost a crown."

João Alfredo planned to arrange compensation to the slave owners for their losses, in spite of the fact that abolitionists were generally opposed to indemnifying slave owners because it would have defeated one of their purposes—to break the power of the *fazendeiros*. It seems likely that Dom Pedro, after he returned to Brazil in August, also intended to provide compensation. Had he done so immediately, he might have worn his crown for the rest of his days, but his failing health had greatly restricted his activity, and he seemed out of touch with conditions in Brazil. It is possible, too, that he had already abandoned any hope that Isabel might succeed him.

Despite the ministry's success in emancipation, when the General Assembly convened in May 1888 the Conservative party was found to be badly divided. João Alfredo asked that the ministry be dismissed. At first Dom Pedro refused, but in June he called on the visconde de Ouro Prêto to form a Liberal government.

Ouro Prêto was an able *Mineiro* who had served as minister of the navy during the Paraguayan War and later as minister of the interior. He introduced a reform program designed to make the republic unnecessary by demonstrating that the monarchical system was flexible enough to accommodate the most advanced ideas. Among the proposed reforms were the extension of suffrage to all literates, federalism, limited terms for senators, religious freedom, and the establishment of agricultural banks to aid *fazendeiros*.

He also began building up the national guard and increasing the size of Rio de Janeiro's police force. Ouro Prêto refused the Chamber's demand that he take up the change of senatorial terms before other issues he considered more important. Nabuco concentrated his efforts on achieving federalism, for he knew that unless some measure of local autonomy was introduced immediately, the empire was doomed. The disgruntled slavocrats merely shrugged; they were indifferent to the fate of the empire, if not eager to see it fall. Republicans intensified their attacks on the ministry, realizing that if the reforms were passed quickly, the chances of establishing a republic were in jeopardy. They aroused the army by emphasizing Ouro Prêto's intentions concerning the police and the national guard. The *Diário de Notícias*, edited by Republican Aristides Lobo, commented that "The events rush headlong toward the republic. . . . Federation would have been the preservative. Delaying it, the cabinet is destined to be . . . the last ministry of the monarchy."

O Paiz, edited by Quintino Bocaiúva, another Republican leader, joined in the assault on the ministry, and neither editor was restrained by the rules of journalism or chivalry. They twisted and exaggerated news stories, and when none were available to be made over for their purposes, they shamelessly invented incidents involving the ministry and the military. This combination of Republican activity and Conservative inactivity doomed Ouro Prêto's efforts to rescue the imperiled monarchy.

In June the Chamber was dissolved and the Liberals handily won the August elections by the customary methods. In the interim the ministry made such economic improvements as were within its power. Ouro Prêto was still oblivious to the depth of military dissatisfaction. He admitted later that he had never suspected that the false rumors could have had any effect on army officers. He had been convinced that the military had won all of the concessions it desired.

One of the rumors spread at this time was that Ouro Prêto was preparing for the abdication of Dom Pedro and the accession of Isabel on December 2, the ailing emperor's birthday. On one occasion Dom Pedro remarked to Deodoro enigmatically, "I expect to see you commanding a great parade soon." The Republicans employed this unexplained comment to confirm the rumor.

Deodoro was by no means committed to the idea of the republic, but his opposition was weakening. During João Alfredo's ministry there had been rumors that the government, in its effort to end military interference, was trying to destroy the prestige of Deodoro and his older brother Severiano. Severiano, adjutant general of the army at that time, died shortly after an insulting encounter with the government: the latter, in publishing a new set of regulations for the military schools, had discarded the general's proposal without telling him. Severiano's death and the unresolved insult greatly intensified Deodoro's bitterness toward the government.

Republican army officers set out to convince Deodoro that only the republic could end the "persecution" of the army. Informed that the army was to be reduced by half, Deodoro exclaimed, "No! I shall not permit this!" The officers were now convinced that in a crisis in which he must choose between the monarchy and the preservation of his beloved army, he would be willing to bring the monarchy to an end.

The sphinx-like Adjutant General Floriano Peixoto, who as a cadet had been called *"o mitrado"* (the sly one), revealed to no one where he stood on the matter of the republic. Ouro Prêto believed his assurances that there was nothing to fear from the army.

Souza Ferreira, editor of the *Jornal do Comércio*, urged Ouro Prêto to use the *Diário Oficial* to deny rumors that he had ordered Deodoro's arrest and the transfer of all garrisons from the capital. Ouro Prêto declined, for if he denied one rumor he would be obliged to deny all. On November 8 the Commercial Association of Rio de Janeiro honored Ouro Prêto for the success of his economic measures in restoring prosperity. On the same day another group met and plotted his downfall. This Republican group delegated Benjamim Constant to convince Deodoro to proclaim the republic when the time came. The uprising was set for November 20, the day the parliament was scheduled to convene.

Republican officers continued to sow seeds of discontent with the monarchy, and rumors of the military plot began to spread among the soldiers. On the night of November 14, with several military units in open revolt, Benjamim Constant decided that the movement must begin at once, instead of on November 20 as planned.

At 3:30 A.M. on November 15 Ouro Prêto sent a telegram to the summer palace at Petrópolis, but it did not reach Dom Pedro. Ouro Prêto went to army headquarters, where Floriano had taken charge of the defenses. As the rebel troops approached, it was clear that there would be no defense. Ouro Prêto turned to the ministers present and exclaimed: "We have been miserably betrayed!"

Deodoro entered the building and informed Ouro Prêto that his ministry was deposed. Only one mishap marred the whole affair, which involved just a small fraction of the army: the minister of the navy, the barão de Ladario, was shot in the leg as he approached army headquarters.

Deodoro led the troops to the naval arsenal to determine the navy's attitude and to observe public reaction. Everywhere he was cheered by the crowds, for many thought they were witnessing a parade. When he learned that the navy was agreeable to the overthrow of the ministry, Deodoro returned home.

Dom Pedro and his family came from Petrópolis early in the afternoon, unaware that they were to face more than a ministerial crisis. Military guards surrounded the palace to prevent the emperor from leaving, but he made no attempt to leave. Had he gone immediately to Deodoro, Dom Pedro could have saved his crown, but he made no such move. "A sad figure I would have been," said Deodoro later, "had the old man, without even a guard, confronted me in the Campo de Santa Anna."

On the afternoon of November 15 Republicans were frantic because the republic had not yet been proclaimed. They wrote a proclamation and drew up a list of officials to serve in the provisional government. In the meantime Deodoro learned that Dom Pedro planned to name him minister of war and to ask Silveira Martins, his enemy, to head the new ministry. This was the news that doomed the empire.

Constant pointed out the peril to all if Silveira Martins headed the government. "The general has the right to dispose of his head," he told Deodoro. But what of his comrades? He convinced Deodoro that he must proclaim the republic at once to save his friends as well as the army. Reluctantly Deodoro signed the two documents. As he admitted later, "I did not wish to proclaim the republic; that was the work of Aristides [Lobo], of Benjamim [Constant], and of Quintino [Bocaiúva]."

Dom Pedro was toppled from his throne by nothing more than the garrisons of Rio de Janeiro and abruptly expelled from the land he loved, but he had served Brazil conscientiously if not always well. He was, from the outset, a hard-working ruler, and there was no court frivolity. Twice weekly he presided over meetings of the Council of Ministers, meetings that began at nine at night and often continued past midnight. He sought to reach agreement among his ministers on important issues, and he refrained from using his veto power. He arose at six each morning to read the newspapers, holding audiences for the public at nine and again at five in the afternoon. Much concerned with improving education, he visited schools, took part in examinations, and regularly attended meetings of the *Instituto Histórico e Geográphico Brasileiro* and other learned societies.

Literature continued to flourish during the latter part of Dom Pedro's rule. Naturalism, a reaction to the excessive idealism of the romantics, gradually superseded romanticism during the last three decades of the nineteenth century. Its practitioners dealt with social themes, generally concerning the cities rather than the interior. The precursor of naturalism, initiating the trend in Brazil even before it appeared in Europe, was Manoel Antônio de Almeida, a "realist before realism." His *Memorias de um sargento de milícias* (Memories of a Militia Sergeant, 1854) was a realistic account of life in Rio de Janeiro during the empire. His approach was malicious and the humor wry, the style simple and unembellished. This promising novelist died at the age of thirty-one in a shipwreck off the Brazilian coast in 1861. Naturalism was not to appear again in Brazil for another twenty years.

French naturalists were extremely influential on the naturalists of Brazil, especially Emile Zola, who had a multitude of disciples and imitators, among them Brazil's Júlio Ribeiro. Some of these French writers had much to say of "superior" and "inferior" races, and they equated miscegenation with "mongrelization." Some Brazilian writers, like Graça Aranha, agreed with this view and expressed themselves pessimistically about Brazil's future possibilities. Arguments refuting this racial theme were often not universally convincing, and as a result Brazilians approached the twentieth century with grave doubts as to their worth as a people and to their future as a nation.

Among Brazil's leading naturalists were the mulatto philosopher Tobias Barreto of Recife, and the writers Júlio Ribeiro, Raul Pompéia, Aluízio Azevedo, and Joaquim Maria Machado de Assis. Aluízio Azevedo is best known for his novel *O Mulato*, the story of a young man who tries to succeed in a society of racial prejudice. The work attacks in crude, but candid language a major problem of Azevedo's time—the problem of miscegenation, which the author suggested was only temporary. Azevedo's other novels include: *Casa de pensão* (Boardinghouse, 1884) a realistic novel of manners setting forth life in a Rio de Janeiro boarding house; and *A Brazilian*

Tenement (1890), considered by some to be the apex of the Brazilian naturalist novel.

Joaquim Maria Machado de Assis was one of the most remarkable and prolific writers of the late nineteenth century. Born in 1839 to a mulatto house-painter and a Portuguese mother, he emerged from the poor section of Rio de Janeiro to become one of Brazil's greatest novelists. Working as a typesetter and proofreader, he began writing verse, articles, short stories, plays, and literary criticism in his spare moments. Eventually he received a government post, married a Portuguese lady, and settled down to an outwardly conventional middle-class life. Inwardly, despite the public's wide admiration for him, he was ever tortured by the fact that he was of Negro descent, physically ugly, and subject to epileptic seizures. His troubled life and almost total disillusionment with mankind are reflected in the fact that in the entire body of his work, which with his letters fills thirty-one volumes, there is only one character who can be called "good," and he is a lunatic. Unrivaled as a writer of short stories, Machado de Assis first won recognition as a novelist with *The Posthumous Memoirs of Braz Cubas* (1881), a cynical and ironic story written, as the preface declares, with "the pen of jesting and the ink of melancholy." Although he did not take an active part in the abolitionist campaigns, his writings sometimes focused on the sadistic treatment of slaves. His *Dom Casmurro* (Mr. Grumpy, 1900) is considered one of Brazil's finest novels. Machado de Assis was instrumental in founding the Brazilian Academy of Letters in 1897, and he served as its president until his death in 1908.

The growth of naturalism in the novel was paralleled by the rise of the Parnassian movement in poetry, which was also a reaction to the excessive sentimentalism of the romantics. The name "Parnassian" came from the French literary review, *Le Parnasse Contemporain*, first published in Paris in 1868. Machado de Assis, as a poet, was precursor of the Parnassian movement in Brazil. The school's verse was governed by the strictest rules of meter and rhyme. These rules were held to be immutable and could not be transgressed; poetic license was forbidden.

Dom Pedro himself was a product of Brazil's flourishing cultural and intellectual life. He knew a dozen languages and corresponded with intellectuals in other countries, such as Henry Wadsworth Longfellow and other New England savants. He was greatly admired in Europe and was received enthusiastically everywhere in the United States during his visit in 1876. At the Centennial Exposition in Philadelphia Alexander Graham Bell showed him a recent invention. "My God! It talks!" Dom Pedro exclaimed, then insisted on becoming Bell's first foreign customer for the telephone.

The ministers who served in his cabinets were less enthusiastic about the emperor, for they invariably resented his use of the moderating power to remove their party from office. (Paradoxically, they were always happy when he used it to remove their opponents.) Dom Pedro remained neutral between the two parties, cultivating the support of neither. As a result neither party felt inclined to support the monarchy when the army challenged it. Eusébio de Queiroz had declared in the 1850s that no one with dignity could serve him twice as a minister, and Silveira Martins complained that the ministers "do only what the emperor decides." Obliged to pass the emancipation laws of 1871, 1885, and 1888, the Conservatives, when accused of betraying their own class, made it clear that it was the emperor's decision, not theirs. Repeatedly attacked in the press after 1868 as "despotic" and "Machiavellian," Dom Pedro never defended himself nor bore a grudge against his attackers.

Whatever his faults, Dom Pedro saved Brazil from breaking up in 1840 and maintained Brazilian unity for nearly half a century. He presided over the transition from absolutism to parliamentary rule which, though imperfect, functioned fairly smoothly because of his intercession. He encouraged such scientific endeavors as the Thayer Expedition of 1865–66, the Hartt Geological Commission, and establishment of the School of Mines in 1875. A number of American scientists remaining in Brazil after the Hartt Commission and the Brazilians who studied with them provided the country with its first geological survey.

In Brazil's relations with foreign nations Dom Pedro was reasonably successful. In the 1840s and 1850s he was concerned over maintaining Uruguay's independence; in the 1860s he insisted on a costly war to oust Francisco Solano López of Paraguay. In the same decade Brazil recognized the belligerency of the Confederate States of America, straining relations with the Union; the emperor also recognized Maximilian as emperor of Mexico, endangering relations with Uruguay and Argentina. Brazil briefly severed relations with Great Britain over a six-day British blockade of Rio de Janeiro inspired by Britain's arrogant minister to Brazil, W. D. Christie.

The monarchy had saved Brazil in 1822, 1831, and 1840, and during Dom Pedro's long reign Brazilians had enjoyed individual rights and freedom from censorship. Dom Pedro was long convinced that the republican form of government was the best, but he did not believe that Brazil, with 80 percent of its population illiterate, was prepared to make republican self-government work. Indeed, Spanish Americans who knew Brazil under Dom Pedro considered it the only real "republic" in South America.

7/The Rise and Fall of the Old Republic

THE PROVISIONAL GOVERNMENT'S FIRST DECREE declared Brazil a federal republic, the United States of Brazil, and authorized the former provinces to organize governments. The second decree named the ministry, which was composed mostly of old-time Republicans: Aristides Lobo, minister of the interior; Quintino Bocaiúva, foreign affairs; Benjamim Constant, war; Admiral Wandenkolk, navy; Rui Barbosa, finance and acting minister of justice. Later Campos Sales and positivist Demétrio Ribeiro were named to head the Ministries of Justice and Agriculture.

On November 17 the royal family was exiled for fear that the emperor's presence might inspire a counter-revolution. Until his death in Paris in December 1891, Dom Pedro, still strong in his devotion to Brazil, continued to hope that he would be recalled.

Widespread fear of monarchist plots led to restrictions on freedom of the press and the use of military courts to try certain civil offenses. Free and unrestrained discussion of political events in the press ended abruptly. Resentment at the violation of Brazil's traditional freedom of the press quickly diminished Deodoro's popularity. Since he gave his ministers free rein, however, and since no minutes were kept of the early cabinet meetings, it is likely that Deodoro was blamed for many things for which he was at most only partially responsible.

A multitude of decrees were passed to introduce the new republican order. Church and state were separated, cemeteries and the marriage ceremony were secularized, and titles of nobility were abolished. Rui Barbosa, the most influential member of the government, had a hand in many of these pronouncements, including the one calling for the destruction of all records pertaining to slavery. This, Rui stated, was to help Brazilians forget that unfortunate part of their past. He did not mention it, but this act also completely ended the ex-slaveowners' hopes for compensation, since the only basis on which remuneration could be calculated was in the official registries of slaves.

The army increased to nearly twice the size it had been in the last years of the empire. Civilians in the government were not particularly happy about this, but they had to admit that they owed the republic to the army. A new national flag was designed, and the positivist motto *"Ordem e Progresso"* was adopted for the nation. Foreigners residing in Brazil on November 15, 1889 were given Brazilian citizenship unless they specifically rejected it.

Those who had believed in the utopian republic that Rui and others had pictured were soon disillusioned. Deodoro had been convinced only that the republic was required in order to benefit the army, but he too was quickly disenchanted. His Council of Ministers was quarrelsome, and tempers flared frequently. On occasion Deodoro saw his authority flaunted; as the highest ranking officer in the army he had never been accustomed to arguing with subordinates. He was also tactless. On one occasion an office-seeker declared that he had been a Republican since 1872. "You must be unfortunate," Deodoro told him; "I have been a Republican only a few months and I am already president." Deodoro soon viewed the whole affair as a sad mistake that could not be undone.

Rui's financial program was the provisional government's chief accomplishment, but even it was abortive. A decree in January 1890 called for government bonds to be substituted for gold as the reserve for bank notes issued. He also changed the philosophy behind the tariff, making it protective rather than merely revenue-raising. By requiring a percentage of customs duties to be paid in gold, he prevented a calamitous drop in the rate of exchange. A wild flurry of speculation and get-rich-quick schemes, known as the *"Encilhamento"* (saddling-up), wrecked Rui's programs, however. Inflation became uncontrollable. Inspired by examples set by the United States, he envisioned a Brazilian industrialization financed by the profits from coffee and rubber sales. His program continued the inflationary policy inherited from the empire and unintentionally encouraged unrestrained speculation in stocks. The cabinet violently opposed Rui's financial decree and demanded that it be negated. Deodoro threatened to resign if the decree was withdrawn. "Swallowing the sword," as they put it, the ministers gave in, but with resentment.

Conflict within the Council of Ministers became chronic.

Aristides Lobo resigned after a clash with Deodoro. Benjamim Constant suggested that Deodoro assume dictatorial powers, but the council would not hear of it. Deodoro grew angry at the army's lack of discipline, for which he blamed Constant. The two old soldiers became so angry that only double heart attacks prevented them from fighting a duel. In May 1890 Deodoro acknowledged his inability to govern the country and sent Rui a letter resigning his authority as provisional president. "The high office with which I have been invested is impossible for me considering that I do not have the patience of Job, nor desire the martyrdom of Jesus Christ," he said. Rui soothed him, however, and persuaded him to remain in office.

Among the issues causing bitter conflict was a campaign to drive robbers from the streets of Rio de Janeiro. Some of the robbers had liaisons with politicians who had protected them effectively in the past. Deodoro was determined that the robbers must go, and although warned that persons in high places would be involved, he promised full support to the police. The robber chieftains were well-known figures and easily found, and soon many of them had been sent off to serve long sentences at hard labor. The expected repercussions also came quickly, for one of the robbers was the brother of the conde de Martosinhos, owner of *O Paiz*, the paper that Quintino Bocaiúva edited. Quintino promised his employer that he would secure his brother's release. Deodoro was adamant. Quintino threatened to resign. Campos Sales interjected that he would resign if the prisoner were released.

The stormy career of the provisional government was marred by many similar quarrels. News of these unfortunate scandals could not be kept from the public, and the government's prestige sank lower and lower.

Deodoro tried to introduce measures that would help revive the economy, only to see his efforts thwarted by his own cabinet. It became increasingly clearer to him that he had been used as the instrument to end the monarchy, and that no one intended him to have much to say about governing the republic. Whatever he did was almost certain to damage his prestige and increase his unpopularity. On one occasion he was warned that army officers intended to attack *A Tribuna*, a monarchist newspaper, but he did not take the warning seriously. When the attack occurred, the army and Deodoro received much abuse in the press. When Deodoro informed his cabinet that he would not sign another measure until they approved of a public works contract for a friend in Rio Grande do Sul, the entire cabinet resigned. Deodoro called on his old friend, the barão de Lucena, to form a new ministry.

A constituent congress was called in 1890 to draw up a constitution. Much of the work was done by Rui Barbosa, an admirer of the constitutions of the United States, Argentina, and the Swiss Confederation. On one occasion Deodoro was examining Rui's work. "Where," he asked, "is the article that authorizes the president to dissolve Congress?" There was no such article.

The republican constitution approved in February 1891 provided for a president and vice president elected for four-year terms; cabinet officials were to be appointed by the president, and senators and deputies were to serve terms of nine and three years. It also contained a bill of rights and provided for freedom of religion. The constitution did not, however, revise the territorial organization of the country, which meant that some states were so weak that the few wealthy and powerful ones could easily dominate the national government. This would soon prove to be a serious omission.

The constituent congress was empowered to elect the president and vice-president for the first term. By this time Deodoro's political ineptness was well-known and distrust of the army was widespread. Deodoro's foes pushed the candidacy of Prudente de Morais of São Paulo, but Campos Sales and others feared that the army would carry out its threat to establish a dictatorship and they supported Deodoro. To the surprise of many Deodoro won, but the enigmatic Floriano Peixoto was named vice president by a much larger vote than Deodoro. Adding insult to injury, on the following day Quintino introduced a resolution declaring Benjamim Constant, who died a few days earlier, as founder of the republic, "a republican without blemish," and "a splendid model of virtue for future rulers."

When Deodoro entered the assembly on the inauguaration day, he was greeted by stony silence; Floriano "the Sphinx" was wildly applauded. The constituent assembly now became the new congress, and the chasm between it and Deodoro grew wider and deeper. Because of the disorder and strife little was accomplished. The barão de Lucena advised Deodoro to secure Floriano's aid in the Senate, over which he was expected to preside. Using ill health as a pretext, Floriano had remained away from the Senate. "If he were to understand the urgency with which we need his support,"

Deodoro replied to Lucena, "he would throw himself openly into the arms of the opposition."

The truth was that Floriano was already covertly conspiring for Deodoro's downfall. When the barão de Lucena approached him, he gave excuses for his absences from the Senate. "I have not been a friend of Marshal Deodoro," he added, "since the day he doubted my loyalty, but I am his comrade. . . . You may assure the Generalissimo that he will always find me at his side in any emergency."

The conflict between Deodoro and the congress became so intense that on November 3 he dissolved it, declared a state of siege, and assumed dictatorial powers. Floriano, Admiral Custódio de Melo, and the deputies from São Paulo heightened the strife by stirring up public opposition to Deodoro. In Rio Grande do Sul federal troops and opposition elements deposed Júlio de Castilhos, one of Deodoro's few supporters. On the republic's second anniversary Deodoro invited Floriano to join him in reviewing a parade. Floriano declined on the grounds that his uniform was "not fit to wear." The truth was that he was too preoccupied with plotting Deodoro's ruin. On this occasion Floriano was obliged to work with others, especially naval officers, who also conspired against Deodoro.

Learning of the conspiracy against him, Deodoro ordered the leaders arrested, including Admirals Wandenkolk and Custódio, but the latter eluded the police and incited the crews of warships to mutiny. On the morning of November 23 with the navy ready for battle, news arrived that Deodoro had resigned to avoid civil war. His bitterness was such that he had all of his medals and decorations thrown into the sea. When he died in August 1892, he was buried—at his request—without military honors.

Floriano remained sphinx-like after he assumed the presidency. Brazilians were to learn much of his cold determination, in some cases more than they had bargained for. Floriano inspired either fanatical devotion or blind hatred. He was from a lower middle-class planter family of Alagoas and cared nothing for wealth and ostentation. Although one of the highest ranking officers in the army, he was careless of dress. Basically an unhappy man, he had no friends and trusted no one. His only love was power, but it remained a lasting passion.

Floriano had a great capacity, almost a natural inclination, for

137

duplicity, as was demonstrated when he convinced Ouro Prêto that the army was loyal. In 1887 he had stated, "As a Liberal, I cannot wish government by the sword for my country; but there is no one who doesn't know, and the examples are there, that it can purify the blood of a corrupt social body such as ours." Floriano was at his best in this statement—deceitful in the first part, but deadly earnest in the second. He cared nothing for either monarchy or republic, for these were merely forms, not the reality of power.

As vice president he had virtually disappeared from public view, shunning his role as presiding officer of the Senate on grounds of ill health and moving silently in the shadows with Deodoro's enemies. The congress considered him useful in its efforts to destroy Deodoro, but it was a serious mistake, as the deputies would learn. When Deodoro resigned, the congress celebrated its victory. Floriano merely smiled.

According to the constitution, a new election should have been held because Floriano assumed office with more than two years remaining in the presidential term. None was held, however. Floriano used monarchist plots as his excuse, and his supporters rationalized his actions by saying that the constitutional provision did not apply to the first term. Although Brazilians had become aroused over Deodoro's violation of the constitution, they were not disturbed by Floriano's equally illegal action.

In his cabinet Floriano included the chief conspirators against Deodoro, Admiral Custódio José de Melo and General José Simeão de Oliveira, as ministers of the navy and war. He replaced all of the state governors who had supported Deodoro, appointing loyal young officers in their places. Rui Barbosa denounced this wholesale dismissal and resigned from the Senate in protest. "Between a dictatorship that in dissolving the federal congress depends upon the weakness of local governments," he wrote, "and another that dissolves the local governments, basing its support on the reinstated congress, there is no appreciable improvement." Opposition to Floriano's dictatorship was widespread, and Rui was the most articulate and courageous opponent.

In January 1892 troops in two forts rebelled against Floriano, and the speed and severity with which the rebellions were crushed should have discouraged all potential rebels. This was Brazilians' first view of Floriano in combat, and it was a chilling sight, for he was fearless. To his countrymen he was the greatest of heroes or the blackest of villains. When thirteen high-ranking officers of the army and navy sent him a request to hold a presidential election, he simply revoked their commissions and retired them. When Deodoro's friends assembled in public and declared that the congress had not accepted his resignation, Floriano personally arrested those he considered dangerous. Soon they were on their way to remote frontier forts, where they were left to repent their error. When Rui Barbosa asked the Supreme Court to issue writs of *habeas corpus* for political prisoners, Floriano merely posed the question, "If the judges . . . grant the politicians *habeas corpus,* I wonder who will grant them the *habeas corpus* they . . . will need tomorrow?"

While many positivists idolized Floriano because he seemed to be providing the republican dictatorship they wanted, others were bitterly opposed to him. Rebellion was openly discussed in Rio Grande do Sul, the traditional hotbed of positivism. Geographically and culturally the *Gaúchos,* as *Riograndenses* called themselves, belonged to the Río de la Plata complex along with Uruguayans and Paraguayans. Gaspar da Silveira Martins, a brilliant and powerful statesman of the empire, had monopolized power in Rio Grande for years. Indeed, when the republic was proclaimed, he was on his way to Rio de Janeiro expecting to succeed Ouro Prêto. Since Deodoro considered him a bitter enemy, Republicans immediately had him exiled. A small group under Júlio de Castilhos then took control of the state.

Castilhos had led the *Gaúcho* delegation to the constituent assembly, where he fought hard to introduce positivist doctrine into the federal constitution. Although most of his proposals were rejected, he was able to introduce positivist doctrines into the state constitution of Rio Grande do Sul. Rio Grande had a one-house legislature which met only to approve the budget. The governor, who could be reelected indefintely, appointed most officials.

Júlio de Castilhos had supported the visconde de Pelotas as state governor in 1889, but Pelotas stepped down and Castilhos succeeded him. By this time he had many enemies and was soon deposed. Floriano named Pelotas governor once more. In June 1892 Castilhos' forces deposed Pelotas and restored their leader, committing so many bloody atrocities against the vanquished that the hatreds became more bitter than ever. Silveira Martins, still a monarchist but willing to fight for a parliamentary regime, crossed over from Uruguay and headed the Federalist rebellion against Castilhos' Republican party and his "positivist dictatorship." The rebels had no plans for opposing Floriano or for restoring the

139

monarchy, yet the situation in Rio Grande do Sul became the crucible test for the republic's survival.

At first Floriano pretended to support Castilhos' opponents in the Rio Grande war, among them Custódio de Melo. Floriano perceived more clearly than any of his contemporaries that the basic issue was between Castilhos, representing positivist doctrines, and Silveira Martins, whose support of a parliamentary republic was probably a first step toward restoring the monarchy. Becoming convinced that Silveira Martins and his policies were more menacing to the republic than Castilhos' positivism, Floriano openly swung his support to Castilhos.

Custódio de Melo resigned as minister of the navy and joined the navy in open revolt against Floriano. Deluded by the easy overthrow of Deodoro, he expected to drive Floriano from office by the same tactics, despite Admiral Luiz Philippe de Saldanha da Gama's warning that "This game will be tougher." Saldanha da Gama was well aware that Floriano would not succumb as Deodoro had done in order to avoid civil war. What Custódio intended to accomplish is not clear, for he made no attempt to gain a foothold on land until too late.

There were many monarchists among the naval officers, and it seemed clear that the navy's goal was to restore the monarchy. Saldanha da Gama, commandant of the Naval Academy, was the most outspoken monarchist, but he maintained neutrality until December 1893, when he called for a national plebiscite on the form of government and threw in his lot with what he knew to be a losing cause.

Foreign governments did not recognize the navy's belligerency and refused to submit to its blockade of Rio de Janeiro. United States warships were placed in positions that made it impossible for the rebels to intercept merchant ships or to fire on the city. The navy rebels thus lost their only hope for deposing Floriano. Finally the officers sought asylum on two overcrowded, unseaworthy Portuguese corvettes. Unable to risk crossing the Atlantic under such conditions, the Portuguese commanders deposited the refugees in Buenos Aires, where about half of the five hundred Brazilians, including Saldanha, quickly joined the Federalist rebels of Silveira Martins. Floriano angrily severed diplomatic relations with Portugal.

Republicans of São Paulo remained loyal to Floriano, and their support was crucial. They recruited and armed a large militia force,

140

and since São Paulo lay between Rio Grande and Rio de Janeiro, the rebels in the south were unable to menace the capital. Floriano and the republic gained a complete victory. Floriano, however, was not a generous victor, for wholesale executions and repressive measures were invoked against his foes. He was hailed, nevertheless, as savior of the republic, and there is no doubt that he did consolidate the republican regime. He also took all of the pleasure out of rebelling against the government.

Paulista support had been a key factor in Floriano's triumph, and the *Paulistas* reaped their reward. Their candidate for the presidency, Prudente de Morais, was able to win and assume the presidential office despite rumors that Floriano intended to retain power. When Prudente became the first civilian president on November 15, 1894, his predecessor was not there to greet him. Floriano, who was in ill health, had already departed; he died the following year. Prudente tried to govern by weakening and meddling in the state governments, resorting to outright intervention when other measures failed. He faced constant opposition from Floriano's partisans as well as from supposed monarchists.

The most bizarre "plot" he had to deal with was the Canudos affair. In the *sertão* (backland) of Bahia was a fanatical band of country people, followers of Antônio Conselheiro, meaning "the Counselor." Antônio was a mystic who reeked of what in ancient times was called the "odor of sanctity." He neither bathed nor combed for years, and as his holy influence extended farther and farther about him, the number of his faithful followers increased. He settled with this devoted band on an abandoned ranch called Canudos. Among the faithful were ex-bandits, who in a holy cause were willing to ply their trade again. Complaints to the governor of Bahia became so frequent that he finally sent a police force to disperse the rabble, but they were frightened off by rifle fire from unseen assailants, a fate shared by several military units. Abandoned weapons and ammunition were appropriated by the *sertanejos*. Finally three large columns were sent against the daub and wattle village. Stung by the earlier defeats the army pounded Canudos to rubble with artillery and took few prisoners.

The country had imagined the simple *sertanejos* to be determined monarchists, although they had not been especially devoted to the empire. President Prudente and some of his cabinet were greeting the troops returning from Canudos when a crazed soldier tried to assassinate Prudente, killing the minister of war instead. While

Brazilians have often condoned violence in certain situations, they have never accepted political assassination. As a result of the assassination attempt Prudente enjoyed one year of peace and popularity.

Prudente's successor was another *Paulista*, Manoel Ferraz de Campos Sales. Whereas Prudente had intervened in the states, Campos Sales believed in federalism and respected state autonomy. He was determined not to be tied to any political party, and the consequences of this policy were unfortunate for Brazil. Campos Sales' federalism and presidentialism led to the formation of state oligarchies and the decline of congressional power. Thereafter it was impossible to control politics or the government through large, national parties, for none existed. But the gravest consequence of Campos Sales' "deals" with state governors—his "politics of the governors"—was the consolidation and entrenchment of the state oligarchies. The nuclei of the state oligarchies were, paradoxically, former monarchists who had laid low for a few years then boldly reemerged. The *coroneis* who headed the oligarchies set up state political machines devoted to minor peculation and the occasional violent elimination of opponents. By 1900 the congressmen were mere pawns of the state oligarchies, committed to support the president's policies. The federal union was thus converted into a multitude of predatory groups concerned more with regional and personal interests than with the welfare of the nation. Campos Sales' policy made *políticos* more important than parties.

The traditional Republicans, whose party roots went back to 1870, failed to organize an effective national party in their moment of glory. The former imperial politicians recovered from their shock and resumed control of their districts, encouraged by Campos Sales' policy of controlling the nation through his influence with state governors. Under these circumstances the power and prestige of the congress vanished.

The tremendous variation in population and wealth among the states made it easy for the most powerful to dominate the others. This meant that São Paulo and Minas Gerais together could control the federal government and alternate the presidency between them. Rio Grande do Sul, the positivist center that had been under the powerful rule of Júlio de Castilhos and Antônio Augusto Borges de Medeiros, also had to be considered. Rio Grande was ably represented in the congress by Pinheiro Machado, whose growing power was based on his personal influence over state oligarchies and over the credentials committees of the Senate and Chamber. He did not tamper with *Paulistas* or *Mineiros*, but if he opposed someone from a less powerful state, the credentials committees would throw out enough of his opponents' votes to defeat him.

Francisco de Paula Rodrigues Alves was the third *Paulista* president (1903–06). An ex-monarchist coffee-grower, he had served ably as minister of finance under Floriano and Prudente. He filled his cabinet with such capable men as Major Lauro Müller, minister of transportation and public works, Leopoldo Bulhões, finance, and the barão do Rio Branco, foreign affairs. These men were chosen on the basis of ability—none was from a large state—and they were given a free hand. "My ministers," said Rodrigues Alves, "do anything they wish, except what I don't want them to."

Rodrigues Alves and his ministers were determined to inject new life into Brazil, especially its capital city. Rio de Janeiro was the scene of much activity as streets were widened and parks enlarged. Yellow fever and smallpox were endemic, the former having been brought from Africa just before the slave trade ended. Dr. Osvaldo Cruz set out to sanitize the city while it was being remodeled. Cruz had studied at the Pasteur Institute in France, and he was convinced that Dr. Carlos Finlay's theory on the spread of yellow fever and methods of mosquito control developed by the United States were both correct and appropriate. Despite complaints of Portuguese merchants and the journalists' sneering comments about Dr. Cruz and his "mosquito swatters," the work went on.

Osvaldo Cruz was astonished at the criticism leveled at the president because of his own efforts to stamp out deadly diseases, and he offered to resign. Rodrigues Alves would not hear of it and encouraged him to continue. In the past sixty years deaths from yellow fever had averaged 10,000 annually. In 1903 the number of deaths in Rio de Janeiro was reduced to 584; in 1904, to 53. By 1906 yellow fever had disappeared. Vaccination for smallpox was made mandatory despite widespread opposition, especially from the positivists. Soon other Brazilian cities were following the lead of Rio de Janeiro in remodeling and sanitation.

Minister of Foreign Affairs Rio Branco, an experienced diplomat who had spent much of his life in Europe, was determined to win international respect for his country. During the rubber boom of the 1890s Brazilian rubber-gatherers had penetrated Acre

Territory, a jungle area in Brazil and Bolivia through which no dividing line had been established. Fearing the loss of the territory, the Bolivian government in 1901 signed a contract giving a United States syndicate the exclusive right to exploit the entire disputed region. Aroused at this threat, the Brazilians in Acre seized control of the territory.

Negotiations with Bolivia resulted in Brazil's purchase of the Bolivian contract, for which it paid £2 million in an agreement to build a railroad around the cataracts of the Madeira to give Bolivians access to the sea. The Madeira-Mamoré Railroad, built at great cost in money and lives by Percival Farquhar, an American entreprenuer, was soon abandoned when the rubber boom ended. Before that time, however, Brazil's revenues from Acre Territory more than offset its investment.

Under Rio Branco's aegis boundary settlements were negotiated with Peru, Ecuador, Colombia, Venezuela, and Dutch Guiana; furthermore, the United States and Brazil raised their legations to the rank of embassies. Joaquim Nabuco, the famed statesman, was named the first ambassador to Washington, where he was eminently successful until his death. He took part in the Third Pan-American Conference in Rio de Janeiro in 1906. Because of his admiration for Nabuco, Secretary of State Elihu Root attended the conference.

Around the turn of the century, with immigration to Brazil reaching about 100,000 persons a year, Afonso Pena, Rodrigues Alves' successor, set up a fairly successful special department to encourage immigration. The Portuguese settled mainly in Rio de Janeiro and northern port cities, Italians chose São Paulo, while Germans were attracted to Santa Catarina and Rio Grande do Sul. Poles and Russians went mainly to Paraná. Lebanese, Syrians, and Jews also joined the stream of immigrants. Each of these groups contributed to the development of commerce and industry, and since the majority of them settled in the south, the southern states continued to advance economically much faster than those in the north. Early in the century overproduction of coffee became a problem never satisfactorily solved, although the government, under *Paulista* influence, occasionally tried to maintain prices artificially.

Afonso Pena courted the support of Governor João Pinheiro of Minas Gerais and Carlos Peixoto Filho, president of the Chamber of Deputies. Peixoto and the group of youthful *políticos* who surrounded him were referred to as the "Kindergarten." They were pitted against the *Gaúcho* Pinheiro Machado and his followers, who were called the *"Morro da Graça"* after Pinheiro's mansion on the Morro da Graça. The Kindergarten won early successes and was gradually isolating Pinheiro Machado, but in October 1908 João Pinheiro died, leaving the Kindergarten leaderless.

When Afonso Pena chose as his successor his minister of finance, David Campista, he persuaded Carlos Peixoto to organize the campaign, during which Peixoto made an oblique, but disparaging reference to the possible candidacy of an army officer. "The Republic," he said, "has demonstrated that it can both govern itself and preserve the civil liberties that keep it from falling prey to conscienceless demagoguery, which is the road to anarchy and violence, the main source of Caesarism and tyranny."

Minister of War Hermes da Fonseca, Deodoro's nephew, immediately resigned, saying that although he was not a candidate he could not agree to the exclusion of military officers. His letter shook Afonso Pena, who abandoned Campista's candidacy but did nothing about Hermes' insubordination. In the panic that followed, the Kindergarten was destroyed and the *Morro da Graça* was once more in command. Afonso Pena died in office and was succeeded by Nilo Peçanha. The army revived its interest in politics and supported Hermes, a *Gaúcho* and friend of Pinheiro Machado.

Pinheiro Machado at first favored Rui Barbosa, who had brilliantly represented Brazil and the small nations at the Second Hague Conference in 1907, where his erudition and fluency in a variety of languages won him and his country considerable recognition. Brazil was, in fact, the only Latin American nation represented. Rui's exchange with a German delegate was one of the high points of the conference and applauded by all but the leader of the German delegation, who considered Rui "most boring."

Although he favored Rui, Pinheiro called a caucus of senators and deputies, who were evenly divided between Rui and Hermes. Refusing the role of tie-breaker, Pinheiro called on the political chief of Pernambuco, who cast his vote in favor of Hermes, for although the *políticos* admired Rui, they doubted his administrative ability. As José Maria Bello, politician turned historian, sardonically remarked, "There arose a theory that great intelligence and vast culture were negative virtues in leaders! In handling public office a mediocre mind, limited knowledge, and everyday common sense were more to be desired." Although the official candidate never lost, Rui ran against him and conducted a whirlwind *civilista* campaign, touring the states and speaking to numerous crowds in an energetic effort to win popular support. One of the greatest Brazilian orators ever, he aroused people over the oligarchs' monopoly of political power, raised the specter of militarism, and urged them to insist on a government that actually represented them. His tirades against militarism and demands for reforms did not win him the presidency, but they aroused a spirit of protest that would grow until it led to the overthrow of the Old Republic, as it was later called. Despite the fact that only a few of the state machines supported him, Rui won a surprising 30 percent of the vote, which reflected the growing independence of urban voters. But Pinheiro Machado's influence over the state machines was decisive. Less than half a million voted, out of a population of some twenty-two million.

A week after Hermes took office the crews of the warships *Minas Gerais* and *São Paulo* mutinied and fired on Rio de Janeiro. Under the threat of naval guns the humiliated congress voted the amnesty demanded by the mutineers. A few days later the government crushed a rebellion protesting corporal punishment in the armed forces.

Hermes' victory in the presidential election was a signal to army officers that the time was ripe to "redeem" their states from the machinations of the oligarchs. By threatening army intervention and other *salvacionista* devices, officers captured the governorships in four of the northern states and undermined Pinheiro's influence in them. The army still nourished belief in "military redemption," dreaming that a few years of army rule would eliminate political corruption and restore morality. Despite Hermes' lack of accomplishment the myth persisted.

Hermes and Pinheiro set out to undermine the state parties that opposed the administration by intervening on the side of parties that were favorable to it. The establishment of the republic had only temporarily dislodged the monarchist *coroneis,* who soon recovered control of the family oligarchies, except in São Paulo and Rio Grande do Sul, where the old Republican party had the greatest strength.

In the backcountry of Ceará, Padre Cícero Romão Batista gathered a band of fanatical followers reminiscent of Antônio Conselheiro's devoted disciples. The town of Joaseiro virtually became his private domain, and even though the church defrocked him, his power remained absolute. Politically ambitious, Padre Cícero aligned himself with Pinheiro Machado, and on one occasion his followers invaded Fortaleza and ran off the governor. There were similar movements elsewhere, such as in the *Contestado,* the territory disputed by Paraná and Santa Catarina. It was led by João Maria the Monk, a former member of Antônio Conselheiro's Canudos followers. João Maria established himself as head of both church and state in the region, and his followers repulsed police sent to disperse them. Eventually a military force of 6,000 men scattered the Monk's followers.

Pinheiro Machado was the dominant figure in Hermes' administration, for the president depended increasingly on him. On one occasion, after Pinheiro had persuaded Hermes to cancel an improper appointment, he wryly commented to Borges de Medeiros that Hermes had again proved to be "open to suggestions in the public interest." Late in 1910 Pinheiro created the *Partido Republicano Conservadora,* which he made into a national party by uniting many of the state machines. With no real national parties, this could have been a significant political contribution if it had endured, but it was a tenuous alliance held together only by Pinheiro's skill.

Pinheiro became the target for those who hated the Hermes regime; his arrogance in manipulating congress made him more feared than loved. He was the only one who might have succeeded in creating an effective national party, but even he could not forge a stable combination out of the divergent elements. He had visions of succeeding Hermes as president. Indeed, he was a logical choice; as spokesman for the state bosses, he was already as powerful as the president. The *políticos,* however, especially those from Minas Gerais and São Paulo, would not accept him. No one closely associated with the lackluster administration could have hoped to win.

In the maneuvering for the coming election the *Mineiros* and *Paulistas* joined forces to support Venceslau Brás Pereira Gomes, Hermes' vice-president but, thanks to Pinheiro Machado's activities, not identified with the regime. Pinheiro threw his support to Campos Sales, but his candidate died the same year. He and others then offered to support Rui if he would abandon his *civilista* goals, but he refused. With the backing of São Paulo and Minas Gerais, Venceslau Brás won the election.

Economically, the worst calamity of Hermes' administration had been the abrupt end of the rubber boom. During the empire an

Englishman had smuggled the seeds of rubber trees out of Brazil and planted them in Kew Gardens, London. The young trees were later shipped to British oriental colonies, where they were largely ignored until shortly after 1900, when a drop in tea prices induced the tea-planters to experiment with rubber. Soon plantation-produced rubber captured the market and Hermes could do nothing to stop it.

Early in World War I Brazil's trade fell off sharply, then exports tripled and prices rose as Allied demands increased. The scarcity of imported goods stimulated production and the volume of manufactures doubled during the war and tripled soon after. The growth of labor unions kept pace.

Although Venceslau Brás hoped to maintain neutrality, Germany's unrestricted submarine warfare forced Brazil into war. Afterwards, at Versailles, there were two issues of concern to Brazil— payment for coffee seized in Germany during the war and the disposition of German merchant ships sequestered by Brazil and leased to France. Both issues were eventually settled in Brazil's favor.

In September 1915 a semiliterate baker named Manso da Paiva Coimbra fatally stabbed Pinheiro in the back as he entered the lobby of the Hotel dos Estrangeiros. In Rio de Janeiro there was little mourning at Pinheiro's passing. The assassin, when captured, declared, "Tyrants have to be done away with. . . . I got the real boss." He indicated later that he had never planned to assassinate the insignificant Hermes.

Soon after Pinheiro's death the *Partido Republicano Conservadora* disintegrated, and the *Mineiro-Paulista* combination again went unchallenged. Former President Rodrigues Alves was elected in 1918, but was unable to serve because of illness. When he died early in 1919, an election was required to fill the office, and both São Paulo and Minas Gerais ran candidates. Borges de Medeiros, seeing an opportunity to exert some influence, instructed the *Riograndense* delegation to support the candidate that both *Paulistas* and *Mineiros* supported, provided he was not from either state. It seemed at first that Rui Barbosa might be a compromise candidate, but Borges proposed Epitácio Pessôa. The *Mineiros* and *Paulistas* agreed on him, and Epitácio went on to win with less than one-third of a million votes out of a population of twenty-six million (the literacy qualification still excluded the vast majority of Brazilians from voting).

148

José Bonifácio de Andrade e Silva. A scientist, humanist, poet, and politician, Brazil's "Patriarch of Independence" was the first in a series of Brazilian political figures who were leading intellectuals as well. Courtesy of the Consulate General of Brazil, New York.

"Old Rio de Janeiro."   *The engraving is by Johann Moritz Rugendas, a nineteenth-century German artist whose visit to Brazil in 1821 provided the inspiration for his book* Picturesque Voyage to Brazil, *which is still popular in Brazil today. Courtesy of the Consulate General of Brazil, New York.*

*"**Christit the Redeemer.**" The statue is located on Corcovado Mountain, nicknamed "the Hunchback." Modern Rio de Janeiro sprawls below; Sugar Loaf Mountain is in the background. Courtesy of VARIG Airlines.*

"Gathering Coffee Beans, Near Rio." This engraving by Rugendas exemplifies the two-class fazenda society. Courtesy of the Consulate General of Brazil, New York.

Modern coffee plantation in the state of São Paulo. *Courtesy of the Brazilian Coffee Institute, New York.*

***Typical plantation house on an* engenho.** *Courtesy of the Consulate General of Brazil, New York.*

Ouro Prêto, Minas Gerais. *The abortive* Mineiro *conspiracy of 1789 unfolded in this colonial city. Once Brazil's richest mining town and a famous cultural center, Ouro Prêto was declared a national monument in 1933. Courtesy of* VARIG *Airlines.*

Eighteenth-century church in the colonial city of São João del Rei, Minas Gerais. Courtesy of the Consulate General of Brazil, New York.

"Christ Carrying the Cross."   *The figure is one of Aleijadinho's woodcarvings depicting the Stations of the Cross in the Church of Bom Jesus de Matosinho, Congohas do Campo, Minas Gerais. The eighteenth-century crippled sculptor's famous soapstone carvings of "The Twelve Prophets" stand outside the church. Courtesy of the Consulate General of Brazil, New York.*

Detail from the main altar of the Church of Saint Francis in Belo Horizonte, Minas Gerais. *The altarpiece was done by the world-renowned Cândido Portinari, who in 1955 executed the murals "War" and "Peace" in the United Nations General Assembly Building. Courtesy of the Consulate General of Brazil, New York.*

Fishermen in Bahia.   *Courtesy of the Consulate General of Brazil, New York.*

Recife, Pernambuco.   *Brazil's third largest city and an important seaport, Recife has been dubbed the "São Paulo of the North" because of its rapid industrial development. Courtesy of the Consulate General of Brazil, New York.*

Congressional office buildings in Brasília.   *The twin towers rise twenty-eight stories above the new capital. The saucer-shaped edifice at the left is the Chamber of Deputies. Courtesy of VARIG Airlines.*

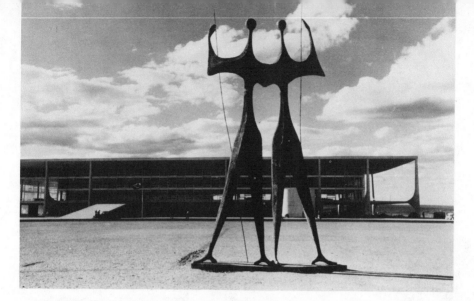

"The Warriors" by Bruno Giorgi.   *The sculpture stands impressively in the Plaza of the Three Powers, Brasília. Courtesy of the Consulate General of Brazil, New York.*

The Palace of Itamaraty, Brasília.   *The building houses the Ministry of Foreign Relations. Courtesy of the Consulate General of Brazil, New York.*

Refusing to deal gently with the armed forces, Epitácio Pessôa named civilians as ministers of war and the navy. Military resentment intensified, and underneath the turmoil dissatisfaction was growing with the republic's ineffectiveness as well as with the excessively dominant power of Minas Gerais and São Paulo. Epitácio spent much of his time trying to maintain or restore order, and his government accomplished little of a positive nature. In part the trouble stemmed from Campos Sales' "politics of the governors." The federal legislature had become merely a meeting place for the representatives of state machines to trade favors in the interest of their states. Opposition to the government was a byproduct of Rui's *civilista* campaign of 1909. As José Maria Bello remarked, "Today we can easily trace the subversive movements that shook Brazil between 1921 and 1930, and that probably would have begun in 1914 or 1915 but for the war, to old disillusionments, honest grievances, reactions to world crises, ambitions, common demagoguery, and love of adventure and disorder." At any rate, in 1921 Brazilians began, perhaps subconsciously, to reject the Old Republic in every way. The elderly were nostalgic for the empire; the young, who had no memory of it, wanted a change, but they were not agreed as to what it should be.

Opposition to the political system was generated by the absence of national parties, the monopoly of government by the two most powerful states, and the chronic, but unavoidable reliance on the state of siege. It seemed to many that republican institutions had become completely ineffective and that the republic was in its death throes. It had never had anything like a popular base, for less than 5 percent of the population was qualified to vote.

Profits from coffee exports had provided funds for industrial enterprise, and by 1920 São Paulo had taken the lead in industrialization. To counter the sharp drop in coffee sales that year, Epitácio yielded to *Paulista* demands for the inflationary issue of large amounts of paper money. The following year the government assumed responsibility for valorization, that is, of maintaining or "defending" coffee prices, as it had occasionally done before. Epitácio also encouraged railroad expansion, and the government acquired Percival Farquhar's Compagnie Auxiliaire, the main line in Rio Grande do Sul, and transferred it to that state.

Epitácio refused to intervene in the choice of his successor. Hence, political activity became more violent than usual. The *Paulistas* and *Mineiros* finally agreed on Governor Artur Bernardes of

149

Minas Gerais. Bernardes was a somewhat controversial figure who had an "almost religious faith in the . . . mission God or destiny had reserved for him." Borges de Medeiros opposed Bernardes, for he wanted a candidate who would promote a sound currency policy. Nilo Peçanha entered the race, supported by Hermes da Fonseca, president of the Military Club, and the army. Army opposition to Bernardes was so strong, in fact, that a revolution was anticipated, and Hermes' statements such as "Political situations change, but the army remains," were not reassuring. Bernardes won, nevertheless, and faced hostility from the army throughout his term.

The election of 1922 further lowered respect for the political system, split the elite groups, and produced renewed hostility between army and government. In July a minor rebellion of young officers—the first of the *tenentes'* (lieutenants) revolts—took place in the Ingrejinha fort of Copacabana. Generally dissatisfied and frustrated, the young officers believed that it was necessary to eliminate regionalism and unite the country. The government, however, reacted quickly to quell the revolt, and all but the "Eighteen of Copacabana" surrendered. Most of the latter fought and died on the beach. Although this act of martyrdom caused a momentary stir, it failed to produce the action desired. Among the survivors was Eduardo Gomes, who was to become a high-ranking air force officer and presidential candidate in 1945.

The July revolt marked for Brazilians the beginning of their contemporary era, for it was the first of a series of incidents that brought the ineffective Old Republic to its end. In Mato Grosso General Clodoaldo da Fonseca was ready to march on the capital if Rio Grande do Sul would support him. Borges de Medeiros refused to encourage civil strife and the march was not made.

Borges—who was to remain active in politics until his death in 1961 at the age of ninety-seven—had been governor ever since the death of Júlio de Castilhos in 1903, and two opposition groups were desperately trying to retire him. A widely circulated story told of the requirement that the governor had to win 75 percent of the vote to succeed himself. A three-man committee headed by Getúlio Dornelles Vargas counted the votes and called on Borges to tell him he had lost. Before they could speak, he told them he knew they had come to congratulate him. Too embarrassed to admit their true purpose, they returned to the vote-counting and threw out enough of his opponent's votes to give him the victory.

Assis Brasil, Borges' chief rival, sought the support of Bernardes and the representatives of Minas Gerais and São Paulo. Bernardes' mediation resulted in the "Pact of Pedras Altas," negotiated at Assis Brasil's ranch at that location. Under the agreement Borges retained the governorship, but the constitution was revised to prohibit the reelection of governors and to make the office of lieutenant governor elective rather than appointive. The opposition in Rio Grande do Sul at last could hope to win office and unseat the dynasty peacefully. By weakening Borges, Bernardes also gained from the pact.

Bernardes was widely unpopular, for he made no conciliatory gestures to his opponents. Like his predecessor, he spent most of his time maintaining or restoring order. The army hated him because of some spurious letters he allegedly wrote. His repressive policies did not even terrorize the opposition. He seemed to be the epitome of everything that was wrong with the political system. The legitimacy of the system was rapidly disappearing, for the government was, in effect, whatever the *Paulistas* and the *Mineiros* wanted it to be. Discontent was widespread, but violence erupted only when the army embraced a particular cause.

On July 5, 1924, the second anniversary of the *tenente* revolt at Copacabana, military rebellions broke out in São Paulo, Sergipe, and Amazonas. The *Paulista* rebels, young officers led by retired General Isidoro Lopes, captured the state capital, hoping to oust Bernardes. When both Minas Gerais and Rio Grande do Sul sent troops to aid in suppressing the rebellion, the rebels gave up the capital and headed west.

In the Missões district of Rio Grande do Sul the young Captain Luís Carlos Prestes, a *Riograndense* and son of an army officer of positivist persuasion, announced support for the *Paulista* rebels and marched to Iguassú Falls where he joined forces with them. For two and a half years the Prestes Column marched through the vast Brazilian interior in a futile effort to generate peasant opposition to Bernardes and the political system. The column marched more than 6,000 miles and was almost constantly harassed by police or troops before going into exile. It became the symbol of defiance to the government, and thereby took its place in Brazilian mythology. The *tenentes'* semimystical belief in the regenerative powers of military activisim—that is, the military's power to introduce reforms and to rid the nation of the blight of the state *políticos*—was already established. Three members of the Prestes Column—Juarez

151

Távora, Osvaldo Cordeiro de Farias, and João Lins de Barros—were later to be instrumental figures in the Vargas era. After the column disbanded, Prestes himself became the leader of the Brazilian Communist party, which had been organized in 1922. He became a legendary figure, the "Knight of Hope," and eventually the peasants were stirred to revolutionary action.

The year that saw the attempt to overthrow the ruling political oligarchy in Brazil by the Copacabana rebels witnessed an assault on the cultural oligarchy as well, for in 1922 Brazil launched a dynamic artistic and literary movement. It was not an instantaneous change of view, for the forces that produced the rebellion had been forming for a generation. Young poets could turn for inspiration to the verse of João de Cruz e Sousa, the Negro Satanist from Santa Catarina, and to the poetry of Menotti del Picchia, whose "Juca Mulato" (1917) helped to counter the feeling of racial inferiority by portraying a mulatto as hero. Another source of inspiration was José Bento Monteiro Lobato, noted for his short stories and the strong national cast of his work. Modernism was further indebted to the work of the widely acclaimed Euclides da Cunha, whose *Os Sertões* (1902), translated under the title *Rebellion in the Backlands*—the incisive portrait of Antônio Conselheiro and the Canudos campaigns—has been hailed as the "Bible of Brazilian nationality," and to the Futurists of São Paulo, who as early as 1912 advocated free verse to liberate poets from classical molds. But it was Anita Malfatti, the daughter of an Italian immigrant, who was to awaken the Modernist movement and break the "retarded and paralytic" tradition of Brazilian painting. After studying at the Berlin School of Art before World War I, she returned to Brazil with an exhibit of postimpressionist paintings; the success of this showing was not repeated in 1917 when she exhibited Cubist-influenced works. The need to defend her united the leading figures of Modernism—Osvaldo de Andrade, Di Cavalcanti, and Mário Raul de Morais de Andrade—and preparations were made for the Modern Art Week Exhibition to be held in São Paulo in February 1922. For poets and sculptors this, Brazil's most significant artistic milestone, represented a break with the past, with its formal rules as well as its classical concepts and academic prescriptions. Poets called themselves *antropófagos* (cannibals) and declared that they intended to devour academicians. For writers, artists, and musicians it was an opportunity to establish a foundation for new artistic and literary attitudes more expressive of Brazil. All literary taboos were cast aside while they endeavored to produce a literature that reflected their own unique land. Modern Art Week had a tremendous, almost revolutionary impact on creative work in all parts of Brazil; cultural centers and literary reviews appeared in many regions.

In 1924 Graça Aranha, author of *Canaan* (1901), who had always been rather conservative, shook the Academy of Letters to its foundations when he said that the members were old men with petrified minds and archaic ideas and literary tastes, incapable of understanding what went on about them. The world, he asserted, belongs to the young. Soon after this Graça Aranha resigned from the academy.

Mário de Andrade, whose ancestors included Portuguese, Indians, and Africans, was the acknowledged leader of the Modernist movement. An active writer, he produced poetry, short stories, novels, and critiques of literature, music, folklore, and other various forms. His "Hallucinated City"—São Paulo—was one of the most widely acclaimed early Modernist poems. He enthusiastically supported pioneering sculptors like Vítor Brecheret, painters like Cândido Portinari, architects Oscar Niemeyer and Lúcio Costa, and the brilliant young composer, Heitor Vila-Lobos, who utilized native themes and instruments in his music. Two of Andrade's important converts to Modernism were Manoel Bandeira, whom he called the "Saint John the Baptist of modernistic poetry," and Graça Aranha.

Andrade's *Macunaíma: The Hero Without Any Character* (1928) led the way in creating something new and lasting out of the rubble, for Modernism implied more than a mere break with style—it signaled a wholesale change in actual themes. For the first time in Brazil, national values replaced foreign ones. Emphasis was on knowing Brazil intimately and telling about it in everyday language, rather than in the inappropriate classical Portuguese. This literary nationalism focused on folklore, the national ethos, and on Brazilian uniqueness as being worthy of pride rather than shame. *Macunaíma* was an apparently formless, experimental work, but no other Brazilian book has included so all-embracing a treatment of the endless varieties of regional life. This literary masterpiece was an allegorical story in ordinary language, and in it could be found the idioms of all localities and all spoken dialects. The classicists looked and shuddered; their immediate reaction was understandably more bewilderment than appreciation. As understanding came, however, so did recognition.

An integral part of the new understanding of Brazilian civilization was the problem of explaining Brazil's three races. After studying anthropology under Franz Boas at Columbia University, Gilberto Freyre took a fresh approach to the questions of racial and cultural differences. He developed a deeper understanding of miscegenation than any of his predecessors. In 1933 he published his ideas in *Casa grande e senzala,* later translated as *The Masters and the Slaves.* This classic work recognized that the mingling of races and cultures produced not "mongrelization," but new and worthwhile social characteristics and values. The inferiority and shame borne by some Brazilians because of the mixed racial composition of the population were shown by Freyre to be clearly unjustified; his work marked a turning point in the growth of national self-confidence of the Brazilian people.

Intellectuals also looked to the past and to Brazil's history. Because little training for historians had been available before the 1930s, the historians of the empire and Old Republic were few in number. Now, influenced by João Capistrano de Abreu, by far the most important of the nineteenth-century historians, Brazilian historians began to view their land as a distinct entity, not as a mere appendage of Portugal. Unlike most works in the Modernist period, Paulo Prado's *Portrait of Brazil* (1928) took a pessimistic, almost fatalistic, view of Brazil's future, as its subtitle "Essay on Brazilian Melancholy" suggests. Among economic historians Roberto Simonsen and Caio Prado Júnior stand out. Social histories of high quality have been produced by Gilberto Freyre, Pedro Calmon, and Sérgio Buarque de Holanda. João Cruz Costa's massive *A History of Ideas in Brazil* (1956; English translation, 1964) is a comprehensive view of the impact of foreign intellectual currents, especially positivism. Unfortunately, because Portuguese is not a widely read language, only those books that have been translated have received much recognition abroad. As the Parnassian poet Olavo Bilac sadly observed, "Portuguese is the sepulcher of literature."

In the late 1920s artists and writers were becoming increasingly conscious of the flaws in Brazilian society and of their responsibilities to that society. It was a confusing, turbulent era the world over, a time of universal economic depression and the rise of new movements, like Benito Mussolini's brand of fascism, which were presumably to take the place of capitalism as a counter to communism. European ideas had an immediate effect in Brazil, and the contest between ideologies convinced Brazilian writers to end their neutrality. As they looked about them, it seemed clear that the Old Republic was a miserable failure, for poverty, malnutrition, disease, and illiteracy were chronic among the lower classes, both urban and rural. Moreover, the malaise of the republic was deep-seated and apparently incurable. Federalism and presidentialism simply did not work satisfactorily in Brazil. The representative system was as make-believe as it had been during the empire, and in the republic even national parties had gone out of existence. During the empire the government's control of elections had resulted in the selection of capable men. Under the republic elections simply reflected popular passions aroused by demagoguery. Governments increasingly had to employ the state of siege, suspending constitutional freedoms and civil rights in order to survive. Under these conditions it is not surprising that few governments accomplished anything constructive and that dissatisfaction continued to mount.

Federalism had degenerated into a narrow, selfish regionalism. Each of the larger states regarded itself as an autonomous body, part of Brazil but independent of it. States formed alliances with others as if they were nations involved in international relations. Through their congressional blocs they could exert pressure on the president. Although the early phases of industrialism and of city growth were beginning to create sources of power outside the control of the state machines, these new urban groups were increasingly frustrated in their political goals.

Because regional interests outweighed all others, it was impossible to build up a genuinely national economy. States collected border taxes like customs duties, in violation of the constitution. State police forces were virtual armies. Deputies and senators were divided not along party lines but by states, and no member of the legislature dared mention a political or administrative matter that was of greater concern to another state.

Owing to the prevailing unrest, continuity in the presidential administration was completely out of the question. Each president, moreover, automatically discarded the half-finished program begun by his predecessor. Thus Bernardes dropped Epitácio Pessôa's public-works program for his own drouth control project for the northeast, and he drastically altered his predecessor's fiscal policy.

By the time Bernardes' administration ended and Washington Luís' began, Brazilians, weary of partisan strife and constant disturbances, hoped that the new president would give the country domestic peace enough for the economy to recover. Washington Luís suspended the state of siege and restored freedom of the press, both hopeful signs. He would have done better, however, to have issued a general amnesty to his predecessor's opponents, for many of them continued to plot against the government.

Washington Luís' cabinet members had been chosen for their political connections rather than for their administrative aptitude. The prime example of this was his choice of Getúlio Vargas of Rio Grande do Sul as minister of finance. In 1924 Vargas had been elected deputy from Rio Grande, and Borges had named him head of the Brazilian delegation. His political training and experience had been in the positivist tradition of the *Gaúchos*. His appointment as minister of finance was in part a conciliatory gesture to Borges de Medeiros, who had long demanded sound currency and stable prices. Vargas himself candidly admitted that he knew nothing at all about finance.

Washington Luís dropped Bernardes' drouth-control projects and introduced his own program of building badly-needed railroads and highways and of reforming Brazilian finances. The government now adopted a "permanent program" of support for coffee. When the New York stock market crashed in 1929, however, Brazil's economy was hard hit.

In this same era the *tenente* revolts seemed to be harbingers of drastic change boding the destruction of the system of state oligarchies. Assis Brasil, who had tried unsuccesssfully to unseat Borges, called for electoral reforms that would include minority representation and an end to the state oligarchies. He came to believe, however, that only by revolution could reforms be introduced into Brazil, and this view increasingly came to be shared by others.

The Pact of Pedras Altas prevented Borges from succeeding himself as governor in 1927, but he remained party chief. Passing over a number of men who had served the party longer, he chose Vargas as the party's candidate for the governorship, assuring him of election. Vargas was victorious and resigned from the ministry. He belonged to the second generation of *Riograndense* politicians, known as "The Generation of 1924." Others of this group were José

Antônio Flores da Cunha, Osvaldo Aranha, Lindolfo Collor, João Neves da Fontoura, Joaquim Maurício Cardoso, and Ferminio Paim Filho. All of them rose to important positions during the Vargas era.

Although it was time for the presidency to rotate to the *Mineiros,* Washington Luís was convinced that only another *Paulista* could carry on his financial reforms successsfully. His choice for the nomination was Júlio Prestes. The *Mineiro* candidate was Antônio Carlos Ribeiro de Andrada, grandson of the independence leader. Another potential candidate was Borges de Medeiros.

Antônio Carlos saw his last chance at the presidency eluding his grasp, and he was determined to defeat the government's candidate. For the first time the *Mineiros* opposed a *Paulista* who had the government's backing, but the economic depression, the political unrest, and the rejection of Antônio Carlos had created a unique situation. Antônio Carlos, Borges, and Vargas made a pact, the so-called "Liberal Alliance." In case Washington Luís agreed to support Antônio Carlos, the vice president would be a *Gaúcho.* Otherwise Antônio Carlos would be out and either Borges or Vargas would be the presidential candidate.

After attempts to arrive at a peaceful solution failed, Osvaldo Aranha—who at the age of thirty-six had already won a reputation for his skill at resolving disputes and was later to serve with distinction at many posts—concluded that Vargas could gain the presidency only by armed revolt, and he began to plan accordingly. Many of the exiled *tenentes* came secretly to join Aranha, who had ordered weapons from Czechoslovakia. Vargas and Borges both held back. (Antônio Carlos was no longer in the running at this point.) Vargas, however, had secretly discussed the plan with Luís Carlos Prestes, the famous *tenente.* Announcing his conversion to Communism, Prestes rejected the offer to join the movement and kept the money Aranha had given him for the purchase of arms.

Convinced that it was impossible to defeat Júlio Prestes, the official candidate, and apprehensive about opposing the president, Vargas astonished Washington Luís by asking for his support. Washington Luís replied that most governors supported Júlio Prestes. Vargas then promised not to campaign outside of Rio Grande do Sul and to accept the outcome of the election if Júlio Prestes did not campaign against him in Rio Grande. Prestes agreed.

The election results were as expected, with Prestes winning

95C,000 of the 1,500,000 votes cast. It seemed as if the "Liberal Alliance" had accepted the outcome and that the revolution would not occur. Then João Pessôa of Paraíba, who had been Vargas' running-mate, was assassinated in July 1930, and that event provided the needed spark. Although there had been much talk of revolution, when it actually broke out on October 3, the government was quite unprepared. The major battle was expected to occur at Itararé on the Paraná-São Paulo border. It was called "the greatest battle in Latin American history, except that it didn't take place." The government's defenses collapsed, and a junta of army and navy officers in Rio de Janeiro deposed Washington Luís and sent him into exile. The whole affair lasted only three weeks. The junta turned the government over to Vargas with the idea that he would hold it only until elections were scheduled. It did not make any conditions, however, and Vargas had other plans.

The era of the Old Republic was over. Except, perhaps, for the administration of Rodrigues Alves, its record was poor. Most administrations had been ineffective. There was a widespread desire for a government that could be respected, and an equally widespread belief that the system could not be changed peacefully. The overwhelming power of Minas Gerais and São Paulo made the federal system a farce and was especially irritating to the *Riograndenses*. Failure to channel political activity into large national parties sharpened factional rivalries and was one of the basic weaknesses of the Old Republic.

The Old Republic was dead, but the new state was yet to be born. Vargas and his followers had evolved plans for overthrowing the government, but they still had no blueprint for the Brazil they hoped to create. Vargas himself was pragmatic and undoctrinaire; he was not committed to any particular "ism" or economic theory. His *Riograndense* background, however, made him scornful of the kind of democratic and representative government that the ineffectual administrations of the Old Republic had fortified. He had not wanted the revolution and had been apprehensive about his political and personal fate if it should fail. Once he picked up the reins of government hastily dropped by Washington Luís, his grasp was firm. Brazil in the 1930s and 1940s would be increasingly different from the Brazil of the empire and Old Republic, although some aspects of both were to survive. In 1930, however, the painful period of transition was just beginning. Few Brazilians had any notion of what might lie ahead.

8/The Vargas Era

GETÚLIO DORNELLES VARGAS—"GETÚLIO," AS BRA-
zilians called him—was born on April 19, 1883 into a family of
well-to-do cattlemen in São Borja, Rio Grande do Sul. Before
turning to law and politics he attended the military academy and
served briefly in the army. Like most *Gaúchos* he was intensely
interested in politics. At the outset of his career, however, his
performance was far from spectacular. His own countrymen called
him "mediocre in everything, cold, reserved, cautious, impersonal. . . ." A remarkable self-control and keen sense of timing
were two of his greatest political assets; he made no false starts or
premature moves. Whatever his goal on a given occasion, Vargas
made a determined effort to win it, relying on his unquestioned
courage, his flexibility, his skill at temporizing, and his unrivaled
patience. He cultivated a reputation for both his *Gaúcho* toughness
and his "proverbial affability." He was controversial while he lived,
and remains so today. No Brazilian, even Floriano Peixoto, has
generated more discussion than Vargas.

A great compromiser, Vargas succeeded in uniting local parties
in a *Frente Única* to cooperate at the national level. As governor of
Rio Grande do Sul he appointed the brilliant young *Gaúcho* Osvaldo
Aranha as state secretary of justice and the interior, and the latter
was able to placate Assis Brasil, whose feud with Borges had
reached classic proportions. The resulting harmony, unique in Rio
Grande, allowed Vargas to devote time to such economic affairs as
establishing the Bank of Rio Grande do Sul. His natural inclination
was to live in peace and quiet rather than amid the atmosphere of
strife characteristic of *Gaúcho* politics. He was able to tolerate
differences and even deficiencies in those around him. He listened
more than he talked, and made decisions after hearing all views
presented, preferably after a consensus had been reached. Uncharitable critics alleged that he did not make decisions at all.

159

As president of the provisional government Vargas included Aranha as minister of justice and domestic affairs and Juarez Távora as minister of transportation in his first cabinet. Távora was soon replaced by José Américo de Almeida, secretary to Getúlio's running-mate, João Pessôa from Paraíba, and a powerful figure in that state. Assis Brasil was named minister of agriculture, so Vargas could keep an eye on him, and the *Paulista* banker José Maria Whitaker was appointed minister of finance to placate the *Paulistas.*

The Ministry of Foreign Affairs went to Afrânio de Melo Franco. A new Ministry of Education and Public Health was created, headed by the *Mineiro* Francisco Campos, who admired the efficiency of authoritarian governments. In December a Ministry of Labor was added, which later was merged with Industry and Commerce. The first to head this new ministry was the *Gaúcho* Lindolfo Collor, who initiated a somewhat haphazard program of labor legislation, restricting immigration, extending retirement and pension benefits, and limiting the alien workers in factories to one-third of the labor force. The minister of labor authorized the creation of labor syndicates which he controlled.

Although Vargas had not fully plotted his course, his major objectives were to make a clean break with the past and to set the government moving in a new direction—the domination of Brazil by São Paulo and Minas Gerais had to be ended if Brazil was to be molded into a nation. He was surrounded by able young men such as Aranha and José Américo de Almeida as well as other *tenentes* returned from exile. Some of them had a genuine desire to eliminate the political evils that had undermined the Old Republic; some were simply eager for power. Most were convinced that Brazilian politics could be changed fundamentally only by an authoritarian government, for the representative democracy of the Old Republic repulsed them. Opposed to the *tenentes* were the liberal constitutionalists who wanted to return to the old system and began agitating for elections.

The exuberant *tenentes* organized the *Clube 3 de Outubro* (the October Third Club), which they expected to grow into a genuine political party. Its members lacked political experience, but the *Clube 3 de Outubro* became so powerful that for a time Vargas discreetly placated its members by agreeing to some of their demands. The *tenentes*' day of power was brief, however, for by 1934 they and their club were on the way to oblivion.

With his usual patience and sense of timing, Vargas submitted to this fragmentation of authority and waited for the proper moment to snatch the reins of government. It was convenient for him that the *tenentes* disliked both federalism and political parties and favored authoritarianism, for these attitudes were compatible with his own well-concealed views. He was, as a result, able to permit them to talk him into doing what he intended to do. This had a therapeutic value for the *tenentes*, and made it easier for him to ease them and the *Clube 3 de Outubro* out of the circle of policy-makers.

The provisional government's first decree incorporated into the regular army the "patriotic" and state units that had served the revolution. Washington Luís' emergency measures were annulled and complete amnesty was declared. The first organic law dissolved the national and state legislatures and granted the president legislative as well as executive authority. The office of interventor was created to supercede state governors when Vargas considered it advisable. The interventors' executive and legislative powers were the same as those the president enjoyed, and they were responsible directly to him. This concentration of power was reminiscent of the empire but quite unlike the Old Republic. A multitude of civil bureaucrats were dismissed and replaced by those faithful to Vargas.

Paulistas and *Gaúchos*, after enjoying independent action during the four decades of the Old Republic, chafed at being dominated by the government in Rio de Janeiro. They demanded that constitutional government be restored. The *tenentes* fiercely opposed doing this until the nation had been purged of the evils they had fought against in the 1920s. Vargas shared their views, but he remained silent and apparently passive, allowing them to make the pronouncements. When obliged to explain the delay in restoring constitutional government, he would say apologetically and with disarming candor that he was not as free to act as he would like to be. In this fashion he skillfully shifted responsibility from himself and encouraged opposition to the *tenentes*, sensing the group's limited usefulness.

Vargas neutralized *tenente* power in other ways as well. When José Maria Whitaker resigned as minister of finance in November 1931 and Aranha, then minister of justice, replaced him, the president named Maurício Cardoso, a *Gaúcho* and a Borges man, as minister of justice. The *Gaúchos* were as eager to see the constitution restored as the *tenentes* were opposed to the measure.

As expected, Vargas' greatest opposition came from powerful São Paulo where Júlio Prestes' loss of the presidency was not accepted gracefully. They demanded a *Paulista* civilian as interventor, for they disliked João Alberto and considered him a wild-eyed Bolshevik. In July of 1931 João Alberto resigned, opening the way for a *Paulista* civilian to be named to replace him. Vargas agreed, and appointed Pedro de Toledo. This gesture still did not mollify the *Paulistas*—having to take orders from Rio, even through a *Paulista*, was more than they could swallow.

Earlier Vargas had appointed Batista Luzardo, a friend of Borges, to be chief of police of Rio de Janeiro, a key position. The *Gaúchos* were convinced that the *Clube 3 de Outubro* actually controlled the president, and they were determined to supercede the *tenentes*. But when João Alberto resigned as interventor, Vargas named him chief of the Rio police in place of Luzardo—a setback to the *Gaúchos* and a delight to the *tenentes*. Following the ancient policy of "divide and rule," Vargas encouraged each group to press its demands, thereby keeping opposing groups at each other's throats.

Aware of the revolutionary conspiracies against him, Vargas proclaimed a new electoral code in February 1932, and soon after announced that the election of delegates to the constituent assembly would be held in May the following year. This news infuriated the *tenentes*, who were determined that Vargas should continue to rule without a constitution indefinitely. If he should falter they would seize the government for themselves. They urged him to disavow the plan to call the constituent assembly. He promised that when constitutional rule was restored it would not mean a return to the former system. He suggested that the *tenentes* continue their peaceful propaganda efforts and warned them bluntly that violence would not be permitted.

Although some of the conspirators were defanged by the announcement of the coming election, Borges sent an agent to check on the possibilities of support from São Paulo and Minas for a movement to oust Vargas. Eager to cooperate, the *Paulistas* rushed ahead with plans for an armed uprising. The *Mineiros* were divided, but former President Artur Bernardes was in contact with the plotters of Rio Grande and São Paulo. Vargas' successful tactics and his apparent preference for the *tenentes* prompted the *Gaúchos* Maurício Cardoso and Lindolfo Collor to resign from the Ministries of Justice and Labor. Both returned to Rio Grande and actively began organizing opposition to the provisional government. The *Frente Única Gaúcha* they created solidly lined up the *Gaúchos* against Vargas.

It appeared that Vargas' enemies in the three most powerful states were thoroughly organized and strong enough to topple him, but he still could not be persuaded to abandon the *tenentes*. Instead he named General Espíritu Santo Cardoso, the *tenentes'* candidate, minister of war. As was usually the case, the action achieved several purposes, for in addition to satisfying the *tenentes*, Santo Cardoso was able to keep the majority of army officers loyal to Vargas.

From Mato Grosso General Bartoldo Klinger loosed a blast at Vargas, who simply put the general on the retired list. Klinger went to São Paulo and took command of that state's militia for the coming challenge to the government. The over-anxious liberal-constitutionalists of São Paulo began the revolt in July without giving their *Gaúcho* and *Mineiro* allies time to prepare. São Paulo mobilized feverishly, but arms were not available for many thousands of volunteers. The revolt was largely a middle-class movement; the *Paulista* workers remained aloof—to them it seemed to be a quarrel of displaced oligarchs.

The liberal-constitutionalists had made a serious mistake in starting the civil war. Their demands for constitutional reforms became thoroughly obscured by demands of a more regional nature that were only of interest to the *Paulistas*. The regional aspect alienated potential allies in other cities, especially in Rio Grande and Minas Gerais. This, compounded by the fact that the revolt was launched before their allies were ready, contributed to the rebels' failure. No help came from Rio Grande or Minas Gerais, and the *Paulista* enterprise was doomed.

Vargas had anticipated trouble from São Paulo and was well prepared. Flôres da Cunha, interventor of Rio Grande, sensed the futility of the rebellion and supported the government. The Minas interventor Olegário Maciel and Benedito Valladares, the rising young statesman, also sided with the government. The fact that Borges de Medeiros and Artur Bernardes headed the rebel factions of their states gave the rebellion the appearance of a reactionary attempt to restore the oligarchs to power. Few Brazilians, even Vargas' opponents, cared to turn back the clock. Borges and Bernardes were arrested and held briefly, and their followers disbanded. The *Paulistas* fought on alone, but theirs was a lost cause.

General Pedro Aurélio Góes Monteiro commanded the govern-

ment forces and quickly blocked the road to Rio. Rio Grande and
Minas both sent troops to be used against the rebels. Government
airplanes bombed the city of São Paulo, an act of inhumanity and
barbarism so deeply shocking to Brazilians that *Mineiro* Alberto
Santos Dumont, one of the inventors of the airplane, killed himself.
Out of respect for his memory, both sides stopped fighting for
twenty-four hours.

After a two-month siege the rebels surrendered. Although about
two hundred *Paulistas* were exiled, Vargas was more eager to soothe
than to punish. He immediately announced that the election would
be held as scheduled, and he instructed the director of the Bank of
Brazil to take over the war bonds São Paulo had sold to finance the
civil war.

The Electoral Code of 1932 provided for some delegates to be
elected by employers' groups in an effort to introduce a measure of
corporatism. The election was held without serious incident. A rash
of new political parties appeared, including the *Acão Integralista
Brasileira*, which issued its manifesto in October 1932. The *Integralistas* were patterned after the fascist parties of Germany and Italy and
displayed the usual trappings—green shirts, heel-clicking, open-
handed, full-arm salutes, and a mysterious symbol. Like fascist
parties elsewhere, the *Integralistas* represented a middle-class reaction to the rise of Communism, then making headway in Brazil
under the guidance of Luís Carlos Prestes. They did not, however,
limit their animosity to Communists. They hated, among other
things, Yankees, Jews, the British, democracy, and sex education.
The *Integralistas* exploited and encouraged the middle-class belief
that the economic problems of the world-wide depression could be
solved only by the methods of the extreme right.

When *Mineiro* interventor Maciel died, Vargas planned to name
Virgílio de Melo Franco in his place. Because of his feud with
Maciel, Virgílio was unacceptable to many *Mineiros*. Flôres da
Cunha and Góes Monteiro warned that if Vargas appointed
Virgílio, the Minas delegation would prevent the constituent
assembly from electing him president. Surprised, Vargas agreed to
delay the appointment.

He called in Flôres, Aranha, Virgílio, and Gustavo Cam-
panema, acting interventor of Minas. Flôres and Aranha were at
odds, but both accused Vargas of evasiveness and breaking his
promise to Virgílio's father, Foreign Minister Afrânio de Melo
Franco. Vargas calmly smoked his cigar and waited for tempers to

cool, but no agreement was reached. When Antônio Carlos submitted a list of eight *Mineiros* who would be acceptable as interventors, Vargas inquired about Benedito Valladares, a member of the *Mineiro* delegation but not well known. Antônio Carlos obligingly added Valladares to the list. He asked Vargas which of the eight men was his choice. "The ninth," Vargas replied, and named Valladares governor of Minas.

Before the constituent assembly met, a preliminary commission under Afrânio de Melo Franco worked on a draft of the constitution. The commission rejected Vargas' request that forty "class representatives" be included in the Chamber of Deputies, to be chosen at large by occupational syndicates. Vargas was determined to introduce a measure of corporatism in the government to counteract the strong sense of regionalism, and he had his way. Workers' syndicates were to choose eighteen deputies; the employers would choose seventeen; the liberal professions three; and the civil servants two. An estimated 5,000 amendments to the constitution were proposed before it was accepted in July 1934. No one was completely satisfied with it, especially Vargas.

The Constitution of 1934 was a mixture of not always harmonious principles. The federal structure remained much as it had been before, but the concept of government responsibility for socio-economic welfare was introduced. New labor tribunals were called for, and the government was authorized to fix minimum wages. The *tenentes* were the chief promoters of the idea of government-sponsored social and economic changes, and although they had no popular following, they influenced thinking on these matters. The constituent assembly became the Chamber of Deputies, approved the acts of the provisional government, and elected Vargas president.

The only *tenentes* who retained political importance after 1934 were those Vargas selected for particular roles. Among the survivors whose political careers were launched on October 3, 1930 were João Alberto of Pernambuco and Juarez Távora of Ceará. Yielding to the urgings of Aranha and the *tenentes*, Vargas named João Alberto interventor of São Paulo, much to the disgust of the proud *Paulistas*. He gave Juarez Távora political control of the north from Espíritu Santo to Amazonas, which earned him the title of "Viceroy of the northeast."

In the state elections the *tenentes* lost out in the northeast and the key southern states. Juarez Távora's candidates lost in Ceará, and

João Alberto was defeated by Lima Cavalcanti in Pernambuco. The only *tenentes* who won were Juracy Magalhães in Bahia and Pedro Ernesto in the Federal District. Armando de Salles and Flôres da Cunha won in São Paulo and Rio Grande, while Valladares retained control of Minas. Flôres, looking ahead to the election of 1937, gave Vargas only conditional support.

One of the issues that united government and military was the independent police and militia forces of the strongest states. Vargas named Góes Monteiro minister of war, instructing him to reorganize the army and especially to bring the state militias under federal control. The most serious problem was Rio Grande do Sul, where Flôres da Cunha had at his disposal the *Riograndense* military brigade, 20,000 strong. Flôres had ordered arms and even tanks from Europe, and attempted to smuggle them into the state. Góes was determined to bring the brigade under his control; Flôres was equally determined to retain it, for without it he could be ousted without difficulty. When Góes attempted to undermine his military strength, Flôres became Vargas' active foe. Having made no headway in his contest with Flôres, Góes resigned early in 1935. Vargas accepted Armando's suggestion and appointed General João Gomes to fill the post. In 1937 Góes was named chief of staff, but he had never been far from the seat of power in the interim.

To counteract the growing strength of the *Integralistas*, who delighted in breaking up left-wing street gatherings with rubber truncheons, one wing of the Communist party organized a popular-front movement, the *Aliança Nacional Libertadora* (National Liberation Alliance). Although it relied on the Communist party organization it attracted a large following of non-Communists from the middle class, partly because of the enduring popularity of Luís Carlos Prestes, honorary president of the ANL. The movement grew rapidly as middle-class liberals joined with activist labor groups in support of the ANL program calling for cancellation of "imperialist" foreign debts, the breakup of large estates, and nationalization of alien-owned corporations.

The *Integralistas* on the right and the ANL on the left were the first nation-wide political movements with clear-cut doctrines. Vargas was pleased by the rise of these two violently opposed, extremist forces. So skillfully and successfully did he manipulate them and encourage them to attack each other that he was able to use them to accelerate his plans for complete takeover.

Between 1934 and 1937 the Vargas regime won over important

segments of society: businessmen and industrialists; the middle class, which benefited by the growth of the federal bureaucracy; and the northeastern states, which were grateful for government assistance. The military supported Vargas because he built up the armed forces and was willing to listen to military leaders, especially Chief of Staff Góes Monteiro, the most influential officer throughout the Vargas era.

Vargas, however, had not placated the intellectuals, whose increasing frustration was gradually channeled into political areas. In the 1930s the Modernist novelists split into new groups: critics of the economic system followed Osvaldo and Mário de Andrade into socialism; others looked to the Vatican for guidance, in what they regarded as a "crisis of faith." Some in the latter group, following the lead of Plínio Salgado, joined the *Integralista* movement. Still another movement—regionalism—sprung up in the northeast. Unlike the earlier traditionalists, whose subservience to European standards and models reflected a "colonial" outlook, and the Modernists, who wanted to deny the past completely and start anew, the traditional regionalists accepted selected parts of their European heritage in their search for a distinctly Brazilian system of values. Like the Modernists, the regionalists rejected classicism and its linguistic restraints and set out to create a Brazilian language that would harmonize with their colorful mode of conversation. Gilberto Freyre launched the traditionalist regional movement in 1925 with his collaborative *Book of the Northeast*, and he organized the first regional congress held in Brazil. In 1928 José Américo de Almeida's *A bagaceira*, translated as *Cane-Trash*, appeared, a gloomy tale of sterile landscapes and wasted, half-dead people—the *fazenda* workers—who lived in vice and filth and, above all, resignation. Like José Américo, other novelists of the northeast wrote from their own experiences, exposing the unbearable conditions which were unknown to or else ignored by other Brazilians. The poverty José Américo exposed in *Paraíba and Its Problems* was echoed by Graciliano Ramos of Alagoas, Jorge Amado of Bahia, and Raquel de Queiroz of Ceará.

At first the "proletarian" novels of the Northeast were scorned in the south, where the "psychological" novel was characteristic. To the southerners it seemed that all of these sociological novels had a monotonous tone of permanent misfortune. By 1935, however, the novelists of the Northeast had been widely accepted in Brazil. Their work was, in fact, the most important literary activity for the next two decades. But the growing censorship of the Vargas regime would soon curtail literary production. Freyre, Amado, and Ramos would be among the writers harassed or arrested by the police.

After 1934 friction between nationalistic factions on the extreme right and left intensified at the same time that strife between pro- and anti-government groups in the states was increasing. The measures taken in 1934 and 1935 to restore democratic processes appeared to be returning the states to control by the rural oligarchs of the Old Republic. This trend was so undesirable to the urban middle class that it preferred an authoritarian government to a "democratic" one. The events of these years had a direct bearing on the highly centralized government that was to emerge in 1937.

The tensions and growing violence between the ANL and *Integralistas* made the military as well as the middle class doubt that a representative, democratic government could cope with the extremists—which was the conclusion Vargas wanted them to reach. He did nothing to stop the violence, for it was preparing the nation to accept strong government in preference to chaos and destruction. The Chamber of Deputies began debating the dangers of leftist movements, and in March 1935 it passed the National Security Law, giving the government ample authority to suppress subversive political activities. Vargas took no public stand on the matter, for there was nothing to be gained by stating his views at the moment. He gave both extremist groups all the leeway they needed to trip themselves, smoked his ever-present cigar, and waited.

The first to stumble was Luís Carlos Prestes. On July 5, 1935, the anniversary of the Copacabana Fort rebellion, he attacked Vargas furiously for failing to pursue the ideals of the martyrs of 1922. Calling for a revolutionary national government to replace the present regime, he concluded with the inflammatory shout: "All power to the National Liberation Alliance!"

The police responded by raiding Alliance headquarters and seizing documents that indicated the Alliance was Communist-controlled and financed. The leaders were arrested and the Alliance lost its standing as a legitimate political movement. The Chamber of Deputies, apprehensive over the "Bolshevik" peril, did not hesitate to grant Vargas the extensive powers he requested. Shaken by the threat to the nation, the deputies had not considered the possibility that he might use the powers for other purposes. The effectiveness of the emergency powers seems to have stimulated his desire for the authoritarian rule that would enable him to unify and reorganize the nation without constant interference from divisive political elements of left, right, or center.

The ANL represented the "moderate" wing of the Communist party. The revolutionary branch had shunned the popular front and was planning to overthrow the government by means of party members who had infiltrated the armed forces. Late in November the revolutionaries staged uncoordinated mutinies in Natal, Recife, and Rio de Janeiro. They began by murdering the senior officers, but were soon subdued. By the time the military revolutionaries rebelled in Rio the army had already been alerted, and the revolt was easily quelled. Poor timing and lack of coordination suggested that the rebellions may have been started prematurely by government agents working within the Communist party. At any rate the uprisings shocked Brazilians and justified Vargas' complete suppression of the revolutionary left. Flôres da Cunha offered 2,000 troops; Plínio Salgado pledged 100,000 *Integralistas*.

The congress hastily extended the government's emergency powers, and when Vargas pointed out the need to declare a state of siege, the legislators agreed. The National Security Law was strengthened and the constitution was amended to enable the president to dismiss bureaucrats without hearings, to give him control over promotions and duty assignments of all officers, and to increase his emergency powers. Police harassed leftists, arresting and imprisoning thousands, including ex-*tenentes* Pedro Ernesto and Luís Carlos Prestes, military personnel, and civilians.

In September 1936 the *Tribunal de Segurança Nacional* (National Security Tribunal) was created at Vargas' request, providing a new and extremely effective weapon against opponents of the government. As Góes Monteiro wryly commented, the tribunal would do what was needed to "quiet recalcitrants." It responded by sentencing Luís Carlos Prestes to seventeen years in prison. His German wife, whom he had married in Russia, had already been deported to Nazi Germany, where she apparently died in a concentration camp.

Despite these events jockeying for the coming presidential election began, for the constitution required candidates holding governmental offices to resign a year before the election. The *Integralistas* were particularly active—they saw victory ahead. The constitution prohibited Vargas from succeeding himself, and they were not worried about other candidates.

169

In Rio Grande Vargas' brothers Protásio and Benjamim harassed Flôres da Cunha. In desperation Flôres made peace with Borges, but it proved to be only temporary. His power depended almost exclusively on his control of the military brigade, but Góes Monteiro was still determined to establish national control over state armies, which in their present state were an insurmountable obstacle to genuine national unification. Minister of War João Gomes blocked Góes Monteiro and the latter's efforts were unsuccessful until General Eurico Dutra—who agreed with Góes—succeeded Gomes.

Governor Juracy Magalhães of Bahia doubted that Vargas intended to allow the elections. Lima Cavalcanti of Pernambuco agreed that Vargas would have to be forced to hold them as scheduled, but this could not be done without the help of the major states. Armando de Salles of São Paulo refused to become involved because he already had Flôres' support for his candidacy, and he expected to win the presidency.

Vargas sent word to Valladares to announce that he supported ex-*tenente* José Américo of Paraíba, and in May all the governors except Flôres and Armando were backing him. José Américo thus found himself in the traditionally winning role of official candidate, although Vargas had not openly endorsed him. Once the main *tenente* advocate of authoritarian policies, he now began to court lower-class voters by pointing out that they could not hope to gain their economic and social rights except by exercising their right to vote.

Manipulating the campaign to suit his own purposes, Vargas encouraged the belief that José Américo was the official candidate, but still did not endorse him publicly. At the same time he allowed speculation over some unexpected move on his part to determine what the public reaction might be. The *Integralistas* finally wearied of waiting for Vargas to declare himself and nominated Plínio.

As the campaign's tempo increased, Vargas' advisers assured him that no other Brazilian could save the country from chaos, and among military and political leaders there was widespread sentiment for his continuing in office. These expressions of support convinced Vargas that he was indeed indispensable, which was that much more justification for what he planned. In February 1937 Góes Monteiro learned from Valladares that Francisco "Chico" Campos, whose authoritarian views harmonized with Vargas' plans, was drawing up a constitution.

During the first half of 1937 Vargas carried on normal election-year negotiations with state governors, lulling many *políticos* into believing that he intended to go through with the election. At the same time he was astutely eliminating state leaders who opposed him, intervening in Mato Grosso, Maranhão, and the Federal District to install dependable men. Discovering a *Gaúcho* plot against him, he sent aid to Flôres' enemies and ordered the military brigade disarmed. An infuriated Flôres remarked that there was only one issue: whether or not Vargas was to be allowed to succeed himself and establish a dictatorship.

Congressional leaders were beginning to detect a pattern in Vargas' maneuvers, and in June they refused for the first time since November 1935 to extend the state of siege another ninety days. Vargas relaxed control over leftist political leaders, but let the *Integralistas* continue believing he favored them.

Having Dutra as minister of war and Góes as chief of staff greatly strengthened Vargas' position, for both favored a centralized, semiauthoritarian regime and resented the continued existence of independent state armies. They saw in the impending change the opportunity to secure a monopoly of military power for the national army, a necessary goal if Vargas was to establish a dictatorship and unify the nation. While Vargas was eliminating or neutralizing his foes, Góes systematically transferred unreliable officers to remote posts and replaced them with others whose loyalty was certain.

In September Vargas sent the *Mineiro* Francisco Negrão de Lima, who happened to be José Américo's campaign manager, on a clandestine visit to release certain state governors from any commitment to José Américo. He was then to sound them out on their attitude toward Vargas continuing as president.

In the meantime the palace conspiracy matured the plan to impose an authoritarian state on Brazil. The important figures in the plot, in addition to Vargas, were Generals Dutra and Góes and the ministers of justice and labor, Campos and Agamemnon Magalhães. Aranha had gone to Washington as Brazilian ambassador in 1934 and was not informed of the plot until after it had been hatched. The only hint he received of the coming coup was in a letter from Maciel Filho: "Vargas' strength," he wrote, "merits a *golpe* to end this foolishness. The navy is firm and dictatorial-minded; the army is the same. There are no more constitutional solutions for Brazil." This last statement reflected the opinion of many in the middle class as well as in the armed forces. In the same month, however, Góes assured the press that rumors of a coup were without foundation.

Meanwhile José Américo campaigned furiously, attempting to widen his appeal with the masses by attacking Vargas and claiming mysteriously that he "knew where the money was." His growing radicalism, however, only aroused fears of another Communist uprising. Vargas sent word to Valladares that both presidential candidates should be dropped in favor of another. There was no need to indicate who the other candidate should be.

On September 30 Dutra announced the discovery of the so-called "Cohen Plan." It was actually a forgery, the work of *Integralistas*, which called for the violent overthrow of the government and the establishment of a Communist dictatorship. A wave of fear swept over the nation, and men of high office urged Vargas to ask the congress to declare a state of war. José Américo labeled the affair an invention designed to cancel the election, but in times of intense excitement men do not recognize simple truths. The Cohen Plan was so effective a device that the congress declared a state of war the day after Dutra's announcement. Plans for the coup were accelerated, and in mid-October Góes ordered the state militias of Rio Grande do Sul, São Paulo, and Pernambuco incorporated into federal units. At last he had Flôres by the throat. Flôres gave up the struggle and avoided capture only by making an extended visit to Uruguay. Armando de Salles mourned the loss of his most powerful supporter, but his sorrows did not end there.

The coup was scheduled for November 15, the anniversary of the fall of the empire and the creation of the Old Republic. The date seemed appropriate, for what was planned was the overthrow of all that remained of the Old Republic and the establishment of something more akin to absolute monarchy. General Dutra had already obtained promises of support from most of the generals of the Rio area, who agreed that the Constitution of 1934 badly needed fundamental revision. Góes Monteiro had read the new constitution to be imposed and was enthusiastic about it.

Francisco Negrão returned from his secret mission on November 1 with agreement from the northern governors (except those of Bahia and Pernambuco, whom Vargas had warned him against visiting) that Vargas should continue as president because of the "confused situation." A few days later the governor of São Paulo, fearing that Armando's campaign was injuring the state, sent word of his agreement.

Plínio had been partially informed of the plan and was permitted to read the new constitution. He was pleased with its corporatist aspect, which he was delighted to think came from *Integralismo*, and he promised that the *Integralistas* would not disturb the peace. Vargas reminded him that José Américo was likely to win the election, which would be most unfortunate for the *Integralistas*. For that reason, he confided to Plínio, the armed forces had decided to "change the regime," and he had agreed with them that a change was in order. He assured Plínio that the Ministry of Education would go to the *Integralistas*. Plínio happily staged an *Integralista* parade as a show of strength. Vargas watched it and smiled. Afterward Plínio spoke enthusiastically of his 50,000 marchers, but Vargas' aides quietly informed him that there had been no more than 17,000 in the parade, including women and children. Vargas smiled again.

Góes Monteiro announced that a change in the administration would not prompt the armed forces to seek a military dictatorship. All they wanted, he said, were basic reforms to strengthen the nation.

José Américo now learned of the Negrão mission and demanded an explanation. Despite press censorship the *Correio da Manhã* reported the mission but concluded quite erroneously that only two governors had approved of the plan. On November 8 Minister of Justice José Carlos de Macedo Soares resigned, for he had finally realized that the "constitutional reform" he had been discussing with army officers was about to be introduced under circumstances not at all like those he had been led to expect. The direction in which the government was moving was at last obvious to others who had also been deceived earlier, and Armando appealed to the military to prevent a "long-prepared plan to subvert Brazilian institutions." He concluded, "The nation turns to its military leaders; in suspense it awaits the gesture which kills or the word that saves."

In the face of these appeals to the army, Campos and Agamemnon concluded that the coup could not be delayed until November 15 simply for sentimental reasons. On the night of November 9 Vargas responded to the call for immediate action. Early next morning federal police and troops blocked congressmen from entering the legislative chambers in Tiradentes Palace. There was no noticeable reaction, except that eighty congress members sent Vargas assurances of their support. Only two state governors—Juarcy Magalhães of Bahia and Lima Cavalcanti of Pernambuco—had to be replaced; preparations for the coup had been extensive and effective.

In a radio address to the nation Vargas decried the "democracy of powers" that had jeopardized national unity, making it "inadvisable" for the congress to continue functioning. The dangers from left and right, he claimed, left Brazil no choice but to create a strong government that could "adjust the political organism to the economic necessities of the country." He also announced suspension of payments on Brazil's foreign debt.

José Américo unobtrusively returned to the Budget Tribunal, but Vargas and his advisers regarded Armando and the *Paulista* liberal-constitutionalists as a serious and divisive threat. Armando was arrested and shipped off to a remote town in the interior, with the understanding that he could leave for Europe at any time, and the sooner the better. Aranha resigned angrily because he had not been forewarned of the coup, but he was persuaded to stay on. Soon afterwards, Vargas recalled him to become the foreign minister, believing that he would serve as a necessary counterweight to Campos.

The Nazi press rejoiced and Mussolini's lackeys gloated that Brazil was following the lead of *Il Duce*. Vargas, however, was simply applying *Gaúcho* methods to the nation, and in a conversation with United States Ambassador Jefferson Caffery, he laughed at the thought of Germans, Italians, Japanese, and *Integralistas* deluding themselves that they had influenced the movement.

Copies of the Constitution of 1937 were distributed to the press after the cabinet had read and approved it. Ambassador Caffrey doubted that democratic institutions would be preserved under it, but withheld judgment. The new constitution omitted individual guarantees. It reduced the state governors to interventors, which made them government officials responsible to the president, and eliminated the exercise of effective power at the state level, power that had contributed largely to the dismal failure of the Old Republic. The presidential term was extended to six years. Regional army commands absorbed the remaining state militias. Many articles on labor activity and social welfare were included, but strikes were outlawed and labor interests made secondary to national economic development. Government planning and intervention in economic affairs were implicit.

The Constitution of 1937 was unique in several ways. It was never actually ratified, but the Vargas regime followed its socio-economic precepts. The constitution should, in fact, be read from back to front. Article 187 stated that "This constitution comes into effect on the day it is dated and will be submitted to a national plebiscite in the form regulated in a decree of the president of the republic." Article 186 stated that "A state of emergency is declared for the whole country." Article 180 was, in effect, the basic constitution: "Until the National Parliament convenes," it stated, "the president of the republic shall be empowered to issue decree laws on all legislative matters of the union." Article 178 said simply that "As of this date the Chamber of Deputies, the Federal Senate, the legislative assemblies of the states, and the municipal chambers are dissolved. The elections for the national parliament will be set by the president of the republic, after the plebiscite referred to in Article 187 has taken place." Articles 168–70 dealt with the state of emergency.

Because the constitution declared a state of emergency, the plebiscite could not be held nor could elections for the legislature be scheduled. Only constitutional amendment could remove the state of emergency, but there could be no amendment until the legislature met! Even though the constitution remained in limbo, it set forth the goals of the *Estado Nôvo*, Getúlio Vargas' "New State," and the government worked to achieve them. The duration of the *Estado Nôvo* was to be a period of fundamental change and rapid economic development.

In the past there had been far too much affection for state symbols and too little for national ones. To remedy this the constitution restricted flags, anthems, coats of arms, and similar trappings to the national level. State flags were burned in a public ceremony. The feelings of old-time *Paulistas* and *Mineiros* can only be imagined.

The new constitution provided for censorship, and the Department of Propaganda was given control over all public communications. The enlarged department, now housed in Tiradentes Palace in the room where the defunct Chamber of Deputies formerly met, broadcast a popular nightly radio program concerning governmental activity. In Rio de Janeiro opponents of the regime called it the "Hour of Silence" and turned off their radios.

All business establishments were required by decree to display photos of Vargas, who promoted the belief that he was mild and essentially good-natured, a kindly father-image. Numerous stories told of his skill in dealing with *políticos*, avoiding crises, and frustrating enemies. Each week he checked up on the latest jokes about him for clues about the public temper. One such joke had him arriving at the gates of heaven, where St. Peter was seated. "St. Peter," he said, "will you go ask if I can come in?" "No," was the reply. "If I do you'll take my seat."

Plínio reorganized his *Integralistas* into the Brazilian Cultural Association, but he had been badly out-maneuvered. He was forced to reject the promised post of minister of education, because it was offered to him on the condition that *Integralismo* be eliminated completely. When Vargas disclosed to him a new decree being prepared by Campos outlawing all parties, uniforms, and salutes, the shocked Plínio urged Vargas to save his beloved heel-clicking, hand-saluting *fascisti*. Vargas good-naturedly agreed to try to persuade Campos to make an exception in the case of the *Integralistas*. He can hardly have been surprised when Campos refused.

Plínio realized that he had not only climbed out on a limb, but had sawed it off. His attempt to reconsider a cabinet post and secure it for Gustavo Barroso was of no avail. The *Integralista* movement was dead; the *Integralistas* had only to be informed of its condition. On December 2 the decree outlawing parties was published. This also meant that Nazi party centers among the Germans of the south would have to be closed and Nazi agents sent home to Germany. Of the 2,800 private German schools in Rio Grande only 20 taught Portuguese—the decree further stipulated that all private schools would now be brought under state control.

Vargas also courted the masses, which no one had ever bothered to do before, except José Américo in his brief flirtation in 1937. Since political power and decision-making had always been in the hands of a small elite group which had totally ignored their existence, the masses responded warmly to Vargas' show of affection. Vague references to mysterious "foreign" or "international" forces evoked a positive response, and he increasingly included such references in his public speeches.

The constitutions of 1934 and 1937 revised the tax structure at the expense of the states, eliminating entirely the major source of state revenues—interstate "export" taxes. In 1938 the *Departamento*

Administrativo do Serviço Público was created. With functions similar to those of the United States Bureau of the Budget and Civil Service Commission combined, the department proved an effective instrument for increasing Vargas' personal control over the whole federal administration. The increased centralization of political institutions reversed the disastrous decentralization of the Old Republic, which had been a response to the overcentralization of the empire.

Vargas had set out deliberately to replace the political domination state machines of Minas Gerais and São Paulo with a strong federal executive. By outmaneuvering the old-style *políticos* of those states and of Rio Grande and Rio de Janeiro, he was able to eliminate the extreme regionalism reflected in the São Paulo rebellion of 1932. The flag-burning ceremony of 1937 was, therefore, symbolic of a fundamental change of the greatest significance for Brazil. In his contest with regionalism Vargas appealed to the growing nationalism. He replaced the traditional political elites of the major states with a web of local alliances that looked to him for direction. Although these alliances were formed on a personal basis, the accomplishment became of lasting value when the state groups transferred their loyalty to the office of president after 1945.

The *Integralistas* recovered from their shock, and under Belmiro Valverde decided to risk everything in a desperate effort to overthrow Vargas. Belmiro, undoubtedly one of Brazil's greatest optimists, imagined that with six hundred dedicated and determined men he could overthrow the regime. On the night of May 10, 1938 he put his theory to the test. *Integralistas* and a few others commanded by Lieutenant Severino Fournier attacked Guanabara Palace, where Vargas and his family resided, and killed or captured the marine guards. The way was now open to charge the palace and overwhelm the defenders, composed of Vargas, his family, and friends, who were armed only with pistols. When Fournier ordered the machine guns readied for action, he discovered that they were still on the truck that had brought them—and the truck was gone. The dedicated and determined men Belmiro had lauded were evidently not the same men who had accompanied Fournier. Facing a few armed men and women was not nearly as much fun as whacking unarmed leftists with rubber truncheons, and it was much more dangerous.

At the same time other parties had been sent to kill or capture top officials. These attackers, however, left the telephone wires intact, and the besieged hurriedly called Police Chief Müller, Góes

Monteiro, and Francisco Campos. When the police dispatched by Müller failed to arrive for reasons unexplained, Benjamim Vargas sent men to the almost defenseless palace. Meanwhile other *Integralistas* had seized a radio station and were broadcasting the fall of the regime. In São Paulo Plínio Salgado, who was not involved in the plot, heard the news and danced for joy.

At 1:00 A.M. Dutra rushed to Guanabara Palace from Leme Fort with one truck and a few soldiers. Panicky *Integralistas* fired at the soldiers, but then began a mad race to the Italian Embassy, where they sought refuge. At 5:00 A.M. rescuers finally reached the palace.

There were many questions about the number of hours it had taken for help to arrive. Müller explained that most of his force was attending the *Estado Nôvo* celebration; he did not dare call out troops, many of whom were known to be *Integralistas*, until he was certain of their loyalty. Others presented more elaborate excuses. Brazilians have never approved of murderous attacks on officials and their families, and consequently Vargas emerged from the scrape stronger and more popular than before. Having crushed the extreme left, he now had the excuse he needed to demolish the extreme right. Later, when he decided that Brazil should enter the war against Germany and Italy, he would be able to point out that he had been the first to take positive action against the fascists.

To Franklin D. Roosevelt's congratulatory message Vargas replied sardonically that advocates of foreign doctrines had attempted a coup against "Brazilian democracy." His speech against fanatics who had acted with "foreign" assistance earned him a vicious attack in the Nazi press of Germany.

Convinced that his brother needed a personal guard loyal to him and his family, Benjamim Vargas recruited a force of tough *Gaúchos* from São Borja who had previously served the Vargas family. Benjamim, known as *"O Beijo"* ("The Kiss"), was himself an unsavory character who had connections with the seamy side of Brazilian life and a reputation for violence. The men he chose were of the same ilk.

The government offered a reward for Lieutenant Fournier, who remained in hiding until late June, at which time army officers secretly drove him past guards at the Italian Embassy and attempted to gain asylum for him there. Under pressure to refuse Fournier asylum, the Italian government persuaded him to sign a letter stating that he left the embassy of his own choice. He was sentenced to ten years in prison, but died before his sentence was completed.

Aranha's brother, a captain in the army, had helped Fournier reach the supposed asylum. Upon learning this, Dutra, no friend of Aranha, demanded that the officers involved be cashiered. Vargas hesitated to offend his minister of foreign affairs, but when Dutra threatened to resign unless action was taken, the officers' cause was lost. Vargas, fearing that Aranha would become the focal point of opposition if he resigned his ministry, forced the latter to withdraw his own resignation.

The attempt on the president's life prompted an amendment to the constitution (after its author interpreted the document to imply that the president had the right to amend it). The amendment specified certain offenses, like an attack on the president, which merited the death penalty—a strong measure since Brazil had abolished capital punishment in the 1890s. The amendment also indefinitely extended the article allowing the government to retire civil or military personnel when this seemed advisable. A related decree allowed the National Security Tribunal to dispose of prisoners at thirty-minute intervals.

After finding a battle plan in Fournier's car, the police arrested at least 1,500 persons implicated in the conspiracy. The government did not consider Armando dangerous, but since plotting continued, especially among his followers, the police resorted to harassment in order to make him see the advantages of going into exile "voluntarily." When he proved slow to learn this simple lesson the government bluntly ordered him to leave the country. Artur Bernardes and Lindolfo Collor followed him into exile. In the spring of 1939 Plínio was also convinced that he should live abroad, and he found employment as a professor in Portugal's ancient University of Coimbra.

When the Nazi press attacked Vargas in 1938 the furor distracted Brazilians from the plebiscite which he had no intention of scheduling. In June of the same year a plan for a German rebellion was discovered, implicating German Ambassador Karl Ritter. Subsequent publicity induced the Nazis to cut off trade with Brazil, a serious blow to the latter since Germany was the main purchaser of Brazilian cotton and second largest customer in coffee. Vargas took steps to restore friendly relations with Germany, and trade was resumed in July. Even though Brazil later declared Ritter *persona non grata*, relations between the two countries continued to improve, and Hitler invited Góes Monteiro to command a German division during field maneuvers. United States Undersecretary of State Sumner Welles learned of the German invitation, and he and Aranha arranged for Roosevelt to invite Góes to Washington for conferences on hemispheric defense. They also arranged for General George C. Marshall to visit Brazil and for Góes to accompany him on the return trip on a United States warship. The two men reached an agreement by which the United States would supply available weapons to the Brazilian army. But at that stage not many weapons were available.

The *Estado Nôvo*, Brazil's "New Deal," was a response to the problem of effectively governing and rapidly transforming the country. By the time World War II began in September 1939, most Brazilians had accepted the regime. Technically Vargas' extended term ended the same year, but he did not mention this fact, for he was hard at work on a five-year plan for large-scale economic development. The plan, announced early in 1940, called for the establishment of a steel plant, an airplane factory, hydroelectric plants, railroads, highways, and a merchant marine.

Although the war interrupted the five-year plan, the steel plant was considered vital to national pride, and to Vargas it was the crucible test of Roosevelt's professed "good neighbor" policy. The United States quickly approved a loan when it learned that the Krupp munitions firm was interested in building the steel plant for Brazil, and in 1941 work on the Volta Redonda steel plant began.

Shortly after Italy invaded France, Vargas addressed the nation. The future, he said, belongs to "vigorous young peoples," and only "stubborn liberals" would resist the march away from "decadent systems." Although this speech was quite applicable to Brazilians who favored the Old Republic over the *Estado Nôvo*, to shocked American observers the comments sounded decidedly pro-Axis. Aranha exercised his considerable talents to convince Americans that Vargas was talking to Brazilians about Brazilians. Vargas cabled Roosevelt that he was merely warning his own countrymen, and that his words might surprise some, but not a "far-seeing mind like that of Roosevelt, who is liberal-minded, progressive, and forward-looking. . . ." Roosevelt apparently found this explanation logical and satisfactory, but criticism in foreign newspapers offended Vargas. He pointed out that he did not permit the Brazilian press to criticize Roosevelt or the United States. In vain Aranha tried to explain the American concept of freedom of the press to him. There was much room for improved understanding on both sides.

The Nazi party still maintained a large staff in São Paulo, which busily distributed Nazi propaganda, much of it anti-American. The Germans were also deeply involved in Brazilian commercial aviation through their Condor airline: the Brazilian VASP and VARIG airlines used Condor planes and repair facilities. The Italian LATI line offered the only direct flights between South America and Europe and was used to transport Axis agents. In the fall of 1940 Vargas decreed that pilots of aircraft registered in Brazil must be native-born Brazilians.

In November 1939 the Brazilian press largely ignored the second anniversary of the *Estado Nôvo,* but it printed banner headlines for the republic's fiftieth birthday a week later. Brazilian newspapers, Lourival Fontes explained to Vargas, had tired of having censors sitting in editors' offices. Vargas pondered this and early in 1940 had the Department of Propaganda enlarged to become the Department of Press and Propaganda, to be directly responsible to himself rather than Minister of Justice Campos, who was not at all happy about the new arrangement. The department was innovative in its censorship techniques. The government decreed a monopoly of newsprint to give its wishes greater weight with the press. Editors were informed what the government did not want them to print, making it unnecessary to read each paper before it was released. If an editor transgressed he was warned. If the transgressions continued he would find himself without newsprint. This new type of censorship was so effective that Juan Perón later borrowed it for use in Argentina.

The Department of Press and Propaganda enjoyed particular success in its relations with foreign correspondents. Favorable reports about Vargas and Brazil brought them royal entertainment in the best champagne-and-dancing-girls tradition. The result was that readers in other countries received a most one-sided picture of the Brazilian government. Perón once commented, "When we are called fascists by the American press we look at our northern neighbor and smile."

In the first years of the war Vargas forbade public expressions of support for the Allies, although Brazilians were overwhelmingly pro-Ally. The ban was cleverly evaded when, on one notable occasion, current diplomats were asked to reenact an event that took place shortly before the fall of the Second Empire, when foreign ambassadors had assembled at the palace. On that day, Dom Pedro, slipping as he entered the room remarked, "The empire slipped, but it did not fall." In the reenactment, when the British and French ambassadors entered, they were greeted with a tremendous ovation.

Because Vargas was not yet certain which side would win the war, censorship followed a confusing line at times. In the early years of the war newspapers were obliged to delete words like "democracy" from Roosevelt's speeches. Later they were filled with Allied propaganda. The official policy in the spring of 1941 was to show enthusiasm for Russian victories; the rest of the year German victories were emphasized. In battles between Britian and Germany the slant was to be pro-British. After the attack on Pearl Harbor Russian victories were not reported unfavorably, but simply played down. The utmost emphasis was given to United States victories, but in the first year or two there were few to report.

In an effort to induce Brazil to stop the activities of Axis agents, the United States agreed to build air bases in the northeast and to supply the Brazilian army with the desired amounts of arms in exchange for raw materials. Brazil had placed orders for German weapons, but when the war began, the orders had not been filled. The Krupp firm shipped part of the arms to Portugal. Soon afterwards, the British navy seized the Brazilian ship *Siquiera Campos* en route from Lisbon with a load of Krupp arms. Pressured by both Brazil and the United States, the British allowed the ship to continue its voyage providing that it would be the last arms shipment, that Brazil would "immobilize" all enemy ships in her ports, and that the LATI flights would cease.

Aranha, with the heated approval of Vargas, Góes Monteiro, and Dutra, agreed to the conditions. Nevertheless, in January 1941 the British forced the Brazilian ship *Bagé* to unload another shipment of Krupp weapons in Lisbon. The Brazilian government explained that the shipment contained parts needed for artillery pieces received earlier. Aranha angrily threatened to resign, accusing Dutra and Góes of being deluded by the Nazis. Dutra denied that he had consented to the British request and handed in his resignation.

While hinting at reprisals against British firms operating in Brazil and branding Aranha as pro-British, Góes secretly asked General Marshall to arrange an acceptable solution. The arms shipment remained in Lisbon, and Vargas persuaded Dutra to withdraw his resignation. Relations in the cabinet, however, were still far from harmonious. Aranha and Góes clashed when the latter connived to bring on violent press attacks against the British. Aranha quietly persuaded Lourival Fontes to convince editors to moderate their views of the *Bagé* incident. Lourival, an admirer of Hitler, nevertheless pointed out to the editors that if the United States were to enter the war it would be on the side of Britain.

In February 1941 Vargas pledged Brazil's support if the United States were attacked by a non-Western Hemisphere nation, but on May Day he sent friendly greetings to Hitler. The government published Vargas' message and Hitler's reply at the same time that Brazil and the United States were engaging in serious discussions concerning strategic materials. The conclusion to be drawn is that Vargas had learned that some of the devices effective in domestic politics could be used, in modified form, in international politics. He also had learned how to help United States officials work themselves into a giving mood toward Brazil.

When the Japanese attacked Pearl Harbor, the Brazilian cabinet agreed without a dissenting vote that Brazil should maintain firm solidarity with the United States. At a meeting of the American states in Rio de Janeiro in the spring of 1942, the foreign ministers agreed on a resolution "recommending" a break with the Axis. Secretary of State Cordell Hull, displaying typical American insensitivity toward Latin American problems and emotions, instructed Sumner Welles to repudiate the agreement. Welles, fully aware of the gravity of such a misguided action, telephoned Roosevelt, who agreed that repudiation would be a critical mistake. In the following days Bolivia, Paraguay, Peru, and Uruguay severed relations with the Axis, and at the closing session of the conference Aranha announced that Vargas had severed Brazil's diplomatic relations with both Italy and Germany.

Vargas decided to take the further step of sending Brazilian troops to the European theater, because the United States gave preferential treatment in arms deliveries to nations with troops involved in the fighting. In February 1943 he flew to Natal to confer with Roosevelt, who was en route home from Casablanca. (The two had met briefly in 1936 when Roosevelt stopped in Rio on his way to a conference in Buenos Aires.) The first contingent of Brazilian troops joined Mark Clark's Fifth Army in Italy in May 1944. A 400-man air force detachment also served in Italy. Both air and ground troops performed with distinction.

Brazilians resented censorship even more after they entered the war. In São Paulo police fired on law students who paraded with adhesive tape over their mouths; the number killed and wounded was never disclosed. Vargas warned that interference with the war effort would not be tolerated. In October 1943 a group of prominent *Mineiros*, including ex-President Artur Bernardes, signed a manifesto also protesting censorship: "If we fight against fascism on the side of the United Nations so that liberty and democracy may be restored to all people, certainly we are not asking too much in demanding for ourselves such rights and guarantees." Vargas reacted angrily. Those who signed the manifesto were dismissed from their jobs and accused of being unpatriotic.

On the night Aranha was to be installed vice president of the Society of Friends of America, police closed the meeting place. It was Vargas' way of pulling the rug from under his long-time friend, whose growing popularity made him seem too good a choice to succeed to the presidency. Aranha accepted the ungentle hint and resigned from the ministry—without Vargas' usual regrets.

Aware, nevertheless, that the dictatorship could not continue after the war ended, in 1943 Vargas began laying the groundwork for a new phase of his political career, the "democratic" phase. Marcondes Filho, the energetic minister of labor, began taking steps to capture the affection of labor by means of new pension and medical benefits. Vargas encouraged Marcondes to organize a Labor party.

Vargas had already become extremely popular with the working class. As José Maria Bello viewed it, "We can suppose that both his sincere revulsion against the harsh inequities in Brazilian society and his clearly demagogic intent caused him to seek among the masses, who were kept permanently worked up by the official propaganda, the support denied or grudgingly given him by the elites." Another view of the regime was that "The government puts the country back one step every day, but at night, while the government sleeps, the country takes two steps forward."

The *Estado Nôvo* gave a powerful impetus to industrialization. The world depression earlier had brought home the dangers of depending on a few crops for export. Work on the Volta Redonda steel plant, the first major step toward industrialization, was followed by the introduction of other mixed public-private enterprises, all before 1945, for after Brazil entered the war, the need for industry became painfully clear. Vargas ordered full economic mobilization under the direction of João Alberto, and the government intensified its intervention in the economy. At the same time economic nationalism was growing strong, and with it resentment against alien corporations operating in Brazil. The armed forces especially wanted to establish national control over those parts of the economy vital to national security. Although the impetus for state-sponsored economic development thus came from the military, the actual policies could be attributed to economists and businessmen like Roberto Simonsen and Euvaldi Lodi.

By 1944 Vargas, like Philip II of Spain, had been in power too long, and even the key figures wearied of his rule. Góes Monteiro, in Montevideo on a diplomatic mission, suddenly decided to resign and returned to Rio. Dutra suggested that he ask what Vargas intended to do about elections. When he met Vargas, Góes announced that he had come to "do away with the *Estado Nôvo*," and suggested that a constituent assembly be convened. Vargas calmly replied that some other procedure more in line with Brazilian reality would be more appropriate. Góes took no action with regard to this threat.

Francisco Campos, who asserted that Vargas' mind went blank whenever a crisis occurred, urged him to speak in support of democracy and freedom of the press. He also suggested modifying the Constitution of 1937 and submitting it to an assembly for approval. Vargas smoked his cigar and listened, but said nothing.

As it became clear to all that the war would end soon and that Brazil would hold elections, various candidates were considered. Juarez Távora, who had been military attaché in Chile, a polite form of exile, joined Juracy Magalhães in support of Brigadier Eduardo Gomes, commander of the air force in the northeast and one of the few survivors of the Copacabana Fort revolt of 1922. Aranha and José Américo also favored Gomes, although Vargas had not indicated who the official candidate would be. He was not Vargas' enemy, Aranha declared, but he was opposed to the regime he represented. Virgílio de Melo Franco journeyed to São Paulo to generate support for Gomes, only to be arrested by Benjamim Vargas' palace guard after his return—a reminder that the dictatorship was not yet dead.

Early in 1945 the Brazilian press began to reassert itself and censorship was gradually relaxed. The *Correio da Manhã* published Carlos Lacerda's interview with José Américo, who supported the principles expressed by a writers' conference in São Paulo—democratic equality and a government elected legally by secret ballot. The Department of Press and Propaganda took no action, so other editors were encouraged to begin gingerly exercising freedom of the press. When United States Secretary of State Stettinius gave Vargas a powerful radio set, it was suggested that this was so he could learn what was going on elsewhere in the world. As talk of elections spread, one paper published a cartoon of a father and his son. "What are elections?" the son asked. "I don't know," the father replied. "Ask grandfather."

Vargas decreed a constitutional amendment, the "Additional Act," calling for the election of a president, federal and state legislators, and state governors. The press immediately charged that the amendment sounded like the continuation of the Constitution of 1937, and that was unacceptable. "Additional to what?" one asked. "To a constitution that doesn't exist?" Vargas replied that the legislators could revise the constitution if they wished, but even Campos was critical. The constitution was not fascist; Vargas had simply misused it. "The time has come," he declared, "for Getúlio to think about Brazil instead of himself."

Agamemnon Magalhães and Valladares suggested Dutra as the official candidate, because he would be obliged to continue the *Estado Nôvo* after so close an association with it. He was so colorless, furthermore, that there was no danger of the people forgetting Vargas. This seemed logical to Vargas, but he was more astonished than gratified by Dutra's hasty acceptance of the role. Dutra promised protection of the working man, complete freedom of the press, and close ties with the United States. When the movement to nominate him began, however, many suspected it as merely a way to draw military support from Gomes.

Vargas granted amnesty to political prisoners, ordered Luís Carlos Prestes released, and opened diplomatic relations with the Soviet Union, which soon led to speculation about some arrangement with the Communists. Gomes suggested that Vargas resign and let the Supreme Court run the country and conduct the elections, but Vargas refused to resign under pressure. When Góes mentioned the possibility of Vargas' candidacy, he replied that he would rather rest than try to work with a congress—he also mentioned his plans for organizing a Labor party.

Since political parties had been outlawed for so long, it was necessary to organize new ones. Valladares and others who had been associated with the regime founded the *Partido Social Democrá-*

tico to support Dutra. The opposition, including José Américo and Flôres da Cunha, established the *União Democrática Nacional.* Police Chief Müller had nearly destroyed the Communist party, but remnants of one branch supported Vargas.

Irritated at Dutra's eagerness for the presidency, Vargas said little in support of that candidacy until Góes pointedly called his attention to the omission. Then he merely stated that Dutra deserved the voters' support. In May he set the presidential election for December 2 and that for governors and state legislators for the following May, as the opposition insisted.

Dutra recalled what had happened to José Américo in 1937 when Vargas and Valladares had deserted him, and he decided to obtain assurance from the army chiefs that they would not allow the elections to be canceled. When he heard that Dutra was meeting with opponents of the regime, Vargas tried to interest Góes in becoming a candidate. To Cordeiro de Farias he suggested that Gomes and Dutra should be persuaded to withdraw in favor of a compromise candidate chosen from among Cordeiro, Góes, and João Alberto—shades of 1937.

No one needed to be reminded of what had happened in 1937, and many concluded that Vargas was planning another coup. Laborers began displaying their slogan, *"Queremos Getúlio"* ("We want Getúlio"), as if he were an announced candidate. The *Queremista* movement gathered momentum, for as usual Vargas did not commit himself either way. Other supporters of the regime began agitating for a constituent assembly in place of the presidential election, in order to allow Vargas to "redemocratize" Brazil. The *Queremistas* changed their slogan to "A constituent assembly with Getúlio."

The "Drop Dutra" talk that had begun to circulate prompted Góes to confront Valladares, who assured him that Vargas had not instigated it. Not satisfied, Góes warned Vargas that if Dutra was dropped, he would need a new minister of war, which implied considerably more than Góes' resignation. Derogatory remarks about Dutra continued; some sneeringly referred to him as an "interim candidate," an oblique reference to 1937.

In September 1945 United States Ambassador Adolph A. Berle made a speech, approved in advance by Vargas, in which he expressed confidence that Brazil would hold elections as scheduled. The speech provoked an outburst from the *Queremistas,* who railed against "U. S. intervention." Later Getúlio would blame the speech for his downfall, though how he reached that conclusion is not clear.

On October 3, the anniversary of the start of the 1930 revolution, Vargas addressed a *Queremista* rally in front of Guanabara Palace. Using terminology he had found effective with the masses, he warned that "powerful reactionary forces, some occult and some public," opposed calling a constituent assembly, something the people had the right to demand.

A week later Vargas decreed that state and local elections would be held on the same day as the presidential election, and that office-holders who ran for reelection had to resign a day before the election. The opposition immediately suspected this as a scheme to give Vargas the opportunity to appoint interim officials who would "manage" the elections.

Vargas' next action convinced even the doubters that he was planning a coup, for he informed João Alberto that he was to become mayor of Rio and Benjamim Vargas would replace him as police chief. João Alberto stormed to Góes, with whom he had agreed that if one left office the other would follow.

Góes penned a vitriolic letter of resignation. Vargas, he wrote, was making a serious mistake. "He can last no longer in a government which, with superhuman effort, I have been maintaining." Góes then sent a coded message to regional army commanders to implement emergency plans prepared earlier. Agreeing that Vargas had forfeited his authority, the generals asked Góes to assume command of the armed forces in order to prevent civil strife. Góes agreed. Dutra persuaded him to rewrite the letter of resignation in less explosive language, for he knew that João Alberto and Agamemnon had gone to Guanabara Palace to protest Benjamim's appointment.

Benjamim arrived at the Ministry of War and attempted to persuade Góes of his willingness to cooperate, but Góes brusquely dismissed him. His next step was to order the marines to take over all communications.

On October 29 Dutra warned Vargas that unless he withdrew Benjamim's name the army would depose him. Vargas refused. "If I am not free to choose even a chief of police whom I can trust," he commented, "this means that I am no longer president." He was certain that Góes would not carry out the threat, but by the time Dutra returned to the Ministry of War, the latter had already called out troops and surrounded Guanabara Palace.

Luís Carlos Prestes offered to intensify pro-Vargas street demonstrations, but Vargas seemed to have adopted a fatalistic attitude. Prestes remained available and ready to act in case the president decided to fight.

Góes named Cordeiro de Farias, one of Vargas' closest associates, chief of staff and ordered him to deliver a message to the president—resign in exchange for full guarantees for yourself, family, and friends. With much pain and no pleasure Cordeiro undertook the unwanted assignment. Vargas at first vowed to resist and let Góes assume the responsibility for killing him and his family. Cordeiro gently pointed out that it was simply a question of Vargas' departing with dignity or assuming the pressure of an impossible situation. The armed forces would cut off water, electricity, and supplies for the palace, which would force him out sooner or later. Vargas finally relented.

"I would prefer that you all attack me and that my death remain as a protest against this violence. But as this is to be a bloodless coup, I shall not be a cause of disturbance." He was satisfied that "history and time" would speak for him. "I have no grounds for ill will against the glorious armed forces of my country," he added. All he wanted was to return to São Borja. For the first time a deposed head of government was not exiled or even deprived of political rights. When Perón was later driven from power, he had to flee for his life; but he had bulging bank accounts awaiting him in Switzerland. Vargas' life was not threatened, nor had he used public office to enrich himself. He simply went to the airport and boarded a plane for Rio Grande.

At the airport Vargas gave João Alberto, again chief of police, a manifesto to the Brazilian people. It was couched in brusque *Gaúcho* language, quite different from the smooth cadences of the speeches his aides had written for him, which had won him membership in the exclusive Brazilian Academy of Letters.

Supreme Court Chief Justice José Linhares, the choice of Góes, Dutra, and Gomes, was sworn in as interim president at 2:00 A.M. on October 30. By then most of the interventors had resigned. One of Linhares' first acts as president was to abolish the hated National Security Tribunal. He also repealed the decree changing the date for the state and local elections, and he suspended all mayors until after the election. Góes still insisted on resigning as minister of war, even in an interim cabinet, but he accepted the newly created office of commander in chief of the army, thus remaining the power behind the scenes.

The *Estado Nôvo* was no more, and its passing was not mourned. Its most enduring legacies were the consolidation of power of both the federal government and the armed forces, and the transformation of the government into a vehicle for national integration. Vargas had also taken the initiative in the modernization of municipal government, which he had put under federal interventors. Centralization displaced completely the traditional local autonomy which had long contributed to disunion and governmental ineffectiveness.

Although there was no official party, the *Estado Nôvo* had the political support of the urban middle class, military, industrialists, landowners, and urban labor. Vargas' popularity with the masses was enormous, even though no one had ever considered him charismatic. An undoctrinaire person, he was willing to borrow freely anything that suited his purposes, whether from the left or right. Although he could not have remained in power for fifteen years without the military's approval, he was not a military dictator in any sense. He dutifully consulted the military on major issues. Fortunately for his plans, the officers also favored national economic planning and administrative centralization.

Vargas' remarkable skill as a manipulator made it seem to some that he was no more than the tool of the military or his political advisers. He appeared bland and sluggish, but could act swiftly and ruthlessly when necessary, suffering no remorse when he felt obligated to doublecross close friends. What is surprising is that after he had done so he was able to retain or regain their friendship. He skillfully played individuals or groups off against one another, so that their energies were spent as wasted effort.

The *Estado Nôvo* was unlike any other state: it did not depend on a political organization, nor did it have a consistent, recognizable ideological basis. It was, in fact, a reflection, on a national scale, of the way of life of Rio Grande do Sul. Under the *Estado Nôvo* Brazil was transformed economically and socially to such a degree that by 1945 there seemed to be little danger of returning to the liberal constitutionalism and ineffectual government of the Old Republic.

Politically, the most significant positive change lay in the relationship between federal and state powers, for the states had been subordinated and the federal government became a virtual national government for the first time. Regional influence, so

190

powerful before 1930, could now be exercised only through national channels. On the negative side, the *Estado Nôvo,* although it inspired the masses to take an interest in politics for the first time, did nothing to increase popular participation in government. Political parties and elections disappeared, and many able men refused to serve the government. Like all authoritarian regimes it could not tolerate the least hint of criticism, so there was no "loyal opposition" nor any means of checking on the activities of individual officials or the regime as a whole. For the most part, however, politicians active during the years 1930 through 1945 seem to have been dedicated men.

Whatever else may be said of it the Vargas regime, or something similar, was an absolute necessity if Brazil was to break with the trends characteristic of the Old Republic. Unless the country could create a truly national government in place of large state domination, it was forever doomed to a troubled existence. Vargas skillfully eliminated state oligarchies and created a network of local alliances that looked to him for guidelines. Despite the unfortunate aspects of the *Estado Nôvo,* it proved to be the vital step that Brazil, the sleeping giant, needed to set it firmly on the road to becoming a modern nation and world power.

9/
Vargas
Returns

WHEN VARGAS RETURNED TO SÃO BORJA, SOME
Paulistas demanded that he and his lieutenants be deprived of their
political rights, but Góes Monteiro had promised him full guarantees for himself and his friends. He declared that he would
personally see to it that Vargas' presence in Brazil did not
jeopardize the government. He added that it would be "inconven-
ient" for Vargas to run for office, and the latter obligingly
announced that he would not be a candidate, meaning that he
would not campaign actively for office.

In 1944 the liberal-constitutionalists, opponents of Vargas and
the *Estado Nôvo*, had created the *União Democrática Nacional,* National
Democratic Union party (hereafter, UDN), hoping that it would
become a coalition of opposition elements that would work toward
reversing the trends of the past fifteen years. Their hopes soared
when Vargas was forced to withdraw before the 1945 election. For
president they nominated Brigadier Eduardo Gomes, who shared
their distaste for the *Estado Nôvo*.

Those who had supported Vargas in the past—the state leaders
and groups he had won over, including landowners, bankers,
businessmen, and urban labor—were expected to support Dutra for
the presidency. The landowners, bankers, and businessmen joined
together in 1945 to form the *Partido Social Democrático,* the Social
Democratic Party, in support of Dutra's candidacy. A combination
of old-style rural *políticos* and businessmen, it was, therefore, a party
without a strong doctrinal base. Urban labor, under the guidance of
Alexandre Marcondes Filho, created the *Partido Trabalhista Brasileiro,* Brazil's Labor party. Realizing the need to secure labor's
loyalty before the Communists did, Vargas patronized both parties.
His sudden departure from the government almost shattered the
Labor party, which had been committed to the *Queremista* movement.

193

The Social Democrats of Rio Grande nominated Vargas for the Senate, despite his statement that he would not be a candidate. The Labor party named him as its candidate for the Senate or Chamber of Deputies in a number of states, as was permissible under the constitution. (When the system of proportional representation was introduced, it became legal for an individual to be a candidate in any number of states. If one was elected in more than one state, he could accept only one post; party alternates were chosen to fill the others). Vargas and Luís Carlos Prestes as well were elected to the Senate and Chamber in a number of states. Vargas was elected senator in Rio Grande do Sul and São Paulo, and deputy in six states and the Federal District. He personally contributed some 300,000 votes to his party, accounting for seventeen of twenty-two Labor deputies elected. Prestes' victories in five states and the Federal District contributed 60,000 votes to the Communist party and four of its fourteen members elected to the congress.

In the presidential race (the vice presidency had been abolished in 1930) little difference existed between the programs of Dutra and Gomes. Vargas' public endorsement of Dutra, however, belated and forced though it was, consolidated Labor's support for the latter and was enough to provide the winning margin. The Social Democrats and the Labor party gave Dutra 55 percent of the vote.* Dutra admitted that Vargas' last-minute support was responsible for his victory.

Dutra, born in Mato Grosso in 1885, had served as minister of war during the *Estado Nôvo* and was one of its founders. He played an equally important role in its demise in 1945. Unpretentious and unaggressive, a man of simple tastes, he could be shrewd as well as tenacious. After his inauguration on January 1, 1946 one of his first acts was to outlaw gambling and close gambling casinos; but horse racing and *jôgo do bicho,* the "animal game" (similar to the American numbers racket), were allowed to continue.

The newly elected legislators also served as a constituent assembly, and their first task was to approve a constitution to replace that of 1937. The Constitution of 1946, largely the work of a group of jurists appointed by the Brazilian Institute of Lawyers, was promulgated in September. Vargas, who had already returned to

---

* This margin represented a relatively greater popular base than in previous elections. Because many more men could meet the literacy requirement and literate women over eighteen were enfranchised, the 1945 electorate, totalling some 5.9 million, was substantially greater than in 1933.

São Borja, was not among the signers. The new constitution provided for a five-year presidential term but prohibited immediate reelection. The vice presidency was restored, and the congress elected Senator Nereu Ramos to fill the vacant post. Each state would now have three senators and an alternate. Although the federalism and presidentialism of the Constitution of 1934 were retained, the government was strengthened in relation to the states, but its right to intervene to force states to comply with federal laws was eliminated. The document also retained many of the socio-economic principles of the Constitution of 1937, and the congress permitted some of the *Estado Nôvo* laws to remain in force. The constitution failed, however, to improve the unfair, archaic tax structure. "Brazil has three problems," a Brazilian once commented. "The first one is . . . its tributary system. I forget what the other two are, but the tributary system is such a calamity that we don't need any more problems."

As president, Dutra governed strictly according to the constitution, without interfering in the congress or the state governments. When asked his opinion on some controversial policy, he would first consult the constitution. The closest he came to interfering with the Chamber of Deputies was when he remarked, "Gentlemen, it is time to do *something*."

At this time there were fourteen parties, most of which had come into existence since 1945. The Social Democratic party was the strongest. In addition to the aforesaid UDN and Labor party were: the Social Progressive party, dominated by Adhemar de Barros of São Paulo; the Popular Representation party, heir to the *Integralistas;* and the Republican party, led by Artur Bernardes and composed of the remnants of the pre-1930 state machines. Since no party could hope for a majority, a number of coalitions—"marriages of convenience"—were formed in the states, but their platforms were generally meaningless. Two parties, for example, might support the same candidate for governor, but back opposing candidates for all other offices. These ephemeral, makeshift unions became increasingly characteristic of politics under the Constitution of 1946 as parties sought to secure election of their own candidates. The fact that the vice-presidential race was separate added greatly to the confusion.

Increasing Communist activity posed a great problem for Brazil after the war. Senator Prestes shocked the nation by stating repeatedly that in case of a war between Brazil and the Soviet

Union, Brazilian Communists would fight on the side of the Russians. As long as the Communist party was small and weak such a threat was not alarming, but membership was growing rapidly. Despite Dutra's dismissal of all known Communists from government employment, Communist activity continued, eventually forcing the administration to conclude that the party must be suppressed for the security of the nation. In May of 1947 the Superior Electoral Tribunal declared the Communist party illegal, and early in 1948 the Chamber, confirming an earlier vote by the Senate, voted to eject Communists from all elected offices. Steps were also taken to exclude Communists from leadership in labor unions. Because of sharp criticism from Russia, in October 1947 Brazil severed the diplomatic relations that had been renewed only the year before.

An unusual postwar problem involved the Japanese, who had come to Brazil after 1899 and settled in the agricultural regions of São Paulo, Paraná, and Mato Grosso. They generally congregated in all-Japanese colonies, called *quistos* (cysts) by Brazilians, where it was possible to preserve their own cultural traits and resist assimilation. During World War II an extremely nationalistic, secret society was organized which engaged in acts of violence against other Japanese who admitted that Japan was losing the war. After the surrender it murdered those who publicly admitted that Japan had been defeated. Several years passed before the Brazilian government could convince them that Japan had indeed lost the war. Despite these problems, the industriousness of the Japanese made them a valuable economic asset, and the government began admitting other Japanese immigrants, many of whom have been active in developing the Amazon region.

Dutra's administration had no clearly defined economic policy, causing the nation to falter somewhat during the early postwar years. A 1948 plan to coordinate government expenditures was never fully implemented, and Brazil soon exhausted the foreign credits it had accumulated during the war. The Constitution of 1946 had called for economic planning on a regional basis, with each regional program to be allocated a specified amount of federal tax receipts. Among the suggested projects were the establishment of a hydroelectric plant on the Rio São Francisco, drouth control in the Northeast, and the development of the Amazon Valley. Commissions appointed to supervise the programs accomplished little. In 1948 the Joint Brazil-United States Technical Commission was formed to make a survey and report on needed developmental projects, particularly with regard to the problems of increasing the food supply and expanding transportation and hydroelectric power. The report it submitted furnished valuable guidelines for such important projects as the São Francisco Valley Commission and the São Francisco Hydroelectric Company, which were established to promote the economic development of the river region and to construct an enormous hydroelectric complex at Paulo Afonso falls, and the less successful National Department for Works against Drouths.

In 1947 Brazil hosted a conference on continental security which was held at Petrópolis, and President Harry S. Truman attended the session—a visit that Dutra later returned. The conference produced the Inter-American Treaty of Reciprocal Assistance—the "Rio Treaty," as it was called—which provided for the mutual defense of Western Hemisphere states against attack.

Dutra maintained close ties with the United States. As Brazilians put it, "We are taught three things in school—believe in mother, God, and the friendship of the United States." As economic nationalism intensified, however, Brazilians, convinced that the alien companies were sending home enormous profits, became ever more resentful of the number of foreign firms in Brazil, most of which were American-owned.

In 1950 rising coffee prices precipitated unfriendly comments in the American press and stirrings in the Senate, offending Brazilians. Brazil had cooperated with the United States during World War II, which should have merited her favorable treatment by the United States government. A Brazilian request for financial assistance was delayed, however, while Argentina, who had not broken with the Axis until after Italy had surrendered and Germany's end was imminent, was given monetary "credits" (Perón did not want to accept a "loan"). This affront, together with the United States' concentration on European problems to the near exclusion of those of Latin America, was another reason for the rise of anti-American sentiment.

During Dutra's administration Vargas appeared only infrequently in the Senate. On his first appearance a resolution was brazenly introduced by Otávio Mangabeira expressing gratitude to the army for its actions on October 29, 1945. Vargas also had to listen to his enemies attacking the *Estado Nôvo*. His interest in politics had not waned, however. In 1947 he tested his political popularity by supporting Carlos Cirilo Júnior against Luís Novelli Júnior for vice governor of São Paulo. The Communists also backed Cirilo. Novelli, Dutra's son-in-law, had the powerful support of Governor Adhemar de Barros, who planned to resign and run for the presidency in 1950, and was seeking an ally to take over the state office. It was a violent campaign: mobs broke up Cirilo's rallies, and Vargas once had to be rescued by the police. When Novelli won, Vargas returned to São Borja, aware that São Paulo under Adhemar was not the proper place to test his popularity.

As the election of 1950 approached Dutra refused to intervene actively in the choice of his successor. He did, however, urge the Social Democratic party to nominate the colorless *Mineiro*, Cristiano Machado, and subsequently tried to bring the moderate parties together in support of a candidate, but the parties were too divided by factional animosities to cooperate. The UDN again nominated Gomes, while the Social Democratic party named Machado. Several of Vargas' former interventors as well as his son-in-law, Ernani do Amaral Peixoto, were Social Democrats and they unofficially swung the party away from Machado to Vargas.

The failure of the moderate parties to agree on a candidate opened the way for the Labor party to nominate Vargas for the presidency. Adhemar's domination of São Paulo was so complete that Vargas needed the support of his Social Progressive party as well. Adhemar, who had presidential ambitions of his own for the future, realized that someday Vargas' assistance might be equally crucial for him. Old differences were forgotten and the Social Progressives also nominated Vargas. Not forgetting that the army had deposed him, Vargas sent out peace feelers to Góes, who assured him that the armed forces would not oppose his taking office if he were elected. The two old comrades had an emotional reunion.

Vargas received around 3.8 million votes or 49 percent of the total, enough to win the presidency by direct, popular vote for the only time in his career. The successful vice-presidential candidate was João Café Filho, also the choice of Adhemar's Social Progressive Party. Café Filho defeated four other candidates and won with less than a third of the votes. A former socialist, he had been exiled in 1937 for protesting Vargas' dictatorship and in 1945 was instrumental in founding the Social Progressive Party in Rio Grande do Norte.

Party affiliation was becoming less rather than more meaningful, causing Brazilians to grow ever more cynical about parties and their leaders. During the 1950 campaign, for example, Vargas found that in Pernambuco the Social Democrats were genuinely behind Machado, making it necessary for him to make an alliance with leaders of UDN in that state. The heterogeneous elements in many parties prevented agreement on strong doctrinal bases. Most parties were held together more by the desire to win office than by agreement on a legislative program.

It may be wondered why Vargas, having served as dictator, would want to be elected constitutional president with only limited powers. Equally curious is the fact that he won the election only five years after the army had deposed him. It seems that Vargas, more deeply offended by his ouster than he admitted, was determined to win to vindicate himself in his own eyes, if not in the eyes of the nation. It is unfortunate that his vanity or wounded pride forced him to seek the office, for he was far less effective as a constitutional president than he had been as dictator under the *Estado Nôvo*. After his victory his interest flagged. The political astuteness that characterized his earlier career had waned, and his administration proved a calamity.

Vargas' first cabinet reflected his political obligations: five posts went to the Social Democratic party, despite its actual nomination of Machado; Labor, the Social Progressives, and the UDN each received one. Despite its rapid growth throughout the country, the Labor party had devoted itself so completely to Vargas that it ignored the need to develop other leadership—certainly not a good sign for the future. Adhemar, to whom Vargas owed about one-fourth of his votes, was allowed to suggest a candidate for president of the Bank of Brazil, a critical choice for *Paulistas* because the bank's president, together with the minister of finance, determined foreign exchange rates and policies. To retain the support of the military, Getúlio appointed General Estillac Leal, an ex-*tenente* and outspoken nationalist, as minister of war.

Unfortunately, these attempts to gain the support of as many groups as possible did little but bring the wrath of the extremists down on the president's head. The reward of a cabinet seat did nothing to stem the frustrated bitterness of the UDN's liberal-constitutionalists, who had long demanded elections in the belief that Vargas would certainly be ignored by the voters. Even the military remained divided in its affections, and in the final analysis its support hinged on Vargas' respect for the armed forces' "inalienable rights" and for the constitution. The administration's enlistment of the influential Góes Monteiro and Generals Zenóbio da Costa and Estillac Leal did not diminish the junior officers' attraction to the UDN extremists and to Carlos Lacerda, Vargas' most vitriolic and unrelenting critic. Lacerda and others denounced the agreement with Adhemar as cynical opportunism. They labeled his reliance on economic nationalism in order to appeal to the middle and working classes as subversive, and indeed the actual economic situation gave their argument a certain validity.

The Brazil over which Vargas was to preside was quite different from what it had been in 1930 or even 1945. Industrial output had doubled since 1945 and, along with rapid industrialization, had greatly strengthened the urban middle and working classes. The literate middle class, comprising only about 10 percent of the total population, in fact represented a much larger percentage of the electorate because of literacy requirements for voting. To secure their support, during the campaign Vargas had stressed his desire to accelerate the pace of industrialization, when what was really needed was a thorough financial housecleaning before even more drastic measures became necessary to set the nation on the road to economic recovery.

After his election Vargas still did not come to grips with the economic situation, and inflation continued to rise. In 1950 and 1951 the cost of living rose a mere 11 percent in Rio, but in 1952 it nearly doubled. In 1950 the Joint Brazil-United States Economic Development Committee was set up, and it made thorough studies of economic problems and possible solutions. In 1952 the National Bank of Economic Development was created. There was still a need for outside financial assistance, but Vargas, with his instinctive *Gaúcho* suspicion of foreign investors, was unwilling to encourage this.

The principle expression of economic nationalism was the creation of *Petroleo Brasileiro, S.A.* or *Petrobrás,* the public-private corporation that in October 1953 was granted a monopoly on oil drilling and refinery building, partly as a reaction to unfavorable United States policies. Oil had been the major symbol of economic independence for Latin Americans ever since the Mexican oil expropriations of 1938. Seen in this light, the creation of *Petrobrás* was symbolically a note sounded for Brazilian economic autonomy. Private refineries were allowed to continue for the time being. Vargas was convinced, however, that private companies were trying to undermine the new corporation. Brazilian nationalistic sentiment regarding the oil industry was so powerful that neither foreigners nor even Brazilians married to foreigners could own stock in *Petrobrás.*

Vargas' concern for the economic state of the country did not apply only to the oil industry. He frequently referred to "exploitation" and the struggle against "international trusts" that were determined to deprive Brazil of her wealth and power. On the domestic front he favored state-owned corporations as basic to investment policies. When Brazil's over-valued exchange rate caused profit remittances to rise sharply in 1951, the government, at Vargas' urging, issued a decree in January 1952 placing a limit of 10 percent on profit remittances. This was invoked, however, only when pressure on the balance of payments made it necessary.

The government kept the printing presses busy running off mountains of *cruzeiros,* and inflation reached proportions so severe that social tensions were exacerbated. In an effort to stabilize the government, Vargas reshuffled his cabinet in 1953. The services of Osvaldo Aranha were once again enlisted, this time as minister of finance. José Américo became minister of transportation and the young *Gaúcho* João "Jango" Goulart was placed in charge of the Ministry of Labor.

Aranha and the president of the Bank of Brazil agreed on the need for a genuine and effective policy to control inflation. They introduced a plan calling for tight control of credit and a multiple exchange system that would allow Brazilian exports to compete in world markets without making imports more costly. Unfortunately, a variety of unforeseen obstacles prevented implementation of that plan. For one thing, the new Eisenhower administration adopted an attitude toward underdeveloped nations less liberal than that reflected in Truman's policies. Eisenhower preferred to emphasize private investments and to play down government-to-government assistance. As a result, the Joint Brazil-United States Economic Commission was terminated after it had already made commitments for financing recommended projects. Although the United States did not cancel long-term commitments, the abrupt policy reversal was a staggering psychological blow to Brazil.

In December of 1953 Vargas again attacked the profit remittances of foreign companies, calling them excessive and implying that those companies were responsible for Brazil's economic morass. He apparently hoped to distract attention from the distasteful austerity measures recently implemented to check inflation and to stem the rising cost of living. By January 1954 these conditions drove workers to riotous protest. Further adding to the economic distress was the fact that high coffee prices were impelling foreign customers to turn elsewhere. A United States Senate investigation of the "exorbitant" prices gave another boost to Brazilian nationalists. American coffee purchases declined so drastically during this period that Brazil's foreign exchange fell below what it had been when prices were lower. Ultranationalists, primarily leftists, blamed the loss of revenue on the "ill will" of other nations, meaning the United States.

Vargas tried to play the role of elder statesman, above party strife, but he discovered that those whom he trusted were not deserving of his trust. The treasury had been poorly managed and looted, and the scandal could no longer be concealed. Even a hasty investigation of the Bank of Brazil during Dutra's administration failed to produce any scandals that would distract attention from Vargas' problems. Opposition in the Chamber and the press became more strident, and the charges of fraud and corruption multiplied.

Opposition to the Vargas administration also centered upon Minister of Labor Jango Goulart, whose collaboration with extremist labor leaders, including Communists, caused the middle class to view him with suspicion and apprehension. Goulart, who was regarded by both friends and enemies as the spokesman for labor when he served as vice president of the Labor party, was more opportunistic than revolutionary or radical. To conservatives and middle-of-the-road Brazilians, however, the distinction was insignificant. Many believed that he was committed to creating a "syndicalist" regime dominated by labor. The army became his most determined critic and foe when he proposed to double the minimum wage for commercial and industrial employees—a measure which would raise the pay of unskilled labor above that of army sergeants.

In February 1954 the junior officers presented to the minister of war a lengthy memorandum known as the "Colonels' Manifesto." The army, it said, was threatened with a crisis of authority which might undermine the unity of the military class and render it ineffective against those who would create disorder. Obsolete equipment, inadequate pay, and inequitable promotion opportunities had damaged the army's prestige and were driving many officers from their military careers. These ex-officers, the colonels hinted, might be susceptible to recruitment by Communists or radical nationalists.

The colonels proposed a simple solution: increased government appropriations for both pay and equipment. Better paid and better equipped, the army would be better prepared to carry out its role as guardian of Brazilian institutions. They mentioned neither Goulart nor the "syndicalist" peril that was ever on the lips of Vargas' foes, but their opposition to the minister of labor was obvious. There were in the document traces of army "honor" that in an earlier era had caused governments to tremble.

The colonels' demands were a warning to Vargas, a serious warning that he could not ignore. They made clear the army's resentment of the social problems caused by inflation and its belief that its own role was threatened. The manifesto reflected middle-class attitudes in general, and it indicated the army's concern for the charges of corruption and radicalism that the press constantly hurled against the regime. The manifesto came as a complete surprise to Vargas, who sharply criticized his minister of war for failing to keep him informed. Bowing to military pressure, he dismissed Goulart, but remained on friendly terms with the ex-minister.

Attacks on Vargas continued unabated. João Neves da Fontoura, foreign minister from 1951 to 1953, charged that Vargas was conducting clandestine negotiations with Perón to form a bloc with Argentina and Chile against the United States. The negotiations, Neves asserted, were carried on through Jango Goulart. Although the Argentine government denied the story, the affair touched off an angry outburst against Vargas in Brazil, for it seemed to support the charge that he was conspiring to establish a "syndicalist" state patterned after Perón's regime. Most Brazilians, convinced that Brazil should follow the United States' lead in foreign policy, were outraged at the thought of joining Argentina in an anti-American bloc.

The UDN seized the opportunity to initiate impeachment proceedings against Vargas, but powerful support for him, especially from the Labor party, convinced them that only the armed forces could remove him from office. Some UDN leaders even approached army and air force generals, hoping to persuade them to stage a coup, but more shocks and subtle persuasion were needed.

In May, over the unanimous opposition of economic experts he consulted, Vargas announced that the 100 percent increase in the minimum wage, proposed earlier by Goulart, would be effected; at the same time he praised his ex-minister of labor as the "indefatigable friend and defender" of the working man. Vargas apparently had concluded that he must cement labor's loyalty, regardless of the repercussions. In the past he had always been prudent and compromising; recklessness was quite uncharacteristic of him. The fact that inflation had brutally damaged the working class and that the 100 percent increase was barely sufficient at best were certainly factors in his decision. His record of political manipulations, however, prompted people to see political motives in whatever he did.

The wage increase instigated an immediate uproar, and attacks on Vargas became even more caustic. At seventy-two the president appeared worn out and quite ineffective; he had lost both his persuasiveness and his gift for manipulation. Talk of deposing him spread among junior officers of the air force. The senior officers, whose defection would be necessary for a successful coup, remained silent at first, for they were not yet ready to take unconstitutional actions. Gradually, however, they began to yield to the increasing pressure of the widespread opposition, and by August the UDN had converted them to its point of view.

The vitriolic Carlos Lacerda was relentless in his determination that Vargas must go and constantly on the attack. No doubt Vargas recalled the happier days of effective censorship under the *Estado Nôvo* and longed for some way to silence his most implacable enemy. Some of his friends, in particular General Mendes de Moraes and Deputy Euvaldo Lodi, talked of "removing" Lacerda. After several abortive attempts on Lacerda's life, young air force officers began accompanying him when they were off duty in hopes that their uniforms would shield him from attack.

Shortly after midnight on August 5 Lacerda and Major Ruben Florentino Vaz approached Lacerda's apartment on Tonoleros Street in the Copacabana section of suburban Rio. A gunman fired on them, killing Vaz and wounding Lacerda. A wave of indignation swept over Brazil. Brigadier Eduardo Gomes charged: "For the honor of the nation, we trust that this crime will not go unpunished." Other air force officers added threateningly, "If the police don't solve this, we will." The warning, however, was unnecessary. Sensing the unrest, Vargas rose to the occasion and urged that the criminals be apprehended. "I considered Carlos Lacerda my greatest enemy," he said. "No man has done so much harm to my government. Now he is my Number Two enemy, because Number One is the man who shot at him." These words, however, were not enough to pacify Lacerda, who never missed an opportunity to strike out against his enemy:

I accuse only one man as responsible for the crime, . . . the protector of thieves whose impunity gives them the audacity for acts like this one tonight. That man is Getúlio Vargas. . . . Ruben Vaz died in the war . . . of the unarmed against the bandits who constitute the Getúlio Vargas government. . . . I am sure the assassins were members of Getúlio Vargas' personal bodyguard.

The driver of the getaway car, which had been marked by bullets in the exchange of gunfire, was soon arrested. He named Climério Euribes de Almeida, a *Gaúcho* in the president's personal guard and a man with a shady reputation and police record, as one of those involved in the attempted assassination.

Thus began the greatest manhunt in Brazilian history. Not satisfied that the government would make a thorough search because of Climério's connection with Vargas, the air force set up its own police-military inquiry. Because the assassin's weapon was a .45 automatic—a gun restricted by law to the armed forces—the act was a "military crime" and a matter for air force action. Vargas and government agencies gave full support.

Using World War II fighter planes, helicopters, cars, and bloodhounds, the police and air force finally trapped Climério in a banana grove. He had quite a lurid story to tell. João Valente de Sousa, subchief of the guard, had given him money for his escape. Gregório Fortunato, chief of the guard and Vargas family friend for at least thirty years, had arranged and financed the assassination. He and José Antônio Soares, the pay-off man, were arrested.

Accused as instigators of the assassination attempt were General Angelo Mendes de Moraes, ex-governor of the Federal District, and Deputy Euvaldo Lodi of Minas. Gregório reported that Mendes had told him that, as Vargas' chief of guards and, in effect, Brazil's "minister of defense," it was his responsibility to save the nation by killing Lacerda. Mendes denied the charge, but his former chauffeur testified that he had also been approached by Mendes to kill Lacerda. According to Gregório, Deputy Lodi had made the same request. Gregório declared that he did not act for money, but was motivated instead by what he considered to be his duty to the nation.

Continuing investigation revealed Gregório's widespread activities in every manner of illegal activity. Though as chief of the guard his salary was modest, influence peddling had proved profitable for him and he had accumulated a fortune. When Vargas learned the extent of corruption among his trusted guards, whose quarters were below his own, he declared, "I have the impression that I am over a sea of mud."

Deep and widespread dissatisfaction led to new demands for Vargas' resignation, even after he disbanded the guard. Even the chiefs of staff of the army and air force and the minister of the navy as well joined their voices to the clamor. Nearly half of the eighty army generals in the Rio area signed a petition demanding that Vargas either resign or take a ninety-day leave of absence. To make matters even worse, Vice President Café Filho informed the congress that he had suggested to Vargas that they both resign, and Brigadier Gomes presented to the officers of the air force a proposal calling for the president's resignation, which became known as the "Brigadiers' Manifesto."

Vargas still refused to yield. "I am too old to be intimidated," he said, "and I have no reason to fear death." General Zenóbio, minister of the army, viewed the situation as critical. The navy had joined the air force, and he did not know how many of his own troops remained loyal. He remained faithful to Vargas to the end.

On August 24 at 2:00 A.M. the cabinet met at Catête Palace at Vargas' request to try to reach some decision about handling the crisis. Zenóbio pointed out the army's "delicate" situation and the possibility of there being a great deal of bloodshed. The ministers of the navy and air force could say nothing: their forces were already solidly in favor of the president's resigning.

The civilian ministers were no more helpful: one suggested handing over the nasty problem to congress; another was willing to let the state governors wrestle with it. These were attempts to evade an unpleasant responsibility. Seeing that the cabinet could not reach a consensus, Vargas decided to take a leave of absence for ninety days.

Immediately after the cabinet meeting ended, at about 5:00 A.M., the admirals and generals assembled. Determined that Vargas must not return to power, they refused to accept the face-saving leave of absence. Zenóbio, realizing that all of his military comrades opposed him, reluctantly accepted their view in order to avoid civil war. What followed was a "revolution of agreement among

206

friends," in the words of Brigadier Epaminondas Gomes dos Santos.

Benjamim Vargas awakened his brother shortly after 8:00 with the news. "Then it means I have been deposed?" Vargas asked. "I don't know whether you are deposed," replied Benjamim, "but it's the end." Vargas sent him on an errand. At 8:30 his family heard a shot and rushed into his bedroom to find him dead, a suicide note on a nearby table.

The suicide note blamed "international groups" for his troubles. The note and a "political testament" he had presumably written earlier were read over the radio with explosive effect. His dramatic death stunned the mobs roaming the streets who had been demanding his resignation. The vague allusions to "international groups" further inflamed them. In a complete turnabout they struck out blindly at his known enemies, the opposition press, and Coca-Cola trucks—apparently tangible evidence of the "international groups" in their midst. The Communist press soon had papers on the streets with headlines screaming "Down with the Americans." Sound-trucks operated by Communist agents steered the mobs to more substantial targets, like the Standard Oil building and the American Embassy. Lacerda fled into exile as frustrated mobs searched for Vargas' enemies.

The president's last act had placed his foes on the defensive. In his self-engineered death he again demonstrated the manipulative skill that had characterized his earlier career. Unfortunately, the note—which in all probability was intended solely to provoke a reaction against his enemies—led to ill-directed and short-lived mob violence.

During Vargas' political career a new Brazil had arisen—a Brazil symbolized by factories and steel plants. The national government had finally gained authority over the states and had assumed a major role in promoting economic development. Although this revolutionizing current was too powerful to have been the work of a single man, Vargas, even after his death, remained the controversial focus of attention. Ultimately the dispute turned from his personality to issues that had prevailed during his periods in office, but political forces remained divided into two principal groups, pro- and anti-Vargas.

His opponents at last had a chance to secure political power, and for the first time men who had opposed the *Estado Nôvo* were able to set national policies. Café Filho gave key cabinet posts to members of the UDN, the party organized to oppose Vargas.

General Henrique Teixeira Lott, a little-known career officer who had signed the "Brigadiers' Manifesto," was named minister of war. It was expected that the government would still pursue Vargas' main economic objectives and take more positive action to check inflation.

These expectations were disappointed. Café Filho, hailing from the underdeveloped state of Rio Grande do Norte, had always been in the opposition and had no credentials as an administrator. Only chance coalition of the Labor party and Social Democrats had resulted in his being chosen to balance the ticket as Vargas' running-mate. As interim president he took a legalistic view of his responsibilities. The ouster of Getúlio Vargas had severely undermined the nation's confidence in republican institutions. Café Filho knew that to restore confidence in them he must stay in power at least long enough to complete Vargas' term; but except for a decree favoring foreign investors who would import machinery for the manufacture of products desired in Brazil, an honest, but empty defense of constitutional processes was as far as he would go. He seemed to be awestruck by the office of president and to doubt his ability to carry out his duties. This attitude, needless to say, did not inspire anyone's confidence in him.

The October elections did nothing to clarify the situation, for no party ran on a clear-cut pro- or anti-Vargas platform; party leaders simply bid for his leaderless following. Although the Social Democratic Party remained the largest, no party appeared strong enough to elect a president without allies. Juscelino Kubitschek, governor of Minas Gerais, supported by both Laborites and Social Democrats, was the first to announce his candidacy. Military members of the government called for a "national unity" candidate to be endorsed by all parties, but Kubitschek refused to withdraw. Adhemar de Barros was the Social Progressive candidate, while the UDN supported General Juarez Távora, *"o tenente do cabelo branco"* (the lieutenant with the white hair).

Juscelino Kubitschek de Oliveria was born in Minas Gerais in 1902. His mother, a schoolteacher of Czech descent, imparted to him a burning ambition to succeed. He worked his way through medical school and advanced study in Europe. During the revolution of 1932 he was in charge of medical services for *Mineiro* troops sent against the rebels of São Paulo, and had gained the friendship of Benedito Valladares, whose political star was then rising. He held a number of political offices and in 1945 helped to found the

Social Democratic party. Following his term in the Constituent Assembly and his work on the Constitution of 1946, he served in the Chamber of Deputies and in 1951 was elected as governor of Minas. His success in encouraging the creation of mixed government-private companies and in accelerating the state's economic development brought him national acclaim and also the endorsement of the Social Democrats for the presidency.

Kubitschek campaigned on a "platform" that invoked the name of Getúlio Vargas, nationalism, and the Brazilians' universal desire for rapid economic development. He stressed industrialization as the key to higher living standards and vowed to move Brazil's capital to the interior. "Fifty years' progress in five" was his campaign slogan.

Jango Goulart ran for vice president on the Labor party's ticket, and a number of minor parties supported him in various states. One of them was the Communist party, whose presence among his supporters seemed to confirm the widespread belief that he was too pro-Communist to be allowed to hold public office. Admiral Pena Bota echoed this belief in an interview granted to Lacerda's *A Tribuna da Imprensa*, adding that neither Adhemar nor Kubitschek had the "moral requirements" for the presidency. The interview was published along with the paper's demands that the congress be dismissed, the elections postponed, and a constituent assembly be called to write a new constitution.

The armed forces were caught between their desire to maintain constitutional government and their fear of another Vargas arising. Zenóbio and others opposing a *golpe* organized the Military Constitutional Movement, which demanded that the verdict of the voters be accepted, no matter how much the military might dislike the winning candidates. This view was not supported by many navy and air force officers nor by the Democratic Crusade headed by General Canrobert Pereira da Costa, president of the Military Club. Although Goulart was the army's main target, Costa protested that Kubitschek's election would restore the very type of irresponsibility and corruption that had prevailed before the military intervened in the previous year.

The election was held in October 1955 and was generally regarded as honest. The electoral reforms of 1953 had created a new system of electoral courts, which removed control of the voting from those in power and guaranteed voters both secrecy and an accurate count of the ballots. The reform had also substituted an official ballot for the individual party ballots used previously. The victors—both of whom won only with pluralities—were Kubitschek, with only 36 percent of the presidential vote, and Goulart, who polled only 40 percent of the vote for vice president. The UDN again claimed that the constitution required an absolute majority. Before the election an amendment had been submitted to the congress providing for the Chamber of Deputies to choose the president if no candidate received an absolute majority, but the amendment had been voted down. The election indicated that the anti-*getulista* opposition, as represented by the UDN, could not win a national election even when its rivals were divided. It also demonstrated that the military, although apprehensive of the new populist politicians, was not sufficiently alarmed to take the government away from them and give it to the UDN.

Nevertheless, strong elements of opposition began to consolidate themselves, making it not at all certain that the armed forces would allow Kubitschek and Goulart to take office. As election results became known, Lacerda and others, especially the UDN, called for a military coup, claiming loudly that Communist votes had decided the election. Carlos Luz, former president of the Chamber of Deputies who had replaced Café Filho as provisional president when the latter was forced to resign after a mild heart attack in 1954, was an unrelenting enemy of Kubitschek and Goulart. He conspired with the military to prevent them from taking office. Furthermore, to add fuel to the flames, extremists among UDN leaders, abandoning hope of legally preventing the *getulista* Labor and Social Democratic parties from staying in power, produced forged letters testifying that Goulart had purchased guns from Perón to arm workers' militias.

The UDN was in a difficult situation: the party existed to oppose *getulistas*, but it also stood for legality. The only way to keep Kubitschek and Goulart from taking office, however, was by an unconstitutional act, a military *golpe*. Apparently UDN leaders decided that they would not actually support a coup, but neither could they bring themselves to hope that one would not occur. General Juarez Távora, UDN candidate, congratulated the winners and denounced the idea of a coup, but the UDN as a whole remained the only party that did not officially and publicly disavow a coup.

Shortly after the election General Canrobert Pereira da Costa died, and ex-*tenente* Colonel Jurandir Mamede, author of the

"Colonels' Manifesto" against Goulart, made a funeral oration that was actually an oblique attack on Kubitschek and Goulart. He spoke of the "victory of the minority," and of the "suicidal insanity" of *políticos* who placed selfish interests ahead of the national welfare. Minister of War Lott, who earlier had forced General Zenóbio da Costa to resign for his public endorsement of the inauguration, now tried to calm tempers. He demanded that Mamede be disciplined for his inflamatory speech on the grounds that military regulations prohibited officers from expressing controversial views in public. As a staff member of the Superior War College, however, Mamede was not under Lott's jurisdiction. His ultimate superior was Provisional President Carlos Luz, who had no intentions of censuring him. Even though it would probably mean Lott's resignation, Luz saw in the situation an opportunity to prevent Kubitschek and Goulart from taking office. The press immediately built the dispute into a major issue, a test of power reminiscent of the 1880s. The excessive publicity made compromise highly unlikely.

Lott, however, decided not to resign and began making plans for a preventive coup to insure that the election results would not be nullified. He commanded troops and tanks in a bloodless movement to oust Luz. Army units surrounded the disaffected air and navy bases and the opposition quickly subsided. Luz, along with Carlos Lacerda, several cabinet ministers, and Colonel Mamede, sought refuge on the cruiser *Tamandaré*, which departed for Santos, where Luz hoped to organize resistance. The army, however, refused to turn against the veteran soldier Lott. Governor Jânio Quadros of São Paulo also declined to become involved. Luz returned to Rio to find that the congress had already declared the presidency vacant, and had named the vice president of the Senate, Nereu Ramos, as provisional president. Luz resigned as president of the Chamber of Deputies and Colonel Mamede was transferred to a remote and isolated post in the interior. Carlos Lacerda decided to visit Portugal for a year. Those who had favored a coup to prevent Kubitschek and Goulart from taking office complained bitterly of the "illegality" of the preventive coup staged to preserve constitutional processes. The sardonic humor of the situation escaped them. It was ironic, however, that legal processes had to be imposed by military power exercised illegally. The affair created a new division in the armed forces and raised serious doubts among some officers as to their real responsibilities toward the constitution.

Lott remained on as minister of war, the power behind the

government. When Café Filho attempted to recover the presidency, the congress, responding to pressure from the army, voted to disqualify him and approved a predated state of siege in order to deny him access to the courts. The state of siege was extended to the end of January 1956 when Kubitschek and Goulart were sworn in as president and vice president. Lott's unconstitutional action to prevent an even more unconstitutional act was responsible, in the final analysis, for enabling the two men to take office. Neither of them had the support of the majority of Brazilian voters.

The governments under the Constitution of 1946 had been ineffective and disappointing, almost as hopeless as those of the Old Republic. Part of the trouble was undoubtedly the constitutional provision for proportional representation, which encouraged the fragmentation of political parties, none of which could command a majority of the votes. No one actually represented the majority of Brazilians—congressmen, like their predecessors in the Old Republic, represented local cliques, not the nation. No sacrifice was made for the nation's welfare.

As a result, as in the 1920s, there was a growing feeling that the system was unworkable and must be changed. Brazilians had become completely cynical about political parties and politics in general. They did not anticipate with much enthusiasm the administration of a man who was, after all, the representative of a minority only, elected by little more than a third of the voters.

10/Decade of Change: 1954-64

DESPITE ITS SHAKY BEGINNINGS, THE KUBI-tschek administration marked a period of tremendous economic development, unmarred by political strife and unconstitutional acts. A remarkable spirit of optimism and expectation was soon generated throughout the nation. The system seemed to be functioning well, and it appeared that at last Brazil had achieved the proper balance between politics and economic development.

Kubitschek's extraordinary skill at improvisation and manipulation enabled him to accomplish all that could be hoped for under the Brazilian political system. Instead of abolishing and completely replacing institutions established under earlier presidents, which might have caused conflict, he created new ones and superimposed them over the others. Pay increases and modern military equipment kept the armed forces happy, and Minister of War Lott lent his support. Kubitschek divided and quieted the opposition by using to his own advantage the vast amount of patronage stemming from his road-building program and the construction of Brasília as the new capital. He succeeded in suppressing extremists at both ends of the political spectrum—the Communist-dominated unions on the left and Lacerda's *Tribuna da Imprensa* on the right.

In foreign affairs Kubitschek's most significant action was his proposal of "Operation Pan America," a program of economic development for all of Latin America to be financed by massive contributions from the United States and supplemented by funds from each nation. Although the United States' reaction to certain aspects of the proposal was initially unenthusiastic, the rise of Fidel Castro was to give United States officials a much clearer perspective. "Operation Pan América" turned out to be the prefiguration of the Alliance for Progress.

Brasília was to be Kubitschek's monument. Moving the capital inland was an old dream discussed occasionally since the 1820s and provided for in the Constitution of 1891. The name had been suggested by José Bonifácio de Andrada during the reign of Dom Pedro I. When Kubitschek discovered that Brazilians were genuinely enthusiastic about the move, he promised to complete it during his term of office. The underlying purpose in building a new capital was to induce Brazilians to look inward rather than outward and to stimulate settlement of the vast, empty hinterland.

Once committed to the Brasília project, Kubitschek focused his attention on it. The corporation NOVACAP was created to supervise construction and to sell city lots to help pay construction costs. Lúcio Costa produced an excellent city plan for the new capital, and Oscar Niemeyer, who called himself a "dormant Communist," supervised the architectural planning. The work began in 1957 and continued day and night without interruption. Concurrently, roads and highways were being built to connect Brasília with all parts of the nation. As the buildings arose and the daring design became clear, it was only natural that not everyone was pleased. The presidential residence, the "Palace of the Dawn," was called both the "most beautiful summer home on earth" and, less charitably, "Niemeyer's cardiogram."

On April 21, Tiradentes Day, 1960, the capital was formally transferred to Brasília and the old Federal District became the state of Guanabara. Since Brasília was far from completed, the nation now had two capitals. Few legislators or diplomats shared the president's enthusiasm for the new capital, but he was insistent that the transfer from Rio de Janeiro be effected officially (if largely symbolically) while he was in office.

Most of Kubitschek's other ambitious production goals were met or even surpassed. Agricultural production had risen 52 percent during the 1950s, while industrial output leapt by a remarkable 140 percent, 80 percent occurring during his administration. Steel production doubled, and at Kubitschek's encouragement an automobile industry was developed, which by 1962 was producing 200,000 cars and trucks per year, the seventh largest volume in the world. The generation of electrical power boomed when the hydroelectric plant at Tres Marias Dam on the Rio São Francisco opened in 1960, and work began on the Furnas plant. The oil industry grew, and the Brazilian merchant fleet became the largest in Latin America. The addition of 11,000 miles of new roads almost doubled road mileage. A population increase from 52 million in 1950 to 71 million in 1960 stimulated industrial growth by expanding the domestic market.

This rapid progress, however, came at a price. The programs were financed largely by deficit spending and by borrowing from abroad. The foreign debt soared from $600 million to $2 billion. Kubitschek's infectious optimism blinded him to the economic consequences of the rapidly increasing public debt and the resultant rampant inflation, which was eroding the real income of wage earners and led to shockingly widespread graft and peculation.

Officials of the International Monetary Fund warned the Brazilian government that IMF funds would be cut off unless orthodox financial practices were adopted. But the nationalists, with the Brazilians' customary defiance of economic laws, considered inflation necessary for rapid industrialization. To their joy Kubitschek broke off negotiations with the IMF in June 1959. It was a reckless act, however, for it meant abandoning efforts to stabilize the currency and left an impossible situation for his successor—runaway inflation and a foreign debt of $2 billion, of which $600 million was to be paid back in 1961.

In the countryside the Peasant Leagues led by Francisco Julião, a lawyer turned Marxist, agitated for land and higher pay. The rural landowners, despite overrepresentation in the congress, felt threatened for the first time. Agitation turned to violence, for Juscelino's program did not include agrarian reform, and the Peasant Leagues were determined to change their situation.

In 1959 growing unrest in the impoverished Northeast prompted Kubitschek to create the *Superintendencia do Desenvolvimento do Nordeste* (SUDENE—The Superintendency of Development of the Northeast). Only after a long struggle was the congress persuaded to allocate the necessary funds and to give SUDENE authority to coordinate and control the activities of other federal agencies in the region. The noted economist Celso Furtado prepared a developmental program for the agency to encourage industrialization, improve agriculture, and relocate surplus population. The unique feature of Furtado's study was his application of economic analyses to problems previously discussed only in social and political terms. He proposed a revolutionary transformation of the Northeast through industrialization, crop diversification, new land-use patterns, and similar devices. Another feature of SUDENE was a tax-credit device which would allow individuals to reduce their income tax liability by as much as 50 percent by investing the tax savings in projects approved by the director. At the outset universal tax evasion foiled the plan, but eventually it became a vital part of SUDENE and similar projects. It was hoped that the program would lessen regional disparities that created conditions favorable to revolution.

As the election of 1960 drew near there was much discussion of the strengths and weaknesses of the Kubitschek administration, especially of the continuing inflation and consequent rise in the cost of living, and also of the widespread corruption in government. Leftists and extreme nationalists protested that the government favored the rich and foreign investors, and that it had neither nationalized basic industries nor even limited the profit remittances of alien companies. Kubitschek was further criticized for concentrating on industrial development to the neglect of agrarian reform.

Lott, the administration's candidate, was opposed by perennial campaigner Adhemar de Barros and by Jânio Quadros, who, after defeating Adhemar for the governorship, had perhaps given São Paulo its most effective and enlightened administration. With a broom as his symbol, Quadros now campaigned on a program of fiscal honesty, an "independent" foreign policy, and the elimination of corruption. In the municipal elections of 1959 *Paulistas* had expressed their contempt for politicians by casting 90,000 votes for "Cacareco," a popular rhinoceros in the city zoo; their presidential candidate for 1960 was almost as rare an animal as Cacareco.

Jânio Quadros burst into national prominence at a time when the suitability of the constitutional system was in question. Because he was free of the old political alignments, which were also being questioned, it seemed that he might be able to transcend the limits set by traditional political maneuverings. Although unorthodox in everything but his ambition, he had, in fact, two valuable assets—his charisma and his record as a winner.

Quadros' appeal as the "anti-politician" who offered a program geared to the 1960s caused many people to place extravagant hopes in him as the Moses who would at last lead Brazilians out of the economic and political desert. His record in previous elections was an unblemished string of victories in which he had used a number of parties, casting them aside as soon as the results were in. He shared the typical Brazilian cynicism about political parties, believing that they would and should always be at his disposal, to be used and discarded at his pleasure.

Quadros was backed by a civilian group known as the *"Movimento Popular Jânio Quadros,"* which took an active part in the campaign. Support also came from the UDN, although Quadros had never been connected with the party. Recognizing his appeal, its leaders, after twenty years of frustration, finally saw a chance to win the presidency and endorsed him. He accepted the UDN's nomination and that of the *Partido Democrata Cristão* (Christian Democrat party), but each party ran its own vice-presidential candidate. Convinced that both depended too heavily upon him, Quadros resigned from the campaign, then resumed his candidacy on his own terms—that both parties agree that he was not bound to them because of their support. Juracy Magalhães, UDN governor of Bahia, warned the voters that Quadros was "unfit" to be president. "At the hour of dismay," he predicted, "the people will remember this convention."

To indicate what he meant by an "independent" foreign policy Quadros visited Castro's Cuba; highly critical press reaction forced him to cut short his visit, but it did not change his views. The Brazilian Communist party nevertheless supported anti-Communist Lott instead of Quadros; agrarian reformer Francisco Julião also urged his Peasant Leagues to vote for Lott despite the latter's opposition to agrarian reform. The logic was that after ten years of Kubitschek and Lott Brazilians would be ready for the revolution. Lott, thinking his victory assured because the "official" candidate had never lost, accepted Communist support. Meanwhile, some pro-Quadros newspapers published the Brigadiers' Manifesto of 1954, with the reminder that the document that "killed Getúlio" had been signed by Lott.

With a plurality of 48 percent, Jânio Quadros became the first *Paulista* president since Washington Luís. Although Lacerda and the UDN had protested the lack of an absolute majority in 1950 and 1955, as Quadros' supporters they took a more realistic view of the matter. The 5½ million votes cast for Quadros were the most any candidate had ever received, and for the first time the opposition candidate had won the presidency. His election meant that a near-majority of voters rejected the *políticos* who for so long had controlled the presidency. Many hoped that Brazil would now have a genuine alternation of parties in power. The successful vice-presidential candidate was Jango Goulart, Lott's running-mate, who won a narrow plurality by linking his name with Lott's in some states and with Quadros' in others. Even with such a vote-getter as Quadros heading its ticket, the UDN could not elect a vice president.

During the campaign Quadros never spelled out the actual steps he would take to implement his program. After the election, with economists anxious to begin work on a blueprint for checking inflation, he blithely left on a trip around the world, an act typical of his cavalier attitude toward politics and his unorthodox approach to government. His absence between the election and his inauguration would undoubtedly make the latter a dramatic event, but less drama and more planning would have been more appropriate to Brazil's condition.

In naming his cabinet Quadros completely ignored the leaders of the *Movimento Popular Jânio Quadros*, who had labored hard for his election. The group could have been organized into a broad base for such future action as marshalling public support, but he gave it even less attention than the UDN received. The cabinet included two UDN leaders: Minister of Finance Clemente Mariani of Bahia and Foreign Minister Afonso Arinos de Melo Franco of Minas Gerais. Clovis Pestana of the Social Democratic party became minister of transportation, and other posts went to lesser figures of smaller parties. Except for Pestana, the ministry was composed of anti-*getulistas*.

After taking office Quadros turned immediately to the problem of inflation, but his extreme solutions made life even more painful for the beleaguered citizenry. By drastically devaluing the *cruzeiro*, he decreased purchasing power, particularly of those living on fixed incomes. Lowering subsidies on imported wheat and oil meant that the retail price of each doubled. To soften the blow somewhat he promised a drive for development once the basis for it could be laid by a period of retrenchment.

Quadros carried out his promise to improve bureaucratic efficiency by bombarding officials with scribbled orders they came to resent. He seemed to make no distinction between matters of national importance and others that might be considered trivial: for example, he personally took time to ban bikinis on Rio's beaches when his attention should have gone to matters of greater significance to the national welfare. His campaign to moralize the administration led to a rash of investigations into financial wrongdoings, one of which connected Jango Goulart's name with unauthorized uses of state pension funds. Rather than deny the

218

findings, the vice president asserted that the affair was publicized for political reasons, an explanation that Quadros testily brushed aside. Because the investigations threatened the dominant Labor-Social Democrat coalition, both parties voted to investigate those who were making the charges. Quadros would have been wiser to have built up cordial relations with power blocs in the congress not controlled by the rural bosses, but he acted as if parties and power blocs did not exist.

During his trip around the world Quadros had been impressed by efforts of developing countries to find a middle way between communism and capitalism. He was convinced that Brazil should assume a neutral position in the Cold War and also develop closer relations with Asia and Africa, even though the latter maneuver was more likely to result in commercial competition than economic cooperation. By negotiating simultaneously with the United States, Western Europe, and the Soviet Union, he hoped to improve Brazil's financial situation. The "Bay of Pigs" fiasco, however, made it an inopportune time to play off one power against the other. Quadros' coolness to President John F. Kennedy's personal representative, who offered Brazil less foreign aid than the president had requested, pleased only the extreme nationalists. For most Brazilians this was a poor substitute for a positive, creative policy clearly in the nation's interest.

Quadros maintained that his foreign policy was "grown-up, vaccinated, and old enough to vote," but it placed him with the extreme nationalists, which did not set well with the military, who thought the policy was madness. The masses were delighted, but the middle class knew that only industrialized nations could furnish the kind of help Brazil needed and they began to doubt the president's judgment. His friendliness to Castro as well as his unfriendliness to UDN leaders incurred the wrath of Carlos Lacerda, who changed from supporter to bitter foe and led the attack against him. Using the same tactics he had employed against Vargas and Kubitschek, Lacerda sought to alarm the middle class and the military over Quadros' approach to foreign relations. When Quadros gave Che Guevara the *Cruzeiro do Sul* award, Lacerda could stand no more. After being rebuffed at a conference in Brasília, he responded on August 24 with an emotional speech, in which he charged that the minister of justice was planning a coup to set up a "Gaullist" regime—a charge that was at least partly correct. Quadros, convinced that he was above the need to have a mass following or to organize a party to mobilize his support, abruptly resigned the next day with little explanation.

In his seven months as president Quadros had shown himself to be as ineffective as he had been effective as governor of São Paulo. He had scorned all parties and made no effort to maintain friends or to win over opponents in the congress, which was completely ill-advised policy. Apparently he had lost the power to make decisions. Even his closest supporters had begun to doubt his judgment, for he remained isolated much of the time, seeking solace by watching films in his private projection room and consuming excessive amounts of alcohol. Since the Brazilian governmental system relied to an extreme degree on presidential guidance, it seemed that the system could not long survive Quadros' unconventional behavior.

Although he has. said little to shed light on his abrupt resignation, Quadros apparently had come to the conclusion that it was impossible for him to achieve the reforms he desired by the methods he had adopted. Much of the time there was no quorum in the legislature, and not a single one of his major bills was passed. Given his cavalier approach to parties and politics in general and the congress' indifference, this was no doubt an expected reaction. His irritating attitude simply hardened his opposition, and the Brazilian congress had a history of doing little of a constructive nature unless inspired by someone like Kubitschek. Quadros, of course, knew of his initially tremendous popularity with the masses and the middle class, but he was not aware that his popularity had declined, and he overestimated their potential militancy and willingness to man the street barricades. He must have been certain that neither the middle class nor the army would accept Goulart as his successor. During the campaign he had withdrawn and was able to resume his candidacy on his own terms. Why not employ the same tactics now? If he resigned, the popular outcry would force the congress to knuckle under, especially if the army reacted positively. He had fortunately sent Goulart off on a good-will mission to the People's Republic of China, making the latter doubly undesirable to the army. To Quadros the timing seemed perfect.

When the minister of justice, apparently the first to be consulted, delivered the resignation to the congress, only a few dozen legislators were present. As it was Friday and already 3:00 P.M., most of the rest were flocking to the airport for a weekend in

Rio. Quadros expected to have several days of grace—time enough for the nation to demand his return. The announcement was made early enough, however, for most of the legislators to be recalled before boarding their planes. Trapped in Brasília because of Quadros' incredible act, they were more surprised than pleased.

Quadros had already left that morning for São Paulo, leaving behind a rather plaintive message:

> I have performed my duty, but I have been frustrated in my efforts to lead this nation on to the path of its true political and economic liberation, the only path that would bring the effective progress and social justice which its noble people deserve. I feel crushed. Terrible forces have risen against me. . . . If I remained . . . I believe that I could not even maintain civil order.

He had purposely created a crisis that pushed the nation to the brink of disaster, expecting to emerge from it with unlimited powers—but he had made a colossal miscalculation.

In a surly mood and urged on by the Social Democrats, the congress quickly accepted the resignation and began a bitter debate over the succession. Labor leaders in Rio and a few governors urged Quadros to return to Brasília, but public demonstrations in his behalf were lackluster and unconvincing. A crowd stoned the United States Embassy, which may have relieved some tensions and frustrations but did nothing to aid Quadros. Attention generally focused on the presidential succession, and the president who had voluntarily removed himself was quickly forgotten. The military ministers had him placed under guard, which prevented him from making any further statements and possibly interfered with his plans. "Where," asked Quadros, "are those six million voters who voted for me?" The congress named Pascoal Ranieri Mazilli, president of the Chamber of Deputies, provisional president in the absence of the vice president.

The military ministers, however, were the real receptacle of power, and Quadros had not misread their sentiments about Goulart. Minister of War Odílio Denys announced his opposition to allowing Goulart to succeed to the presidency, and the other military ministers agreed. Provisional President Mazilli informed the congress of this, apparently expecting it to provide the legislation necessary to exclude Goulart, as it had done in the cases of Carlos Luz and Café Filho. If it had met in Rio, where Lacerda and most of the military upheld the military ministers, the congress might have yielded to the pressure. This time, however, it refused, for the armed forces clearly were not at all united behind the military cabinet members.

The military ministers issued a manifesto stating their reasons for opposing Goulart: he had given key labor posts to Communists; as president he might allow the armed forces to be infiltrated and undermined. Unstated was the major reason for military opposition—apprehension that under a labor-dominated regime the armed forces would no longer be the most powerful group in Brazil. The military, however, was not united in its stand; Quadros' departure had been too sudden and unexpected to hold out any real possibility that the armed forces could reach a consensus in time to prevent Goulart's return.

General Lott, now retired from active service, expressed the hope that the vice president would be allowed to assume the presidency according to the constitution. When the minister of war ordered Lott's arrest, other "pro-legality" officers in Rio remained discreetly silent. Then General Machado Lopes, commander of the Third Army, issued a statement from Pôrto Alegre in support of Goulart. Leonel Brizola, Goulart's brother-in-law and governor of Rio Grande do Sul, had pressured Lopes into making the announcement. He also organized mass demonstrations to suggest to the military ministers that they might be starting a civil war. With the threat of civil strife looming large, the commanders of Brazil's three other armies vacillated. Minister of War Denys, seeing serious trouble ahead, looked for a face-saving compromise.

Civilians, too, were divided in their opinions. To many of them constitutional principles and processes were more important than politics, and they did not feel that an elected official should be denied office on the basis of predictions concerning his future actions. Others agreed in principle, but were apprehensive over seeing Goulart assume full presidential powers.

On September 2, to avert the threat of civil violence, the congress presented a compromise which offered at least a temporary solution. It passed an amendment establishing a parliamentary system, thus enabling Goulart to assume the presidential mantle without the authority that customarily went with it. A congressional delegation hurried to meet him in Paris, where he had flown after leaving China. Although not happy about the limitations on his authority, he agreed to the change so as not to lose his chance at the presidency. The military ministers accepted the new arrangement on September 4, and Goulart arrived in Brasília the following day. Under the new system the president nominated the cabinet ministers; the Chamber of Deputies accepted or rejected them, and it could remove them without the president's approval. The compromise solution was evidence that the political system was still malleable enough to stave off an open break between the military and rising populist *políticos* such as Goulart. It was prematurely hailed as a victory for civilian democracy; Goulart was granted a "probationary" term and won widespread sympathy.

Before the end of the year, *Electrobrás,* which had been debated for many years, was established, giving the government authority to coordinate the public and private production of electricity. The project, reminiscent of *Petrobrás* and Vargas' support of it, represented a victory for the nationalists, who resented the presence of alien companies in any of the public utilities. They scored another victory when Goulart limited profit remittances of foreign companies to a maximum of 10 percent, as Vargas had done earlier.

Except for these measures, however, the parliamentary regime was a complete failure. The public was indifferent to the government, and no powerful group made an effort to see that it functioned properly. Problems inherited from the Kubitschek and Quadros administrations required incisive governmental action. Hastily passed to quell the immediate threat of strife, the compromise solution which denied Goulart full presidential powers diminished the possibility of such action and thus was not altogether in the best national interest. From the time of his inauguration, Goulart maneuvered to discredit the government and recover full power, and he was supported in his actions by Kubitschek, who intended to run again in 1965. His efforts were crowned in a plebiscite held in January 1963, when Brazilians voted to return to the presidential system by a five-to-one margin.

For the first six months after receiving full presidential powers, Goulart struggled to solve national problems by maneuvering to broaden his political base and thereby secure greater leverage over the congress. He attempted to remove the military's doubts by stressing anti-Communist, anti-Fidel policies and tightening bonds with the United States. He also promoted officers who would be favorably disposed toward him. Goulart even succeeded at this time in straddling the fence between the moderate and radical factions of the left. To the center and trade unions he held out the promise of economic reforms. When Celso Furtado, who had served ably as

223

director of SUDENE, drew up a three-year plan to slow down inflation while maintaining economic growth, Goulart went further: he proposed what he called "basic reforms"—breaking up the large estates with compensation for the expropriated lands to be paid in government bonds instead of cash, as required by the constitution. The administration could not be all things to all men for very long, however.

By padding payrolls of such institutions as *Petrobrás* and allowing Communists to attain key positions in labor unions, Goulart intensified Brazil's problems. Corruption, widespread during the Kubitschek administration, flourished under Goulart. One officer who surveyed corruption, inefficiency, and Communist infiltration was immediately removed from his position—Goulart was apparently satisfied with the status quo or was afraid to do anything about it.

The president's overtures toward the United States also backfired. When he sent his finance minister to Washington to negotiate a loan, extremists accused him of "selling out." To secure the bulk of the nearly $400-million loan, the Brazilian government would have to carry out an effective program of financial stabilization by orthodox procedures, and the finance minister assured Washington officials that wage increases for civil servants would be held to a maximum of 40 percent. Goulart did not wish to risk alienating the military, however, and the cabinet quickly overturned the policy by approving a 70 percent increase for both the military and the bureaucracy. Under pressure, the congress followed suit several months later.

Also foiled was a mutually satisfactory solution to the problem of foreign-owned utility companies that Goulart had discussed with President Kennedy. When Governor Brizola of Rio Grande do Sul, Goulart's brother-in-law, expropriated a subsidiary of ITT, the United States Congress added to the 1962 Foreign Aid Bill the Hickenlooper Amendment, calling for the curtailment of aid to nations expropriating American-owned properties without adequate compensation. Goulart was again accused of "selling-out" when the Brazilian government negotiated a generous agreement with the American and Foreign Power Company, the largest foreign-owned utility. Under pressure from the left he reneged on the final settlement on the pretense that the purchase price had not been agreed on.

The center also viewed Goulart with suspicion. Some of his

proposed reforms, such as extending the vote to illiterates and enlisted men in the armed forces, were coupled with complaints that the congress would never pass the bills. Since the president had made no effort to secure the support of individual deputies, they were certain that he was preparing to dispense with the legislature as Vargas had done. Many agreed that reforms were needed, but their distrust of Goulart was so strong that they refused to support him. His agrarian reform bill was simply held for a year without rejection, approval, or amendment. The congress was at least partly responsible for creating the prolonged impasse between itself and Goulart and for forcing him to adopt a more extreme position than he wished. Too many of the deputies were more interested in blocking the president's efforts than in solving critical problems.

Meanwhile, Francisco Julião's Peasant Leagues were spreading violence throughout the countryside. Chinese and Hungarian agents, ostensibly members of trade missions, provided instruction in guerrilla warfare and terrorist tactics. In the past rural labor had always been inarticulate and leaderless; now its growing militancy was alarming the middle class as well as the landowners. On the defensive as usual, Goulart turned more and more toward the extremist views of Governor Brizola, the spokesman for the radical left. Brizola had promoted the organization of "committees of eleven" all over Brazil. These committees were to watch over the government at every level and presumably would become something akin to local soviets at the proper time. He also demanded even larger wage increases than those to which the congress had already reluctantly yielded and insisted that alien-owned companies be confiscated without compensation. With the government overcommitted to "basic reforms," financial stabilization, and economic growth all at the same time, the extremists saw a chance to gain power by sowing discord. Goulart was a suitable instrument for their purposes.

Radical nationalist views took hold among the noncommissioned officers of army units in the Rio area. A group of them who had been in contact with leftist leaders staged a brief mutiny in Brasília and tried to seize control of the government. They managed to hold a Supreme Court justice and the president of the Chamber of Deputies for a few hours—long enough to alarm the congress. The mutineers claimed that they were only trying to dramatize the plight of the noncommissioned officers, who were denied the right to run for office. Goulart, still courting the ranks of

225

the armed forces, refused to condemn or approve the rebellion, raising suspicions among the military that perhaps it was for some sinister purpose of his own that he was willing to see discipline undermined. Recalling the mutiny of Communists in the armed forces in 1935, the officers alerted themselves for other signs of defection.

The military ministers, concerned over the frequent strikes and political violence in the countryside, urged Goulart to ask congress to declare a state of siege. When the congress hesitated to comply to his request, he withdrew it on the pretense that conditions had improved. Actually, conditions were steadily worsening.

Lacerda declared that Goulart remained in office only because the military refrained from deposing him. A plot to kidnap Lacerda engineered by some of Goulart's military friends not only failed, but prompted a large number of officers to join in a conspiracy against the president. Among them was highly respected Chief of Staff Humberto Castello Branco.

Painfully aware that his term would soon end, Goulart tried to appraise the effect of the unpopular fiscal measures, but his understanding of economic affairs was too limited. Comprehending clearly only the negative political impact of the restrictions, he convinced himself that enacting his reforms was more important than checking inflation—even though the cost of living rose 70 percent in 1963 and was doing so twice as fast in the first few months of 1964. He dismissed his minister of finance and Celso Furtado, who were responsible for the unpopular measures and had no political followings of their own. Goulart proved to be an insecure and ineffective administrator, involved in problems beyond his grasp; he simply abandoned the program for combining financial stability with economic growth and concentrated on his "basic reforms." He was convinced that the advice of his radical friends was correct: he must somehow either get around the congress or cow it into submission; conciliatory measures that pleased no one had to be abandoned and a positive stand adopted that would inspire the "popular forces" to take action. At the suggestion of Luís Carlos Prestes he scheduled a series of mass rallies to stir up support for his reforms, which he then planned to enact by decree. If the congress opposed him, he would call for a plebiscite and let the "popular forces" demonstrate their power.

On March 13 a mass rally was held in Rio, in Lacerda's state of Guanabara. Lacerda decreed a holiday hoping to distract the crowds, but at least 150,000 attended the rally, which was broadcast on radio and television. Somewhat apprehensive about his new and perilous course, Goulart arrived late, but just in time to hear Brizola call for a constituent assembly to be elected in place of the congress.

Surrounded by Communists and extreme nationalists, Goulart signed two decrees at the rally that were part of his basic reforms. The first nationalized private oil refineries. The second declared all underutilized land over 1,200 acres and located within six miles of federal highways subject to expropriation; also subject were properties over 70 acres that were within six miles of federal dams or irrigation projects. "I am not," Goulart declared, "afraid of being called a subversive for proclaiming the necessity of revising the present constitution, which no longer conforms to the wishes of our people. It is antiquated because it legalizes an economic structure that is already obsolete, unjust and unhuman." He indicated further that he planned to issue other decrees concerning rent control, tax reform, and the enfrancisement of illiterates and enlisted men.

The rally and Goulart's actions made it clear that he had abandoned the policies of the moderate left for those of the radical left: the principle of private ownership was noticeably under attack. The expropriation of privately-owned oil refineries was an oblique appeal to all nationalists, since oil was the symbol of economic nationalism. It had the advantage of avoiding difficulties with other nations, because the refineries were owned by Brazilians. The agrarian decree was an attack on a genuine problem; it was made outside the constitutional processes because the congress had failed to act on his agrarian reform bill. Since the constitution required immediate cash payment for sequestered property, and since there were no funds available, the conclusion was that he planned outright confiscation without compensation. Goulart planned to issue new decrees at other rallies, which meant that he intended to govern unilaterally, without recourse to the congress.

After the March 13 rally Goulart still lacked organized mass support for his attack on the congress, but the demonstration convinced the radical left that it was all powerful. At the same time the rally succeeded in solidifying Goulart's opposition, particularly in the armed forces. Many officers concluded that the president was a threat to national security and must be removed. The moderates held back, but the military was fast approaching a consensus. The change was significant because the military was in a position to make key decisions in the event of a major civilian crisis.

One week after the Rio rally Chief of Staff Castello Branco circulated a memo to his subordinates pointing out Goulart's clear intention to use the government-dominated trade unions as his support for subverting constitutional government. Calling a constituent assembly would be a prelude to dictatorship. The "historical role" of the military as defender of constitutional order must not be compromised, he concluded. The memo was a blunt warning to Goulart to turn back before it was too late. Military and civilian conspirators awaited only some action that would justify expelling him from office.

They did not have long to wait. Sailors staged a rally in Rio in support of Goulart, and when ordered to cease political activity and return to duty, many refused. They were not subversive, they declared. The subversive ones were the "dark forces" which had driven one president to suicide, forced another to resign, and had opposed Goulart's taking over the presidency. The high-ranking officers at once recognized themselves as the "dark forces." When Goulart granted amnesty to the offenders, the minister of the navy resigned and was replaced by a more pliable man. No one doubted any longer that Goulart was purposely undermining military discipline to prevent the military from taking action against him. When a general who had not yet joined the conspiracy pleaded with him to renounce the Communists and the leftist Workers' Command, he replied, "I cannot cast aside the popular forces that support me." He seemed bent on dictatorship or self-destruction.

On March 30 the Workers' Command called for a general strike to paralyze the nation, but workers generally ignored the call. On the same day Goulart addressed a meeting of sergeants in Rio and implored their support, declaring that the only breach of discipline was on the part of the officers who had tried to prevent him from becoming president. This was what the generals had been waiting for. They closed ranks, and on the next day tanks and troop trucks rolled out of Minas Gerais toward Rio and were joined by forces sent from Rio to oppose them. Early next morning the minister of justice broadcast a frantic plea to the "people" to come out and fight off the *golpistas*. Few responded. Goulart flew to Brasília, hoping to make a stand there. Having assumed that the army would not intervene at all since it initially had not prevented him from taking office, he was astonished at the magnitude of the revolt.

Aware that his cause was lost, he flew to Pôrto Alegre before going into exile in Uruguay. On the same day the Senate declared the presidency vacant, and as they did when Quadros resigned, they again named Ranieri Mazilli provisional president. Effective power, however, rested with the three military ministers, who had appointed themselves the Supreme Revolutionary Command.

Brazil had been in serious financial and political difficulties when Goulart assumed the presidency. When he was ousted, the nation was on the brink of disaster. Goulart had been unable to cope with the complex situation, and conditions had steadily worsened. It was simply his and the country's misfortune that he had become president at such a time. Without the sincere cooperation of the congress, however, no president could have cured the nation's mortal ills. The calamities that occurred in the 1950s and 1960s are as much an indictment of the congress as of any of the nation's presidents.

The military uprising reflected growing resentment against the corruption and ineffectiveness that characterized representative democracy in Brazil. The armed forces had expelled Vargas only to see the voters return him to power. They had expelled him a second time, only to see his followers and policies continued in office by the will of the electorate. This time the military was determined to provide direction for the hopelessly misguided Brazilian voters.

The revolution of 1964 was the most serious of such actions since 1889, for the bankruptcy of democratic and representative government in Brazil was laid fully exposed. State political officials and party leaders encouraged or approved Goulart's overthrow by the military—tacit acknowledgment that representative democracy could not solve the nation's problems constitutionally. Anarchy or military rule were the alternatives. In the face of these extreme options, *políticos* had no choice but to yield authority and the responsibility of leadership to the armed forces. Painful decisions had to be made, and most *políticos* were quite willing to postpone governing according to a constitution until after the military made these decisions and cleared up the mess. One of the *linha dura* ("hard-line") generals made a statement, however, that should have given them cause for reflection: "If the *políticos* think we risked our lives for everything to go on just as before," he said, "they are making a capital mistake." As when Vargas proclaimed the *Estado Nôvo*, few Brazilians had any idea of what the Supreme Revolutionary Command and the future had in store for them.

229

11 / Under Military Rule

THE FAILURE OF THE MODERATE DEMOCRATIC left to organize an effective political base, together with the political irresponsibility of the early 1960s and the belief that Jango Goulart had "sold out" to the Communists, finally exhausted the military's patience. It now seemed certain that Goulart had begun to create a labor-dominated government that would bypass the congress and enable the radical left to monopolize power in which the upper echelon of the military had always had a share. Thus the army had gradually been forced to reach a consensus: Brazil's political system was unworkable in a time of rapid change; if the nation was to be saved from Communism, the task could not be left to populist politicians like Goulart and Leonel Brizola who, whether legally elected or not, could not be trusted to preserve constitutional government. Having ousted Goulart and seized power for itself, the military next had to determine what its course of action would be.

The hard-line officers were basically fervent nationalists who preferred an authoritarian regime to ineffective democracy. Having intervened several times in the attempt to start the country moving in a new direction only to see the government restored to its previous condition, they looked to long-range fundamental changes as the answer. Many older officers still thought of the army in terms of its traditional role as "moderating power," and it would require time and pressure before the hard-liners could convert them to the idea of retaining power much longer than usual, if not indefinitely.

In contemplating a course of action the military heeded the advice of the well-known democrat Eugenio Gudin, who pointed out that Brazil needed not a perfect system, but one that was appropriate to the degree of political development the nation had achieved. The governments elected after the *Estado Nôvo*, as well as the political system in which they functioned, had proved disappointing; no one mourned when the system was overthrown. The

231

Supreme Revolutionary Command promised to retain democratic institutions, but the hard-liners were convinced that abolishing direct elections and restricting political activity were necessary to weather the painful economic readjustments ahead. The military apparently was not alone in this belief: indeed, complaints against the regime were to reflect concern over economic injuries resulting from the government's efforts to check inflation rather than over its curtailment of political activity.

According to the constitution, a vacancy in either the presidency or vice presidency had to be filled by an election within thirty days. Some *políticos* began to speculate about possible choices, but this was a futile exercise. The hard-liners had already indicated that elections would not be held until political conditions had been changed to their satisfaction. At first moderates seemed to think this could be accomplished in a year or two at most, but experience was soon to show that this timetable had to be revised.

The hard-liners pressured the congress to expel "unacceptable" members and to pass stiff emergency laws against subversives. The military ministers, also under pressure from the hard-liners, demanded that congress give the president ample power to purge the government of "undesirables," whether appointed or elected. Still unaware of the extent of the military's determination to clean house, and unwilling to abdicate their position or to perform the demanded operation, the legislators produced their own emergency-powers act.

The lawmakers soon learned that their freedom of action had been drastically curtailed. On April 9, 1964 the Supreme Revolutionary Command issued what came to be known as the First Institutional Act, written by Francisco Campos, author of the Constitution of 1937. The preamble stated the position of the military government:

A victorious revolution is invested with the right to exercise the constituent power . . . it explains itself . . . it remains clear that the revolution does not endeavor to be legitimized by Congress. . . . To demonstrate that we do not intend to radicalize the revolutionary process, we decided to maintain the Constitution of 1946. . . . In order to reduce even more the full powers invested in the victorious revolution, we resolve equally to maintain the National Congress.

The First Institutional Act was virtually an amendment to the constitution that removed some of the obstacles to presidential effectiveness, especially the lack of leverage over congress, that had frustrated Quadros and Goulart. Now the president could submit constitutional amendments which the congress would have only thirty days to consider. Passage required only a simple majority. The president was given exclusive authority to submit expenditure bills to the congress, which in turn was prohibited from increasing the amounts requested in the bills. On his own authority the president could declare or extend a state of siege for thirty days. Until June 15 he would also wield the awesome power of "cassation," or suppressing the political rights of "undesirables," for ten years. Furthermore, he could cancel the mandates of local, state, and national legislatures. The constitutional guarantees on civil-service job security were suspended until November 9, allowing the bureaucracy to be purged without having to go through the usual legal processes. Congress was charged with electing a new president and vice president within two days after the act's publication, and military officers on active duty were declared eligible for elective office.

The act's temporary nature and early expiration date of January 1966 reflected the military's continued intention to restore civilian government quickly as well as its inherent dedication to constitutional processes. It also demonstrated that the military chiefs had not yet fathomed the magnitude of the task they had assigned themselves.

This First Institutional Act was the military's response to the weakness of presidential authority. The act, along with sixteen other Institutional Acts and seventy-seven Complementary Acts issued in the first five years of the military regime drastically changed Brazil's political rules. Sensing the strength of the myth of constitutionalism in Brazilian political history, the military retained the constitution. The document remained a symbol only, however; it was violated whenever the military chiefs deemed it advisable to do so. The Institutional Acts came to be the real constitution. The traditional "politics of compromise" that had been discredited by Goulart was simply discarded by the military. Intervention by the armed forces was the price *políticos* paid for the chaotic conditions their irresponsibility had created.

General Humberto Castello Branco, chief of staff and a major coordinator of the military movement against Goulart, was the logical presidential choice of the moderate revolutionaries, civilian as well as military, for they believed that he could hold back the hard-liners. The congress dutifully elected him president, and, to convince itself that it was still an independent body, it elected a *Mineiro* civilian member of the conspiracy as vice president. Castello Branco made his own position clear. "We have just toppled a government of the extreme left," he said. "We will not form a government of the extreme right." As mediator between hard-liners and moderates, however, he was in a difficult position. The hard-liners demanded that he suspend the political rights of some 5,000 Brazilians, but by the June deadline only 378 individuals had lost their rights—a victory for the moderates. Castello Branco refused to yield to the hard-liners' demands that he extend the deadline to November, the cut-off date for the purge of the civil service.

Among those proscribed were ex-Presidents Kubitschek, Quadros, and Goulart, six governors, and fifty-five federal deputies (whose expulsion increased the percentage of conservatives in the legislature). Military courts of inquiry ordered at least 9,000 people to appear and answer charges of corruption or subversion. The decision in each case was purely arbitrary; those summoned were allowed neither to defend themselves nor to plead their cases. The Superior Institute of Brazilian Studies was closed and the National Student Union dissolved. Labor unions were purged of Communists, and the Peasant Leagues were outlawed.

Many among the small group of army and air force officers who took over the government in 1964 had participated in the Brazilian Expeditionary Force in World War II. Castello Branco, operations officer of the Expeditionary Force, and United States General Vernon Walters had become close friends during the Italian campaign. The latter's presence as military attaché to Brazil at the time of the coup inspired many rumors about the United States' role in the takeover. Indeed, where the old regime was undeniably anti-American, the new one was unreservedly pro-American; it is doubtful, however, that the Brazilian armed forces needed American advice or encouragement about the fate of Jango Goulart. Nevertheless, the officers, who had been impressed with United States technology during the war, now felt that cooperation between the two countries was vital for Brazil. They considered American investment essential for rapid industrialization.

There was another side to the Italian experience—the first-hand observation of the debacle of Fascist Italy. As one officer noted, "In the ten months we lived in Italy, we could appreciate in all its implications the tragic condition that a nation is reduced to when it is deprived of its basic liberties and allows an authoritarian regime to govern." This may have induced the regime to put such an early expiration date on the First Institutional Act. The experience certainly strengthened the military's initial resolve to return democracy to Brazil as soon as this was feasible.

Many of the officers at the center of the 1964 movement had attended the Superior War College, established in 1950 to solve problems of national security in its broadest sense. The college emphasized the need for order, planning, and rational financing in government, and its program of study concentrated on national development and internal security. This training ultimately convinced the college's military graduates that they were far better prepared and more competent than the *políticos* to handle problems of national development. Unlike the Superior Institute of Brazilian Studies, which emphasized nationalism and government domination of the economy, the War College looked to private enterprise as the key to rapid development. More than half of its students and staff members were civilians representing large businesses. This made for a similarity of views concerning national development between the military elite and industrialists. The officers thus did not abandon democracy as a goal, but it was superseded by a more immediate priority—the development of private industry.

Castello Branco and his close associates, except for Minister of War Costa e Silva, were all "scholar colonels" in the Brazilian tradition, the intellectuals of their services. All of them had attended foreign schools. Because military schools were the only ones to make this educational opportunity available to brilliant men from poor families, many took advantage of it, although they had little interest in the art of war. They insisted that the armed forces play a larger role in economic and political affairs. Castello Branco's government united these political conservatives with young professionals dedicated to economic development. Economic stability was the first order of business.

The generals soon discovered that under Goulart corruption had been a greater national menace than Communist infiltration. Smuggling and payroll padding were among the greatest evils, and it was found that Goulart's staff had engaged in nationwide influence-peddling while the former president himself had speculated in land. One shocked general remarked, "If everything wrong with Brazil were removed there would not be very much left."

235

Obviously the military chiefs had been optimistic when they envisioned straightening out the economic mess in the eighteen-month duration of Castello Branco's term. Castello Branco who disliked politics, reluctantly agreed in July 1964 to extend his term an additional fourteen months until March 1967. But even this would prove to be insufficient time, since the revolutionary government tried to maintain as many of the democratic processes as possible, and these produced frustrating delays.

Government regulations and fees had always presented serious obstacles to business. The Campos Planning Ministry combined some of the levies as well as reduced the cost and simplified the process of securing permits and licenses. Restrictions on exports were lifted to restore reserves of foreign currencies. To check inflation the government fixed both wages and prices. These austerity measures were bitterly protested, but they proved effective and prepared the way for unparalleled economic prosperity. Another measure that eased the financial instability was the new policy of devaluing the *cruzeiro* one or two percent whenever necessary, eliminating the population's fear of being caught with a large supply of sharply devalued currency.

In April 1965 the United States intervened in the Dominican Republic. Convinced that a genuine Communist threat existed there, Brazil's Foreign Minister Vasco Leitão da Cunha approved of the United States' action. As ambassador to Cuba he had tried to persuade the Cubans to avoid alignment with Moscow even though they had adopted a socialistic system. His failure made him determined that another Cuba should not be allowed to rise in the Caribbean. Castello Branco recognized an opportunity to gain credit with the United States at little risk, and Brazil sent the largest Latin American contingent to the Dominican Republic. Brazilian General Hugo Panasco Alvim, commander-in-chief of the occupation forces, contributed to a settlement there.

Early in 1965 the mayoral election in São Paulo had been won by the candidate backed by Jânio Quadros, much to the hard-liners' chagrin. Minister of War Costa e Silva warned that any enemy of the revolution elected in the July gubernatorial races would not be allowed to take office. The government issued an "ineligibility law" that excluded from candidacy anyone who had served as a minister under Goulart after he received full presidential powers. The Statute of Political Parties established the means for a long-range overhaul of political activity, including plans for eliminating the multitude of minor parties. The act was never implemented, however, for after the 1965 gubernatorial election the government took more drastic steps.

Candidates of the Social Democratic party were victorious in two of the eleven gubernatorial contests—those in Guanabara and Minas Gerais. Making matters even more disagreeable to the hard-liners, the *Mineiro* candidate was backed by the cassated Juscelino Kubitschek. Furious over the two defeats, they demanded that Castello Branco annul the elections, backing up their demand by alerting several military units for a march against him. On October 27, 1965 the government responded with the Second Institutional Act, a compromise measure which extended the temporary powers of the first act. By yielding partially to the hard-liners' demands Castello Branco was able to allow the two opposition governors to take office. In return all political parties were to be dissolved, the president was to be elected indirectly by the congress in 1966, and governors were to be elected by state legislatures. The president was empowered to cassate anyone he considered dangerous to the government. The number of justices in the Supreme Court was enlarged from eleven to sixteen in an effort to block frequent rulings to liberate political prisoners. Like the first, this act was temporary, to run only until the end of Castello Branco's term.

Two parties replaced the dozen that had been dissolved. The official government party was the *Aliança Renovadora Nacional* (ARENA), which Brazilians promptly dubbed "Yes." The "opposition" party, the *Movimento Democrático Brasileiro* (MDB), they named "Yes, Sir." The artificial two-party system created by fiat did not generate much enthusiasm in an electorate that regarded even genuine parties with contempt. Paradoxically, the Communist party, which embraced a platform of extreme nationalism, was rendered more palatable at this time because of widespread concern over the huge foreign debt; the party gained wider acknowledgment, if not acceptance, as a truly Brazilian, rather than alien, party.

Still facing the military government were all of the unsolved postwar problems that had intensified under Goulart's vacillating policies: stabilizing the economy, servicing the substantial foreign debt, restoring a satisfactory rate of economic growth, instituting agrarian reform, and improving education. Castello Branco emphasized the need to create the conditions required by Brazil's

237

international creditors, which meant a painfully severe program to check inflation. The Agrarian Reform Law was passed, introducing a progressive land tax to discourage inefficient use of agricultural land. A computerized cadastral survey of all rural landholdings was begun by the Agrarian Reform Institute to determine boundaries and subdivisions, the first such survey in Brazil.

As the months passed the regime realized that securing political support for a stringent economic program would be extremely difficult under a constitutional government; genuinely effective measures to check inflation were sure to be resented. The ineffectiveness of the party structure and its inability to influence sources of political power in times of crisis regarding government policy raised serious doubts that the varied and conflicting interests could ever be harmonized in an open system. The military became increasingly aware of the enormity of its task, as well as why Quadros and Goulart, both of whom lacked Kubitschek's ability to accomplish the maximum possible under the system by manipulation, had been so troubled and ineffective. Because of its determination to attain more concrete goals, the regime's intention to retain as many democratic and constitutional processes as possible was gradually compromised. Even after the various Institutional Acts it was still frustrated by the attitude of the electorate's support of "undesirable" candidates.

ARENA met opposition in the gubernatorial elections of 1966, and as a result the government purged Rio Grande do Sul's legislature and removed the corrupt Adhemar de Barros, last of the civilian revolutionaries in relatively high office, from the governorship of São Paulo. The government tightened the reins even more when faced with difficulties in enforcing its anti-inflation edicts.

In 1966 the Third Institutional Act was passed providing for indirect election of governors and for nomination of state-capital mayors by governors. The only bodies still chosen by direct election were the federal and state legislatures. Brazilians, who seldom lose their sense of humor, conjugated the new act thus: "I vote, you vote, he votes, we vote, you vote, *they* veto."

The government refrained for a time from imposing censorship, but Brazilians never knew exactly what to expect from the regime on any given occasion. Reports and rumors that the government had interfered to prevent its enemies from seeking office were difficult to substantiate. When the press did occasionally report abuses, the government usually took corrective action. As all politicians knew, the military could have suspended the constitution, the congress, and elections if that had been its desire.

By the end of Castello Branco's term the economy showed signs of recovery and the growth rate had risen from -1.5 to $+4$ percent a year; inflation had been reduced to about 40 percent, half what it had been in 1964. In spite of the improvements, however, some criticism of the military regime was voiced. Carlos Lacerda criticized the government for failing to secure mass support for its reforms and predicted that although it had been accepted out of fear of communism, in the end it would lead Brazil to a Communist regime because the people had no democratic alternative. Unlike earlier presidents who were stung by Lacerda's attacks, Castello Branco remained unmoved. Also among the outspoken were the workers, who protested their loss of purchasing power, and a few intellectuals, who protested the loss of liberties.

Literary activity continued despite the precarious position intellectuals occupied as a result of the tense political situation and the ever-present fear of censorship, harassment, and arrest. The novel of social protest that originated in the 1930s persisted through the 1960s. In some works, such as those of José Lins do Rêgo and Raquel de Queiroz, the protest is implicit rather than explicit. In the novels of Graciliano Ramos and Jorge Amado, however, the protest is manifest. Novels written to expose the deficiencies of the political system were characteristic of the *Mineiro* Mário Palmério and Oscar Dias Corrêa. Their concern was with fundamental causes of political defects, not with any political party or doctrine. Dias Corrêa's *Brasílio* (1968), for example, was a satire on political activity during the Vargas era. Antônio Callado's *Big Stir at the Cananéia Plantation* (1964) has at its core an unmistakable call to action—the usually passive peasants should organize, acquire arms, and do battle with the *fazendeiros*.

In the 1960s the short story became the center of attraction. Writers of the sixties were influenced by such masters of the genre as Machado de Assis, whose stories dealt with the imperial court and were written in the literary language of Portugal, and the Modernists Mário de Andrade and Alcântara Machado, whose work reflected strong regional and realist tendencies. The stories of Guimarães Rosa, particularly those in his *Sagarana* (1946), provided the link between the socially conscious stories of the rural interior and those of the cities. His method of giving rural characters universal human qualities was borrowed by more recent writers whose stories center in the cities and deal with a variety of social types living under the impersonal conditions of industrialized societies everywhere. They portray the erosion of human values in the overpowering urban environment and the loneliness and isolation of people surrounded by thousands of others like themselves. Love or the yearning for it is a predominant theme. Samuel Rawet, Rubem Fonseca, and Clarice Lispector are among the trend's leading figures.

Protest also appeared in the theater at this time. Dias Gomes led the way in writing protest plays with *Keeper of Promises* (1960) and *Revolution of the "Beatos"* (1962). He and Ferreira Gullar collaborated on *Dr. Getúlio, His Life and His Glory* (1968), the story of Vargas' election in 1950 and his subsequent suicide, which represents him as friend of the poor, the hero of leftists, and the nationalist who defends his people against American corporations. Dias Gomes' efforts to bring the theater to the people and to indoctrinate them at the same time make his plays more effective as propaganda than as drama. Another playwright of protest is Jorge Andrade, whose *Senhora na Boca do Lixo* (Lady in the Police Station, 1968) exposes corruption among the upper classes and sharply contrasts the treatment of upper- and lower-class people by the police.

Two theatrical groups—the *Grupo Opinão* of Rio de Janeiro and the *Teatro de Arena* of São Paulo—have been most active in both theatrical protest and innovation. Among the issues of protest are dishonesty and corruption in politics, the closing of congress, censorship, the exploitation of peasants by *fazendeiros,* and the American support for the military government, as well as their attempts to gain control of the riches of the Amazon region. Because many priests encourage protest, the church does not receive much criticism.

The selection of Costa e Silva to succeed to the presidency was an unmistakable indication that many military officers had not been happy with all of Castello Branco's policies, particularly his encouragement of private enterprise and his welcoming of foreign capital. The MDB "opposition" members of congress abstained from voting, and Costa e Silva won the election without difficulty. Unlike his associates with whom he had served in the Expeditionary Force and attended the Superior War College, Costa e Silva was no "scholar colonel"; but neither was he an outright hard-liner. He was less eager than Castello Branco to restore orthodox financial measures, balance the budget, and encourage American investment, and he wanted to exclude foreign capital from new industries like petrochemicals. He also favored a more independent foreign policy than his predecessor. His ministers shared his views, so some of Castello Branco's policies were abandoned. Measures to check inflation and encourage economic development were retained, however; Castello Branco had insisted on a commitment to the latter as the condition of his support for Costa e Silva's candidacy.

The general public, still soured by the ineffectiveness and corruption of civilian politicians, was willing to accept government by professionals under military supervision. Many hoped that the new president would relax controls, for he appeared more jovial than his austere predecessor and was certainly more responsive to public opinion. He proved to be indecisive, however, until he yielded to pressure by the hard-liners and, in effect, became their agent.

In order to incorporate the various Institutional and Complementary Acts, a new constitution was promulgated in January 1967 centralizing control in the hands of the president. When Castello Branco was killed in a plane crash in July of that year, it was thought that Costa e Silva would be freer to follow his own moderate inclinations. Unrest became widespread as students rioted against the government and even church leaders joined the growing chorus of demands for radical change. Priests and students were arrested in increasing numbers. The military refused to abandon its program for national development.

Costa e Silva did not help matters at first. His hesitancy and indecisiveness resulted in independent actions being taken by the Supreme Court and the congress, both virtually handpicked by the military. The Supreme Court granted writs of *habeas corpus* to leftist student leaders and the congress voted down the government's request to lift the immunity of a deputy who had urged the people to boycott Independence Day parades in protest.

Student demonstrations against the government intensified, uniting many moderate officers behind the hard-liners. When Costa e Silva refused to crack down at once on all protesters, military units were alerted once more and tanks rumbled into position as unit commanders sent ultimatums to the president. Their demands were met in the Fifth Institutional Act issued on December 3, 1968. It gave the president dictatorial powers in "defense of the necessary interests of the nation." It also disbanded the federal and state legislatures, suspended the constitution, imposed censorship, and led to the cassation of hundreds of individuals. In the wave of arrests that followed, Juscelino Kubitschek and Carlos Lacerda were among those detained by the police. Lacerda had proposed that he, Kubitschek, and Jango Goulart unite in a coordinated opposition movement, but the movement was outlawed and soon collapsed.

Late in 1967 an urban guerrilla movement had formed, composed of Communists, disaffected students, and army deserters. Its goal was to goad the military regime into repressive acts that would lead to anarchy and the government's overthrow. The terrorists robbed banks, raided arsenals, bombed bridges, foreign consulates, and newspaper offices, and kidnapped foreign diplomats as hostages for the release of some of their number who had been arrested. The guerrillas' strategy was at least partly successful, for their violent acts were repaid by increasing violence and repression. Off-duty policemen formed "death squads" and waged a private war of extermination against the terrorists. These squads have been held responsible for more than a thousand killings and disappearances. The number of complaints about torture and police brutality soared at this time. Neither the complaints nor arrests were to decline substantially until the terrorism began to subside.

In August 1969 Costa e Silva suffered a stroke and had to relinquish the presidency. The military ministers assumed power, shunting aside the civilian vice president. When urban guerrillas kidnapped United States Ambassador Charles Burke Elbrick in early September, the military ministers immediately agreed to meet their demands that fifteen of their number be freed from prison and that the guerrillas' antigovernment manifesto be published. The incident prompted the government to restore the death penalty for acts of violence and subversion. It had first been abolished in 1891 and then revived briefly by Vargas following the *Integralista* attack on him.

The military ministers, after careful deliberation, decided on the *Gaúcho* General Emílio Garrastazú Médici for president and Admiral Augusto Rademaker for vice president. ARENA was revived for the occasion and congress was allowed to meet to "elect" the president. A constitutional amendment concentrated power even more in the president's hands and drastically reduced congressional immunity, making congressmen liable to prosecution.

Médici took charge of the 1964 movement after Costa e Silva, yielding to pressure from the hard-liners, had severely damaged it by harassing students and professors. The nation's economic welfare was his major concern. Considered dedicated and incorruptible, he was quick to inspire confidence in businessmen. Inflation declined to about 20 percent, one-fourth of what it had been in 1964, and Brazil entered into the greatest economic boom of its history.

Under Médici Brazil has acquired foreign currency reserves upwards of $1 billion, and the nation is experiencing a growth rate of about 9 percent a year. By 1970 foreign investments had risen to $5 billion, and Brazil was able to extend credit to a number of its neighbors. Manufactured goods—including such articles as steel, earth-moving equipment, freighters and tankers, computers, and refrigerators—provided 17 percent of the value of exports. The tonnage of Brazil's merchant fleet has doubled in the last few years, making it equal to the combined fleets of the rest of Latin America.

The government took some steps to see that the benefits were widely shared. It raised the minimum wage and began building schools at a record rate, with $5 billion having been allocated for use in classroom construction by 1973. Educational reform had long been discussed in Brazil, but until the 1960s little had been done about it. The considerable number of public schools built between 1965 and 1970 reduced the proportion of private schools in the system from 70 to 42 percent over the five-year span. By 1970 the Ministry of Education, which in the past had been fortunate to receive 5 percent of the national budget, was receiving 12 percent. Teaching salaries were raised substantially for the first time, and an anti-illiteracy campaign begun in 1970 produced 600,000 more literate adults within a year.

When the University of Brasília was established soon after the capital had been transferred, its founders abandoned the ancient custom of isolated faculties or professional schools in favor of departmental organization by disciplines. The wasteful duplication of professors in different faculties teaching the same subjects was thus eliminated. After the 1964 movement many faculty members had been dismissed. The government then undertook a serious review of education, that seems to be continuing. The regime was intent on changing the old-style university which, by failing to produce scientists and technologists, contributed little to society; it sought to establish a modern institution with a closer relationship to government and industry and a greater ability to provide the kinds

243

of education and professional training that the expanding economy required. Salary scales were increased drastically, making full-time faculties possible for the first time.

Another remarkable change has been in income-tax collection. Beginning in 1967, the government introduced automated record-keeping for tax returns and began to enforce the tax-evasion law. The following year 600,000 Brazilians paid an income tax; three years later the number had increased to 5,000,000, and collections had risen accordingly. The income-tax provision of SUDENE, which allowed individuals to invest up to 50 percent of their income taxes in approved projects, was also augmented. The program resulted in the building of two hundred new factories in the northeast, providing jobs for 150,000. Other provisions now make it possible for men to begin business enterprises in approved industries with only 15 percent of the capital needed, the remainder being financed by revenue from the income-tax provision. The same device is used to promote reforestation projects and development of the fishing industry in the Amazon basin.

Long a Brazilian dream, the exploitation of the riches of the Amazon region has begun in earnest, with Médici giving it highest priority among developmental projects. He promised that development of the Amazon would raise Brazil to the status of a great power and that Brazilians would take pride in their long-delayed conquest of the world's greatest wilderness. By its completion in 1973, the Trans-Amazon Highway, expected to cost the government some $100 million, will extend more than 3,000 miles from the northeast coast to the Peruvian border—an enormous and costly, but vital undertaking. The network of roads on either side of the new highway are opening half of Brazil's territory to settlement for the first time. Cynics predict that the new road will only link the "poverty of the northeast with the misery of the jungle"; however, the fact that in less than a decade after completion of the Belém-Brasília highway the population along the route soared from 100,000 to 2,000,000 has encouraged many to believe that a similar growth will follow the Trans-Amazon Highway.

Today's pioneers of the Amazon basin are located in *agrovilas*, townships laid out and constructed by the government. Those who want to settle there are given 250 acres, a house, and a "survival" allowance until their first crops are harvested. Eventually these embryonic towns will be provided with schools and recreational facilities.

Among the Amazon basin's rich resources already being exploited are its iron ore reserves, the largest known in the world. Bauxite, manganese, tin, and other ores are being mined by both domestic and foreign corporations, but primarily the latter. Timber operations are extensive, as are cattle raising, tree farming, and the planting of such crops as rice. A boomtown atmosphere pervades the region, and land speculation is widespread. A lawlessness reminiscent of the mining camps and oil towns of the American West is characteristic of the region. Some land companies are even forced to maintain private armies. The government seems to consider this lawlessness merely one of the prices it must pay for development of the region. The regime appears determined to push Amazon development as rapidly as possible, whatever the cost.

The sudden opening of the jungle has had calamitous results for Brazil's remaining Indian tribes. The government has been unable to prevent land companies from enslaving or exterminating Indians whenever they were in the way of progress. The Chavantes, once famed for their prowess in defending their land beyond the Rio das Mortes, have been dispossessed of their land and dispersed, their number reduced to a few hundred. It has been estimated that only about 100,000 Indians remain, and they are not expected to survive the century.

Until 1910 brutal mistreatment of Indian tribes was not uncommon in Brazil. In that year Cândido Mariano da Silva Rondon, an army officer of Indian ancestry, founded the government agency known as the Indian Protective Service. Having witnessed in his early years of service the army's heartless handling of Indians in the interior, Rondon finally persuaded the army to let him try dealing peacefully with the wild tribes. He succeeded in creating one of the most unique organizations in the history of the Western Hemisphere. Those who worked with Rondon had to swear that they would never kill, even in self-defense. He made many expeditions through the unexplored wilderness, establishing peaceful contact with unknown tribes and collecting an enormous amount of scientific data.

After Rondon's death in 1958, however, the Indian Protective Service changed from benevolence to exploitation. The service was disbanded and its functions transferred to other agencies after a government investigation revealed that it had become a "sinkhole of corruption and indiscriminate killing" and an accomplice in schemes to defraud the Indians of their lands. Since its demise only a few dedicated individuals have made an effort to continue Rondon's work, hoping to save the Indians from extinction and to help them adapt to a totally new way of life. *Projeto Rondon*, a Brazilian "peace corps" which enlists university students in voluntary service, was established with these goals in mind. The number of students involved in the project has been increasing annually.

In December 1971 Médici made a long-delayed visit to Washington, at which time President Nixon lauded Brazil as a model for the rest of Latin America to follow. The ensuing talks were among a series of "vitally important" discussions that Nixon was then holding with the nation's "closest friends" before his trips to Peking and Moscow—an indication that the United States regarded Brazil as being in the same category as Canada and its European allies. Nixon's statement that Brazil was the "natural leader" of Latin America brought down a torrent of protest from other Latin American nations. On his return to Brazil Médici felt obliged to reject the role publicly, expressing a desire that Brazil's "progress be won without harming other peoples, without any pretension to hegemony, without leadership or imperialism. . . ."

Unfortunately Brazil's spectacular economic boom is not without its dark side. The military regime has fallen gradually, though almost reluctantly, into a posture of repressiveness, beginning in 1965 when a number of government-backed candidates were defeated in the gubernatorial elections. By throttling legitimate dissent, the regime has left its opponents no other recourse than violence. When he first assumed the presidency, Médici spoke of a return to free elections. After a few years in power, however, pressure from hard-liners has apparently changed his attitude. In the spring of 1972 he announced that state governors would not, as he had indicated earlier, be chosen by direct popular vote in 1974. This surprised many *políticos*, who had been encouraged to expect a gradual return to more conventional political processes. Médici's rationale was that campaigning for the governorships would "interfere" with the election of a new president in January 1974. The government also feared that campaigning would jeopardize the stability necessary for continued economic expansion.

There were widespread fears that Médici's announcement meant the end of the military's "gradual and controlled withdrawal" from political activity. The government has stated, however, that direct elections will be allowed whenever the two new parties stop being dominated by the cult of "personal ambition." In any case, the cancellation of direct gubernatorial elections indicates the regime's unwillingness to risk the growing prosperity by increasing civilian participation at this time.

For nearly a decade the military has labored to remake politicians and the political system, but this obviously has not been enough time. Will ten more years, or twenty, be enough? The army, traditionally dedicated to constitutional government, is troubled by this. Some officers, weary of the attempt to maintain the fiction of constitutionalism, have begun to feel their efforts an exercise in futility. They would prefer the army to return to its role as the "moderating power," but can discover no avenue of escape. Tensions and frustrations generate an increasing desire for a frankly authoritarian regime.

By mid-1972 the achievements of the military government were uneven, registering spectacular successes in economic development with much less impressive gains in political restructuring. Centralizing the government, however, has brought about an enormous increase in the regime's effectiveness. Its allocation of national resources is far more productive than ever before. Additional political and social reforms are essential if the military's goal of stable and effective constitutional government is to be achieved. Thus far, however, the military's reformist faction led by General Afonso Albuquerque Lima has not been able to exert much influence. At this stage there seems to be in the making a contest between reformists and hard-liners which, if it occurs, will certainly affect the government's future course of action. Those who still value democratic government and freedom of speech above economic prosperity continue to oppose the government, but most Brazilians, delighted at the unprecedented economic growth and development made since 1964, are not eager for the military regime to return the government to civilians.

Epilogue

IN THE 150 YEARS SINCE INDEPENDENCE, BRAZIL has undergone a remarkable transformation. For centuries a producer of raw materials for European commerce, Brazil had maintained a colonial economy to some degree until the military seized power in 1964. Since that time the nation's economic transformation has been astounding. Brazil has begun to export manufactured items and is on the way to making adequate use of its natural resources—a goal that has long been left unfulfilled. These achievements have opened the way for other advances in international affairs, and Brazil has risen to the status of a major nation.

Today Brazil's major unsolved problem is to devise an effective and acceptable political system—since independence neither monarchy nor republic has functioned properly. Monarchy guided by Dom Pedro II seemed from a distance to be working smoothly: because he changed the party in power and held elections occasionally, there seemed to be a relationship between the two. The relationship was, however, superficial at best, and opposition to the monarchy grew steadily from the 1860s onward. The half-century of Dom Pedro's personal rule, furthermore, accustomed Brazilians to depend more heavily on an individual than on the political system. This dependence carried over into the Old Republic, where its effect was far from salutary—presidents were not monarchs, and they did not have at their disposal the moderating power that made Dom Pedro's wishes so effective.

The introduction of federalism during the Old Republic resulted in the splintering of the party system into a multitude of local cliques and state organizations. The old Republican party had failed to establish itself on a national basis, and no other genuinely national party arose. The *coroneis,* who had provided local government throughout the colonial era, dominated rural areas and decided the outcome of many elections. The national congress came

249

to be composed of representatives of local and state oligarchies who made "deals" among themselves without thought of program, party, or nation. Campos Sales' "politics of the governors" intensified the problem. The Old Republic was thus doomed almost from the start, and the nation found itself trapped in a sterile political situation from which there was no peaceful escape.

Under the circumstances nothing much could be accomplished toward accelerating economic development. Despite expressions of discontent from the Prestes Column and others, no one seriously considered socio-economic reforms. Part of the trouble was that federalism had been introduced without any effort to balance the grossly unequal parts of the federation. As a result the wealthiest and most populous states were able to alternate the presidency between them, and the interests of the poorer states were ignored. Customarily *Paulista* presidents abandoned the programs begun by their *Mineiro* predecessors and vice versa. Euclides da Cunha's description of elections—"a euphemism which with us is the most striking instance of the daring misuse of language"—reflected the cynicism of his countrymen toward the political process.

Under the dictatorship of Getúlio Vargas and the *Estado Nôvo*, Brazil accomplished more in the way of economic development than it did during the entire Old Republic. Brazilians admitted the need for economic progress, but many felt that the price—dictatorship, censorship, the lack of civil liberties—was too high. As soon as Vargas was ousted in 1945 a new constitution was promulgated, restoring democratic, representative government and limiting the authority of the president, but these measures did not prevent the nation from once again embarking on the road to political and economic stagnation.

Brazil has never found a form of representative government that has worked properly and effectively. For one thing, because of the literacy requirement, the electorate has never been large enough to be truly representative: until 1946 only about 2 percent of the population were enfranchised; by 1960 the percentage had risen to nearly 20 percent, but this figure was still inadequate. The Constitution of 1946 was clearly not the solution to Brazil's political problems. It led to the splintering of parties, none of which could command an absolute majority. Except for the administration of Juscelino Kubitschek, all of the others under the Constitution of 1946 were ineffective, and few of the presidents had received an absolute majority of the votes. Kubitschek's achievements, moreover, resulted from his rare talents for manipulation and for generating optimism, rather than from a smooth-working political system; he left a financial shambles which his immediate successors were unable to rectify.

With the ouster of Jango Goulart and the military's seizure of power, Brazil turned another corner. The armed forces' decision to stay in power indefinitely was reached only gradually, but when it was, Brazil's economic situation began to improve markedly. The financial stabilization program showed early signs of success and the confidence of the business community began to return.

The Superior War College—which has embraced industrialization as one of its major goals—is the key to Brazil's recent, unprecedented economic growth. Civilians from industry have been equally involved in the War College, both as faculty and students. Because most high-ranking government officials since 1964 were graduates of the War College, they had already established rapport with industrialists and were far better informed than most *políticos* on the economy and its problems. They were also more dedicated than *políticos* to solving these problems, and they did not allow the political system to obstruct their plans. At present the college's main concern is the ecological future of the Amazon basin.

The present solution, government by the military, is considered temporary, to be phased out one day in the future. There is nothing, however, to suggest that if a civilian regime were installed today it would be an improvement over those of the past. One might almost conclude that representative democracy is not the best system for Brazil, and that a semiauthoritarian regime is needed to keep the economy flourishing. In the final analysis, realization of Brazil's greatness depends on its people's creating for themselves a viable political system—a system effective enough to foster and sustain economic stability and democratic enough to promote an atmosphere of liberty and order in which efficacy and participation are guaranteed to all major sectors of the population.

Chronology

1494	Treaty of Tordesillas moved the Line of Demarcation to 370 leagues west of the Cape Verde islands, which placed part of Brazil within the Portuguese sphere.
1500	Pedro Alvares Cabral landed on coast of Brazil and claimed the land for Portugal.
1503	Royal dyewood contract with Fernão de Noronha; beginning of New Christians' interest in Brazil.
1532	Martim Afonso de Sousa founded São Vicente, first Portuguese settlement.
1549	Tomé de Sousa became first governor-general; brought Jesuits to Brazil.
1565	Founding of São Sebastião do Rio de Janeiro.
1567	Mem de Sá expelled French from Guanabara Bay.
1580–1640	The Spanish Captivity, era of Spanish rule of Portugal and its empire.
1621	Maranhão separated from Brazil.
1624–1654	Period of Dutch occupation of northeastern captaincies.
1680	Founding of Colônia do Sacramento in the Río de la Plata.
1690s	Gold discovered in Minas Gerais.
1750	Treaty of Madrid; principle of *uti possidetis* established in determining boundaries.
1759	Marquis de Pombal expelled Jesuits from all Portuguese possessions.
1772	Maranhão reunited with Brazil.
1808	Royal family, fleeing French, arrived in Brazil.
1815	Brazil raised to rank of kingdom, coequal with Portugal.
1821	Dom João VI annexed the *Banda Oriental* as *Cisplatina* province.
1822	*Grito de Ipiranga* (September 7), Brazil's declaration of independence under Dom Pedro I.
1824	First constitution adopted; United States recognized Brazil's independence.
1825	Portugal and Great Britain recognized Brazil's independence.

1825–1828	Rebellion in *Cisplatina* aided by Argentina; Uruguay established as an independent state.
1831	Dom Pedro I abdicated in favor of infant son, Dom Pedro II; regency established.
1835–1845	*Farroupilha,* or War of the Ragamuffins, in Rio Grande do Sul.
1840	Dom Pedro declared of age; regency ended.
1850	Queiroz Law ended slave trade.
1852	Brazilian troops aided in overthrow of Juan Manuel de Rosas of Buenos Aires.
1865–1870	Paraguayan War (War of the Triple Alliance against Paraguay).
1868	First military intervention led to fall of Zacarias ministry.
1871	Rio Branco Law of Free Birth—first step toward abolition of slavery.
1888	Complete abolition of slavery without compensation.
1889	Fall of the empire and proclamation of the republic.
1891	Republican constitution promulgated.
1893–1895	Naval mutiny and civil war in Rio Grande do Sul crushed.
1896–1897	Canudos campaigns against Antônio Conselheiro.
1909	Rui Barbosa's *civilista* campaign—beginning of disillusionment with Old Republic.
1917	Brazil declared war on Germany.
1922	Modern Art Week in São Paulo, initiating the Modernist movement; Copacabana revolt and beginning of *tenente* movement.
1924–1927	Prestes Column traveled through the interior.
1930	Overthrow of the Old Republic and beginning of the Vargas era.
1932	Rebellion in São Paulo crushed.
1934	Second republican constitution promulgated.
1937	*Estado Nôvo* proclaimed under third republican constitution; beginning of the Vargas dictatorship.
1942	Brazil declared war on the Axis powers.
1944	Brazilian Expeditionary Force entered European theater.
1945	*Estado Nôvo* ended with ouster of Vargas.
1946	Fourth republican constitution promulgated.
1950	Vargas elected president; Superior War College established.
1954	Vargas' suicide; Café Filho assumed interim presidency.
1956	Juscelino Kubitschek inaugurated.
1960	Capital transferred to Brasília; former Federal District became state of Guanabara.
1961	Inauguration and resignation of Jânio Quadros; parliamentary system adopted and João Goulart inaugurated.
1963	Parliamentary system ended by national plebiscite.

1964   Goulart deposed; military regime established under General
            Humberto Castello Branco; Cassation of "undesirable" poli-
            ticians began.
1967   General Artur da Costa e Silva succeeded to the presidency;
            new constitution proclaimed.
1969   Costa e Silva disabled, replaced by General Emílio Garras-
            tazú Médici.
1973   Opening of the Trans-Amazon Highway.

Glossary

(Portuguese Terms Used in the Text)

Agregados   Free, rural working class, colonial era.
Agrovila   Township laid out by government for settlement of interior, twentieth century.
Aldeia   Village, applied especially to Indian communities under control of Jesuit priests.
Arroba   440 kilograms.
Aviso   Warning, used for certain army regulations.

Bala e onça   "Rough and ready"—term applied to *Paulistas.*
Balaiada   Name of a revolt in Maranhão, 1838–41.
Banda Oriental   Eastern Shore of the Río de la Plata; modern Uruguay.
Bandeira   Expedition to the interior in search of slaves or mines.
Bandeirante   Member of a *bandeira.*
Berlinda   Light carriage.
Boca do inferno   "Mouth of hell," applied to Gregório de Mattos, seventeenth-century poet.

Cabanagem   Revolt in Pará, 1835–40.
Caboclo   "Copper-colored," term applied to Indians in colonial era, rural peasants today.
Candomblé   African religious cult in Bahia.
Capangas   Henchmen of *fazendeiros,* colonial era.
Capitania   Captaincy, huge grant of land, colonial era.
Capitão mor   Administrative and military assistant of colonial governor; commander of local militia unit.
Caramurús   Name applied to Portuguese faction during *Cabanagem.*
Carioca   Resident of Rio de Janeiro.
Casaca   Frockcoat; term for politician.
Civilista   Term applied to Rui Barbosa's presidential campaign of 1909.
Colégio   Academy, secondary level, colonial era.
Concelho   Portuguese chartered community.
Conselho da India   Council introduced during the period of Spanish rule.
Conselho geral   General meeting of citizens and officials.

257

Conselho Ultramarino New name for *Conselho da India* after Spanish rule ended.

Coronel (plural **coroneis**) Colonel, title given to major landowner of a region, which became synonymous with *fazendeiro;* also, political boss of a region.

Correição Official inquiry, punishment.

Côrtes Portuguese assembly similar to parliament.

Crioulo Creole, Portuguese born in New World.

Cristãos Nôvos New Christians or recent converts to Catholicism.

Cruzado Portuguese coin.

Cruzeiro Brazilian coin introduced in 1942.

Degredado Exiled criminal.

Devassa Official inquiry.

Dízimo Tenth or tithe on agricultural production.

Donatário Donatary, recipient of a captaincy.

Emboaba Unflattering term *Paulistas* applied to outsiders who came to goldfields.

Encilhamento Term applied to a brief period of financial speculation after the fall of the empire, literally "saddling-up."

Engenho Sugar mill.

Escola Mineira *Mineiro* school of poets, late eighteenth century.

Exaltados "Radicals" of 1820s and 1830s who wanted a federal republic.

Farrapo Name applied first to cowboys of Rio Grande do Sul, later to all *Riograndenses.*

Farroupilha War of the Ragamuffins, 1835–45.

Fazenda Large plantation.

Fazendeiro Plantation owner.

Fidalgo Portuguese nobleman.

Filantrópicos Name applied to Brazilian faction during the *Cabanegem.*

Gaúcho Term for cowboy in the South; came to be applied to all Riograndenses.

Golpe Coup.

Golpista Participant in a coup.

Inconfidência Mineira Conspiracy in Minas Gerais, broken up in 1789.

Irmandade Semireligious brotherhood.

Jôgo do bicho "Animal game," a popular gambling game that began as a means of attracting people to the Rio de Janeiro zoo.

Lingua geral Language generally spoken.

Linha dura   "Hard line," term applied to a group of officers who believe the military should govern without interference from civilians, 1960s and 1970s.

Macumba   African religious cult in Rio de Janeiro.
Maiorista   Participant in the majority movement, which favored declaring Dom Pedro II of age, 1839–40.
Mamelucos   Term applied to the halfbreed *Paulistas,* colonial era.
Marrano   Unflattering term applied to converts from Judaism.
Mascate   Term applied to peddlers in Pernambuco.
Mazombos   Portuguese born in Brazil, creoles.
Mineiro   Resident of Minas Gerais.
Moderados   Term applied to liberals of 1820s and 1830s who favored a constitutional monarchy.
Muleque   Slave boy given to the son of a fazendeiro.

Orientalista   Uruguayan (from *Banda Oriental*).
Ouvidor geral   Chief justice, colonial era.

Padroado   Royal patronage, colonial era.
Paulista   Resident of São Paulo, province or state.
Pequenino   "Very little one," applied to children of slaves, colonial era.
Político   Brazilian term for politician.
Praça   Plaza.
Praieira   Name given to a rebellion in Pernambuco, 1848.
Procurador   Provincial representative, colonial era.
Provedor mor   Chief treasurer, colonial era.

Quilombo   Colony of runaway slaves.
Quinto   Royal fifth collected on minerals.
Quistos   "Cysts," term applied to all-Japanese colonies in Brazil, twentieth century.

Reinóis   Portuguese born in Portugal.
Relação   High court, colonial era.
Residência   Judicial hearing at the end of an official's term, colonial era.
Ricos homens   Upper class in Portugal, late Middle Ages.
Riograndense   Resident of Rio Grande do Sul.

Sabinada   Name given to a revolt in Bahia, 1837–38.
Senado da Câmara   Municipal government; town council.
Senhores de engenho   Mill or plantation owners.
Sertanejo   One who lives in the *sertão.*
Sertão   Interior backlands, especially of Bahia.

Tenente   Lieutenant, applied to a group of reformist officers, 1920s and 1930s.

Tumbeiro   Brazilian term for slave ships.

Vaqueiro   Term for cowboy in the Northeast.

Visitação   Official inspection or inquiry.

Xangô   African religious cult in Pernambuco.

Suggested Readings

The study of Brazilian history and civilization by American scholars has become significant only in recent decades, which will explain why the majority of the books listed below were published since 1945. The preponderance of recent books indicates that we have only lately recognized Brazil's growing stature among nations.

For many years the only general history in English was the translation of João Pandiá Calógeras, **A History of Brazil** (Chapel Hill: University of North Carolina Press, 1939), which concludes with the early years of the Vargas regime. The first full-length general account is **A History of Brazil** (New York: Columbia University Press, 1970), by one of the most productive of current American Brazilianists, E. Bradford Burns. Valuable introductory studies are: Gilberto Freyre, **Brazil: An Interpretation** (New York: Alfred A. Knopf, 1947) and **New World in the Tropics** (New York: Alfred A. Knopf, 1959); Rollie E. Poppino, **Brazil, the Land and the People** (New York: Oxford, 1968); José Honório Rodrigues, **The Brazilians, Their Character and Aspirations** (Austin: University of Texas Press, 1967); and **Brazil and Africa** (Berkeley: University of California Press, 1965); William L. Schurz, **Brazil, the Infinite Country** (New York: E. P. Dutton, 1961); and Charles Wagley's excellent **An Introduction to Brazil** (New York: Columbia University Press, 1963).

On society in general, some of the most important works are: Fernando Azevedo, **Brazilian Culture** (New York: Macmillan, 1950); Roberto Havighurst and J. Roberto Moreira, **Society and Education in Brazil** (Pittsburgh: Pittsburgh University Press, 1965); Donald Pierson, **Negroes in Brazil: A Study of Race Contact at Bahia** (Chicago: University of Chicago Press, 1942); and T. Lynn Smith, **Brazil: People and Institutions** (Baton Rouge: Louisiana State University Press, 1946 and later editions).

Economic histories include: Celso Furtado, **The Economic Growth of Brazil: A Survey from Colonial to Modern Times** (Berkeley: University of California Press, 1963) and Howard S. Ellis, ed., **The Economy of Brazil** (New York: Columbia University Press, 1970). João Cruz Costa, **A History of Ideas in Brazil** (Berkeley: University of California Press, 1964) is in a class by itself, as are the historiographical study, **Perspectives in**

261

Brazilian History (New York: Columbia University Press, 1967), edited by E. Bradford Burns, and also Burns' **Nationalism in Brazil, A Historical Survey** (New York: Praeger, 1968).

Books on colonial Brazil are few, but there are several first-rate studies of various aspects of colonial history. Dauril Alden, **Royal Government in Colonial Brazil, With Special Reference to the Administration of the Marquis of Lavradio, Viceroy, 1769–1779** (Berkeley: University of California Press, 1968) is the most detailed study of a particular period. C. R. Boxer, **The Dutch in Brazil, 1624–1654** (Oxford: Oxford University Press, 1957), **The Golden Age of Brazil, 1695–1750: Growing Pains of a Colonial Society** (Berkeley: University of California Press, 1962), and **Salvador de Sá and the Struggle for Brazil and Angola, 1602–1686** (London: The Athlone Press, 1953) are readable and instructive books by Britain's eminent Brazilianist. Gilberto Freyre, **The Masters and the Slaves. A Study in the Development of Brazilian Civiliation** (New York: Alfred A. Knopf, 1946) is a Brazilian classic. **The Bandeirantes: The Historical Role of the Brazilian Pathfinders** (New York: Alfred A. Knopf, 1965), edited by Richard M. Morse, presents a variety of views of the earliest Brazilian expansionists. Mathias C. Kiemen, **The Indian Policy of Portugal in the Amazon Region, 1614–1693** (Washington: Catholic University of American Press, 1954) and Alexander Marchant, **From Barter to Slavery: The Economic Relations of the Portuguese and Indians in the Settlement of Brazil, 1500–1580** (Baltimore: The Johns Hopkins Press, 1942) concern Portuguese-Indian relations in the sixteenth and seventeenth centuries. Caio Prado Júnior, **The Colonial Background of Modern Brazil** (Berkeley: University of California Press, 1967) is an economic historian's broad view of the colonial era and its legacy.

Although there are a number of thorough studies of various aspects of the empire, the period between 1808 and 1822 has not been fully treated. The era of Dom Pedro I is covered in Sérgio Corrêa da Costa, **Every Inch a King: A Biography of Dom Pedro I, First Emperor of Brazil** (New York: Charles Frank Publications, 1964); Bertita Harding, **Amazon Throne: The Story of the Braganzas of Brazil** (London: George G. Harrap and Co., 1942); and C. H. Haring, **Empire in Brazil: A New World Experiment with Monarchy** (Cambridge, Mass.: Harvard University Press, 1958), which also covers the regency period.

Other significant studies of the empire are : Leslie Bethell, **The Abolition of the Brazilian Slave Trade: Britain, Brazil, and the Slave Trade Question, 1807–1869** (New York: Cambridge University Press, 1970); Gilberto Freyre, **The Mansions and the Shanties: The Making of Modern Brazil** (New York: Alfred A. Knopf, 1968); Richard Graham, **Britain and the Onset of Modernization in Brazil, 1850–1914** (Cambridge: Cambridge University Press, 1968); Charles J. Kolinski, **Independence or Death! The Story of the Paraguayan War** (Gainesville:

University of Florida Press, 1965); Henry Koster, **Travels in Brazil** (Carbondale: Southern Illinois University Press, 1966); Alan K. Manchester, **British Preeminence in Brazil: Its Rise and Decline** (Chapel Hill: University of North Carolina Press, 1933); Anyda Marchant, **Viscount Mauá and the Empire of Brazil** (Berkeley: University of California Press, 1965); Carolina Nabuco, **The Life of Joaquim Nabuco** (Stanford: Stanford University Press, 1950); Charles W. Simmons, **Marshal Deodoro and the Fall of Dom Pedro II** (Durham: Duke University Press, 1966); Robert J. Toplin, **The Abolition of Slavery in Brazil** (New York: Atheneum, 1972); and Mary W. Williams, **Dom Pedro the Magnanimous** (Chapel Hill: University of North Carolina Press, 1937).

Recommended for the period between the fall of the empire and the 1930 revolution are: José Maria Bello, **A History of Modern Brazil, 1889–1964** (Stanford: Stanford University Press, 1966); E. Bradford Burns, **The Unwritten Alliance: Rio-Branco and Brazilian-American Relations** (New York: Columbia University Press, 1966); Euclides da Cunha, **Rebellion in the Backlands** (Chicago: University of Chicago Press, 1944); Warren Dean, **The Industrialization of São Paulo** (Austin: University of Texas Press, 1969); Gilberto Freyre, **Order and Progress: Brazil from Monarchy to Republic** (New York: Alfred A. Knopf, 1970); June E. Hahner, **Civilian-Military Relations in Brazil, 1889–1898** (Columbia: University of South Carolina Press, 1969); Lawrence F. Hill, **Diplomatic Relations Between the United States and Brazil** (Durham: Duke University Press, 1932); Joseph L. Love, **Rio Grande do Sul and Brazilian Regionalism, 1882–1930** (Stanford: Stanford University Press, 1971); and Charles W. Turner, **Ruy Barbosa: Brazilian Crusader for Essential Freedoms** (New York: Abingdon-Cokesbury Press, 1945).

On the Vargas era there are three recent works: John W. F. Dulles, **Vargas of Brazil: A Political Biography** (Austin: University of Texas Press, 1967); Robert M. Levine, **The Vargas Regime: The Critical Years, 1934–1938** (New York: Columbia University Press, 1970); and Jordan M. Young, **The Brazilian Revolution of 1930 and the Aftermath** (New Brunswick: Rutgers University Press, 1967). It seems likely that there will be many more books on Vargas in the future.

Books on recent Brazilian history are appearing in increasing numbers. For a deeper understanding of the period from 1945 to the present the following are especially helpful: Werner Baer, **Industrialization and Economic Development of Brazil** (Homewood, Ill.: Richard D. Irwin, 1965); Eric Baklanoff, ed., **New Perspectives of Brazil** (Nashville: Vanderbilt University Press, 1966) and **The Shaping of Modern Brazil** (Baton Rouge: Louisiana State University Press, 1969); Vladimir Reisky de Dubnic, **Political Trends in Brazil** (Washington, D.C.: Public Affairs Press, 1968); John W. F. Dulles, **Unrest in Brazil: Political-Military Crises, 1955–1964** (Austin: University of Texas Press, 1970); Celso

Furtado, **Diagnosis of the Brazilian Crisis** (Berkeley: University of California Press, 1965); Irving L. Horowitz, **Revolution in Brazil: Politics in a Developing Society** (New York: E. P. Dutton, 1964); Octavio Ianni, **Crisis in Brazil** (New York: Columbia University Press, 1970); Riordan Roett, ed., **Brazil in the Sixties** (Nashville: Vanderbilt University Press, 1972); Ronald Schneider, **The Political System of Brazil: Emergence of a Modernizing Military Regime** (New York: Columbia University Press, 1972); G. Edward Schuh, **The Agricultural Development of Brazil** (New York: Praeger, 1970); and Alfred Stepan, **The Military in Politics: Changing Patterns in Brazil** (Princeton: Princeton University Press, 1971).

There are a number of studies of Brazilian literature, beginning with Isaac Goldberg, **Brazilian Literature** (New York: Alfred A. Knopf, 1922). More recent works are: Afrânio Coutinho, **An Introduction to Literature in Brazil** (New York: Columbia University Press, 1969); David M. Driver, **The Indian in Brazilian Literature** (New York: Hispanic Institute, 1942); Fred P. Ellison, **Brazil's New Novel: Four Northeastern Masters** (Berkeley: University of California Press, 1954); Wilson Martins, **The Modernist Idea: A Critical Survey of Brazilian Writing in the Twentieth Century** (New York: New York University Press, 1970); John Nist, **The Modernist Movement in Brazil** (Austin: University of Texas Press, 1967); Samuel Putnam, **Marvelous Journey: Four Centuries of Brazilian Literature** (New York: Alfred A. Knopf, 1948); Raymond S. Sayers, **The Negro in Brazilian Literature** (New York: Hispanic Institute, 1956); and Erico Veríssimo, **Brazilian Literature: An Outline** (New York: Macmillan, 1945).

Among the available translations of Brazilian literary works, the following are representative: Manoel Antônio de Almeida, **Memoirs of a Militia Sergeant** (Washington, D.C.: Pan American Union, 1959); Jorge Amado, **Dona Flor and Her Two Husbands: A Moral and Amorous Tale** (New York: Alfred A. Knopf, 1969), **Gabriela, Clove and Cinnamon** (New York: Alfred A. Knopf, 1962), **Home is the Sailor** (New York: Alfred A. Knopf, 1964), **Shepherds of the Night** (New York: Alfred A. Knopf, 1967), and **The Violent Land** (New York: Alfred A. Knopf, 1945); José Pereira Graça Aranha, **Canaan** (Boston: The Four Seas Company, 1920); Joaquim Maria Machado de Assis, **Dom Casmurro, a Novel** (Berkeley: University of California Press, 1966), **Epitaph of a Small Winner** (New York: Noonday Press, 1952), **Esau and Jacob** (London: P. Owen, 1966), **The Hand and the Glove** (Lexington: University of Kentucky Press, 1970), **The Psychiatrist and Other Stories** (Berkeley: University of California Press, 1963), and **What Went on at the Baroness':** **A Tale with a Point** (Santa Monica: Magpie Press, 1963); Aluízio Azevedo, **A Brazilian Tenement** (New York: Robert McBride Company, 1926); Raquel de Queiroz, **The Three Marias** (Austin: University of Texas Press, 1963); and Graciliano Ramos, **Anguish** (New York: Alfred A. Knopf, 1965) and **Barren Lives** (Austin: University of Texas Press, 1965).

Index

Brazilian personal names are indexed according to the final name, following current Brazilian library practice. For example, although he was known as José Bonifácio, José Bonifácio de Andrada e Silva will be found under *Silva*.

271